HELEN RING ROBINSON

To Patricia,

Patricia Hill Dascoe

December 12, 2011

TIMBERLINE BOOKS

Stephen J. Leonard and Thomas J. Noel, editors

HELEN RING ROBINSON

COLORADO SENATOR AND SUFFRAGIST

Pat Pascoe

UNIVERSITY PRESS OF COLORADO

Published by the University Press of Colorado
5589 Arapahoe Avenue, Suite 206C
Boulder, Colorado 80303

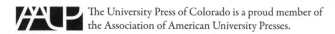 The University Press of Colorado is a proud member of
the Association of American University Presses.

The University Press of Colorado is a cooperative publishing enterprise supported, in part, by Adams State College, Colorado State University, Fort Lewis College, Metropolitan State College of Denver, Regis University, University of Colorado, University of Northern Colorado, and Western State College of Colorado.

∞ The paper used in this publication meets the minimum requirements of the American National Standard for Information Sciences—Permanence of Paper for Printed Library Materials. ANSI Z39.48-1992

Library of Congress Cataloging-in-Publication Data

Pascoe, Pat.
  Helen Ring Robinson : Colorado senator and suffragist / Pat Pascoe.
    p. cm. — (Timberline books)
  Includes bibliographical references and index.
  ISBN 978-1-60732-146-0 (hardcover : alk. paper) — ISBN 978-1-60732-147-7 (e-book)
  1. Robinson, Helen Ring, 1860–1923. 2. Women legislators—Colorado—Biography. 3. Legislators—Colorado—Biography. 4. Colorado—Politics and government—1876–1950. 5. Colorado. General Assembly. Senate—Biography. I. Title.
  F781.R63.P37 2011
  328.73092—dc23
  [B]
                      2011030828

Design by Daniel Pratt

20 19 18 17 16 15 14 13 12 11   10 9 8 7 6 5 4 3 2 1

CONTENTS

FOREWORD

Helen Ring Robinson (1860–1923) was the second woman state senator in the United States. An activist senator serving from 1913 to 1917, she pushed through the Colorado legislature a minimum-wage law for women and tenaciously fought for other causes, including repeated but unsuccessful efforts to pass a law allowing women to serve on juries. A popular and eloquent proponent of national women's suffrage, she traveled and lectured through the country.

Robinson proclaimed government and politics "in need of motherliness" and welcomed women's roles as the "housekeepers" needed to clean up government and make it more efficient. As Robinson was in the middle of many pacifist, reform, and women's issues of the early twentieth century, this biography provides unique national as well as local perspective on progressive age battles. Sadly, Robinson is a little-known public figure—even her marriage is a puzzle.

The University Press of Colorado's Timberline Series is proud to publish the second full-length biographical study of a female Colorado legislator. We are especially proud to have an illustrious state senator in her own right, Patricia Hill Pascoe, do the researching, writing, and polishing. As a state senator, Pascoe was devoted to the same causes—women, families, children, health, and education—that state senator Helen Ring Robinson embraced.

Pat Pascoe is also a scholar, a Phi Beta Kappa with a PhD in English literature from the University of Denver. After graduating, Dr. Pascoe taught English at Kent Denver and Metropolitan State College of Denver. She also worked as a professional writer, specializing in education and politics.

First elected to the state senate from Denver in 1988, Pat Pascoe served twelve years until term limits prevented her running again. In the legislature she sponsored many bills on education improvement (preschool, child care, truancy, bilingual education), freedom of press for students, teen pregnancy, wood-smoke pollution reduction, planned growth, organ donations, marital maintenance, spousal protection, domestic partners, and other topics. She chaired the Senate Public Policy and Planning Committee and the Senate Education Committee. Her fellow Democrats elected her caucus chair.

Pascoe writes and speaks widely on women in politics, sometimes in the costume and character of Helen Ring Robinson. After five years of researching her heroine, Senator Pascoe has produced an intimate, knowledgeable look at a woman who made a big difference. This warm, readable biography resurrects a forgotten but major role model not only for women but also for anyone interested in politics, reform movements, and Colorado's past.

THOMAS J. NOEL,

coeditor with Stephen J. Leonard of the Timberline Series
Professor of History and director of Colorado Studies, Public History,
and Preservation at the University of Colorado of Denver

PREFACE

The fascinating story of Colorado's first woman senator came to my attention when I sponsored a resolution in the Colorado State Senate to celebrate the 100th anniversary of Colorado women receiving the right to vote in 1893. A Legislative Council staff person, Elizabeth Haskell, found interesting information about her, so that I could read my resolution as if I were Helen Robinson making a return visit to the senate. The resolution passed, and I was captivated by her story.

As I learned more about Helen, I realized that she and I led parallel lives. Both of us had rather humble beginnings, became high school English teachers, wrote articles for newspapers and magazines, married lawyers, and were elected to the Colorado State Senate from Denver. We lived in the same Denver Capitol Hill neighborhood. We were both members of the Denver Woman's Press Club, and both of us served as president of that club, though a hundred years apart. In our senate careers, we both focused on education and on the treatment of women and children.

When progressive Democrat Helen Ring Robinson was elected to the Colorado State Senate in 1912 at age fifty-two, she was the second woman in the United States to be elected to such an office. In this role, she had more impact on Colorado and the nation than any other woman of her time, in part just by modeling what a woman office-holder could do. As what she called "the housewife of the Senate," "Senator Mrs. Robinson" worked for social and economic justice through bills that would establish a minimum wage for women and children, the right of women to sit on juries, and the protection of children committed to the state home. This biography reviews the events of each of the legislative sessions in which she served (1913, 1914, and 1915). During her four-year term of office she made a place for herself on the world stage as a worker for woman suffrage. When her term ended in early 1917, she labored first for world peace and then for the American war effort.

Helen's humble background gave her a deep understanding of the struggle of ordinary people trying to make a living. Her father was a laborer supporting a large family, and her siblings worked in the textile mills. Fortunately, Helen was an excellent student, which provided her with the opportunity to improve her situation—to attend Wellesley and become a teacher.

Throughout her adult life, Helen made her way in the world with a pattern of self-sufficiency and independence unusual for women in the late 1800s and early 1900s. She set very high aspirations for herself and courageously pursued them in every area of her life. Although she was an attractive woman, she resisted marriage until she was about forty-two and apparently supported herself throughout early adulthood with her teaching and writing. Seeing her parents' struggles to support nine children, three of them younger than she, might have discouraged her from an early marriage and the many children that often brought.

Helen moved to Colorado in 1893 to teach English at Colorado College in Colorado Springs. Two years later she moved to Denver, where she taught at Wolfe Hall and then at the Miss Wolcott School. Presumably her teaching career ended when she married Ewing Robinson, a Denver attorney, in 1902. Ten years after her marriage she ran successfully for the Colorado State Senate. Though many sources claim she was the first woman in the country to be elected to such an office, she was, in fact, the second.

In addition to her legislative work, Helen was a creative and inspired writer and orator and a devoted advocate of woman suffrage who was chosen to represent the United States at conferences in Madrid and Geneva.

Helen Ring Robinson's story offers us not only the inspiration of her personal accomplishments and her passion for the public good but also insights into the turbulent history of Colorado politics. She modeled the leadership role wives and mothers were beginning to assume in the public life of the community.

ACKNOWLEDGMENTS

In the long process of writing this book, I have been grateful for the patient assistance of many librarians, especially the knowledgeable staff of the Western History and Genealogy Department of the Denver Public Library. Other helpful librarians assisted me at the Colorado History Museum Library, the Colorado State Archives, the Legislative Council Library in the Colorado State Capitol, the Library of Congress, the Minnesota Historical Society, the Providence Public Library, and the University of Colorado at Boulder Libraries Archives.

Thanks to these individuals who made it possible to gather the information about Helen Ring Robinson: Virginia P. Dawson (History Enterprises, Inc., Cleveland), David Erickson, Marcia Tremmel Goldstein, Diane Hartman (Colorado Bar Association), Elizabeth Haskell (Legislative Council staff), Jim McGuiggan (website), Charlie Pike (director of Legal Services, Colorado General Assembly), Jessy Randall (curator and archivist, Colorado College, Special Collections), Wilma R. Slaight (archivist, Wellesley College), and Robert I. Woodward (archivist, St. John's Cathedral, Denver).

Stephen Leonard, Thomas Noel, and Todd Laugen generously recommended many excellent historical interpretations of the progressive movement and the struggle for women's suffrage. Todd Laugen kindly shared his manuscript on the progressive movement in Colorado.

This book was improved by my thoughtful editors David Horne, Elspeth MacHattie, Cheryl Carnahan, and Donna Potempa.

Though Helen had no descendants, I was able to talk with Fred Weybret, the husband of Helen's stepdaughter's daughter, Alcyon Martia Weybret, and communicate as well with another Robinson relative, Ann Hofstetter Delaney. I appreciate their assistance.

Without the support and encouragement of my extraordinary family, Sarah, Mark, and Max, Ted, Will, and especially Monte, this book would not have been possible.

HELEN RING ROBINSON

1

ORIGINS

Twenty years of teaching provided the skills that propelled Helen Ring Robinson into the Colorado State Senate. She became a scholar, an excellent speaker, and a fine writer, and she developed a lifelong interest in the education of young people. Though she only attended Wellesley for one year, her studies there were impressive. In the early years of her career she taught in New York and at a private school in Cleveland before coming to Colorado to teach at Colorado College. Then she taught at two private girls' schools in Denver. When she married lawyer Ewing Robinson, her teaching career ended, but her writing career began. Drawn into a fight over a water company monopoly, she became involved in progressive political campaigns that led to her election to the state senate in 1912.

We do not have a clear picture of Helen Ring Robinson's birth and family or of her experiences as a child and young woman. Even her birth date and her parents' exact identities are uncertain.[1] She was born Helen Margaret Ring in the early 1860s to Thomas Warren Ring and Mary Ring.[2] Two biographical references contemporary with Helen's rise to political office asserted that she was the daughter of Thomas and Mary (Prescott) Ring and was born in Eastport, Maine.[3] Maine is also cited as Helen's birthplace in several census reports, including the 1870 census.

In the 1870 census, Helen is listed as the sixth child in a family of nine children, of ages ranging from twenty-one down to four, all living in Providence, Rhode Island, though several—including Helen—were born in Maine: Rebecca, Matilde, Etta (or Baronetta), Judson B., Eva A., Helen, Ellsworth, Gustavus, and Annie L. Helen's age is given as ten years old, putting her birth date at about 1860. From the children's birthplaces and ages, it appears that the family moved from Maine to Rhode Island sometime between 1864 and 1867. Helen's father's occupation is listed as "labor," and the value of his personal property was put at only $300. Three of Helen's sisters, who were twenty-one, seventeen, and fifteen, worked in the cotton mill. Helen, age ten, and four of the other children were attending school.[4]

HELEN'S EDUCATION

Helen graduated from high school probably around 1877 or 1878. In a later visit to Providence, she acknowledged graduating from Providence High School but refused to give the date, and she claimed to have forgotten the name of the elementary school she had attended.[5]

By the time of the 1880 census, Mary Ring was a widow,[6] and Helen was listed as a restaurant cashier. At some earlier time, though, she apparently taught school because records at Wellesley College verify that Helen attended Wellesley in the 1880–1881 school year as a "teacher special." This made her part of a program for women who were already teachers. The object of the program was to "aid teachers of ability who find their usefulness impaired and their salaries limited by the deficiencies in their education." They often needed courses in ancient or modern languages or science, the course description says. The "teacher specials" were given flexibility in the courses they could take. Helen's courses suggest her very impressive scholarly abilities: three terms of Latin, German, Bible (Sunday), French, botany (junior course), history (junior course), and English literature (junior course), first and second terms only.[7]

The tuition at Wellesley at the time was $250 per year. Of the 372 students, 49 were teacher specials, but it is unclear whether Helen or the other teacher specials received any scholarship aid. As Mary Ring was by that time a widow with nine children living with her and her deceased husband had been a laborer, it is unlikely that the family could have paid for Helen's education. The college has no record of her attendance in the following years, in 1881–1882 or 1882–1883, as claimed in a later Colorado College Bulletin.[8] But in this period, any college education at all was remarkable for a woman of modest means.

Some sources assert that Helen also studied at Barnard and Oxford.[9] However, there is no record of her matriculation between 1889, when Barnard opened, and 1893, when she journeyed west to Colorado Springs.[10] Colorado College claimed she attended Columbia College Annex in 1886.[11] Just one source claims she studied in Paris.[12]

The details of Helen's career and personal life between 1881 when she left Wellesley and 1890 when she was in Cleveland are yet to be discovered. She was said to have been a teacher for a number of years in Yonkers, New York. In the period 1890–1893 she was associate principal of the Hathaway-Brown School in Cleveland, just before her move to Colorado Springs.[13] An 1891–1892 catalog from the Cleveland school lists her as "Miss Helen Margaret Ring, Natural Sciences, Direct supervision of instruction in Academic Department." She traveled to Colorado for the summer of 1892, sending back letters to "inform her friends that she is enjoying the climate and life of Colorado." She returned to Cleveland for the 1892–1893 school year, but moved to Colorado at the end of that school year.[14]

THE MOVE TO COLORADO

Helen's courage was clear in her decision to go west without the assistance of any relative, as far as we know.[15] She apparently had not married by this time, her thirty-third year.[16] She may have migrated in part seeking a suitable husband, since the proportion of single men to single women was very favorable in 1890; in Colorado it was 146.7 men for every 100 women, and in Denver there were 60,744 single men to 45,969 single women, or 1.3 men for every woman. From a woman's point of view, the Colorado numbers represented an excellent ratio.[17]

It is tempting to suggest that her motive for moving to Colorado was her interest in women gaining the right to vote, an issue that was to appear on the Colorado ballot in the fall of 1893, the very year she began teaching at Colorado College in Colorado Springs.[18] However, she later claimed in a suffrage speech that when she "went from the East to the West I was an anti-suffragist and used to make anti-suffrage speeches." She was converted to the suffrage cause in Colorado, she said.[19]

A combination of factors probably drew Helen to Colorado Springs. The 1886 *Colorado College Catalogue* says the population of Colorado Springs was 5,000 "and that its society is largely made up of eastern people," so perhaps Helen had connections there. Seven years before Helen went there, the catalog boasted only one professor of English literature and no instructors.[20] From 1892 on, Colorado College offered a summer school of science, philosophy, and languages. For five summers it brought distinguished scholars to the campus, including the poet who wrote "America the Beautiful," Katherine Lee Bates, an English professor from Wellesley College who taught in the 1893 Colorado College summer session. Bates wrote the stirring poem that summer. It is possible that Helen knew her from her year at Wellesley. The following summer Woodrow Wilson, then a political science professor at Princeton University, gave a lecture course on American constitutional government at Colorado College.[21]

Helen was listed in the 1894 *Colorado Springs Directory* as "Helen Margaret Ring, Instructor in English and Elocution," one of three instructors in English on the faculty at Colorado College.[22] She apparently taught at the college only for the 1893–1894 school year. In the fall of 1894, she put an advertisement in the *Colorado Springs Gazette* offering herself as a tutor in "all English Branches" and in Latin and German. She gave her address as 112 E. San Rafael Street, which was across from an area called "College Reservation" in Colorado Springs.[23] Whether this tutoring of Colorado College or high school students provided her with enough income to support herself is unclear.[24] In any event, she was teaching in Denver by the following school year.

There were many ties between Colorado College and Denver. At the 1893 college commencement, just before Helen moved to Colorado Springs, the speaker was the Honorable Joel F. Vaile,[25] who later married Anna Wolcott—a 1881 Wellesley graduate, a teacher and principal at Wolfe Hall, and later the founder of the Miss Wolcott School, both in Denver. Anna, like Helen, was originally from Providence. After her move to Denver, Helen taught at both schools. In April 1894 the Reverend H. Martyn Hart, dean of St. John's Cathedral in Denver where Helen was to become a member, spoke. Most intriguing for the possible influence on Helen was a series of lectures that year by Professor William M. Hall titled "Government in the United States." These were the topics: the difference between the US Constitution and other laws, party organization, elections, and the organization of states. Although there is no certain evidence that Helen attended these lectures or the lecture course by Woodrow Wilson, it is possible that they may have spurred her interest in politics.[26]

WOLFE HALL AND THE MISS WOLCOTT SCHOOL

Perhaps at the invitation of Anna Wolcott, Helen moved to Denver in 1895, where she became a teacher at Wolfe Hall, an Episcopalian girls' school. She was listed as a member of the Episcopal St. John's Cathedral for the years 1897–1898.[27] Wolfe Hall was a rather small finishing school that prepared girls for eastern colleges or local women's colleges. In 1887 the school had 145 students of both elementary and secondary age, of whom 30 were boarders; a faculty of 14; and a graduating class of 19.[28] Enrollment in the high school portion of the school where Helen later taught dropped from 8 in 1892 to 5 in 1893, the year the silver depression hit Colorado.[29]

The elegant building of Wolfe Hall, called a Ladies Seminary in the city directory, was located on Clarkson Street between 13th and 14th Avenues in Denver, directly facing the block where St. John's Cathedral was to be built. Today, Morey Middle School sits on that site.

Helen taught at Wolfe Hall in the academic years 1895–1896, 1896–1897, and 1897–1898.[30] The 1896 school annual, *The Banner*, listed her as Helen Margaret Ring, one of four faculty members in the Academic Department. After her name, in parentheses, the book gives her college as Wellesley and then her subjects: English, history, and literature.[31] The curriculum, at least in 1893–1894, two years before she came, indicated that English literature and composition were taught during each of the four years of high school. The annual names the history classes offered—ancient history and church history, both electives, and a special class called History of Art.[32] Helen also sponsored a weekly current events discussion in her room and a semi-monthly Senior Literary Club that at one point was reading *The House of Seven Gables* by Nathaniel Hawthorne.[33] *The Banner* suggests a gift from Santa Claus for Miss Ring: a bottle of red ink, implying that Miss Ring was highly critical of the girls' compositions. She may have lived at the school part of the time, but in 1897–1898 her address on the St. John's Cathedral membership list was "The Belview," per-haps the translation of "The Belvoir," a "family hotel" at 737 E. 16th at Clarkson, just two blocks from Wolfe Hall.

Evidently a popular teacher, Helen was named an honorary mem-ber of the Wolfe Hall class of four girls in 1897. Among the students at Wolfe Hall was Fredericka LeFevre, whose parents, Judge and Mrs. Owen LeFevre, became close friends of Helen and her future husband.[34]

The first evidence of Helen's lecturing career was a praised lecture she gave during her years at Wolfe Hall. A newspaper report of an

"Educational Afternoon" that featured a number of speakers declared that Helen "gave the cleverest talk of the day." As the article reported, Helen said:

> Knowledge was not power in itself; it was only power when it enabled a person to live, in the highest sense of the word. It was not what Christ knew, but what He was which drew all men unto him. Whatever trained the faculties of the child so that he became a fully developed being, was the thing he should study. It might be that mathematics would do this; but the world had long since abandoned the opinion that there was any means of grace in the multiplication table.

The way to train the faculties of the child, she suggested, was to have him study literature, thus stressing the importance of human connections and concern for the suffering of others demonstrated later in her preface to *Uncle Tom's Cabin*. She added: "Literature was the only continuity in history; the only thing that made history mean anything more than a list of wars and conquests, and statistics showed that seventy-five per cent of children left school absolutely without the ability to distinguish between good literature and bad; between Roman candles and stars."[35]

Mae Bradley, a reporter who interviewed Helen later in her career, wrote an anecdote about her teaching days. According to Bradley, when Wolfe Hall was threatened by a nighttime fire, "a girl knocked timidly at the sleeper's door and announced politely, 'I beg your pardon for disturbing you, Mrs. Robinson, but the school is on fire.'"[36] The story is suspicious because Helen was not "Mrs. Robinson" until four years after she left Wolfe Hall, but the characterization of Helen as a stickler for manners rings true.

In 1898 Anna Wolcott left Wolfe Hall, which was having financial difficulties, to found her own school. She took faculty members with her, including Helen Ring,[37] and a who's who of trustees. The first board consisted of Mrs. C. B. Kountze, Mrs. D. H. Moffat, Mrs. W. S. Cheesman, Mr. A. Coors, Mr. H. R. Wolcott, Mr. J. F. Campion, and Mr. F. O. Vaile.[38] Charles Kountze, a banker, owned large tracts of real estate; David Moffat, another banker, was one of the investors in the Denver Pacific Railroad; Walter Cheesman also owned real estate and was another founder of the Denver Pacific Railroad; Adolph Coors founded Coors Brewery; Henry Wolcott, a lawyer, was the brother of Senator Edward O. Wolcott and founded the city's first golf course, Overland; John Campion held silver mines; and F. O. Vaile, later the general counsel of the Denver and Rio Grande Railroad, was a law partner of Senator Edward O. Wolcott. Among the students at the Miss Wolcott School was Helen Brown, daughter of Margaret "Molly" Brown.[39] A new school building at 1410–1414 Marion, which still stands today, was finished just in time for the 1898–1899 school year.[40] Miss Wolcott was principal until 1913, when she married Joel Vaile, a law partner of her brother Edward O. Wolcott.[41]

Miss Helen Margaret Ring was named head of the high school's Academic Department. One hundred pupils were enrolled, while only forty remained at Wolfe Hall. There were about five graduates a year from the new school until 1903, when the number jumped to sixteen, and 1904, when there were twenty-three.[42] While she was teaching at the Miss Wolcott School, Helen gained membership in Denver society circles, at least at the lower levels. She was listed in the less exclusive list in *The Social Year-Book* in 1898.[43] She was not yet a member of the Artists' Club, which she joined later, and the Wellesley Club was not formed until the next year.

Helen probably quit teaching at the Wolcott School when she married in February 1902, in part because married women were not often teachers in that era. At least, she was not listed in the school's 1904 annual.[44] An article about her marriage reported that she had been an instructor within the past year, first at Wolfe Hall and then at the Miss Wolcott School.[45] In the Wellesley Club listing in the *Social Year-Book* for 1901–1902, Helen's address is the Miss Wolcott School, where she was teaching, at least until her marriage. In any event, her marriage allowed her the financial independence to write for newspapers and magazines and to play an active role in campaigns to advance the cause of woman suffrage and economic and social justice for women.

EWING ROBINSON

Being thrown from her horse and breaking a rib led to Helen's meeting Ewing Robinson while she was convalescing, according to a newspaper article. Helen, who loved horseback riding, was in the southwestern United States studying the Indians of Arizona and New Mexico.[46] Ewing, a widower, may have been drawn to Colorado to join his cousin, Roy Robinson, who for a time was a journalist in Silverton.[47]

Ewing was a widower whose first wife, Cora M. Ballard, died of typhoid in 1897 after they had been married just two years and when their daughter, Alcyon, was only sixteen months old.[48] This must have been a heartbreaking experience for Ewing, which might explain his carelessness in handling the probate of Cora's estate. In January 1900 the National Surety Company asked to be released from liability for its bond because Ewing, the administrator of Cora's estate, had not obtained or filed a proper receipt for his daughter's share of the estate.[49] He may have been preoccupied with the care of a toddler, and he may not have considered the small amount of money Cora left to their infant daughter very significant.

(George) Ewing Robinson, born in January 1857, was the son of a Washington County, Ohio, attorney, Samuel Bushfield Robinson, born about 1815, and Collina or Caroline Robinson, born about 1826. Ewing's father was relatively prosperous, with property valued at $15,000.[50]

In 1880, Ewing, about twenty-three years old, was a telegraph operator in Creston, Iowa.[51] According to his obituary, he graduated from the Law School at Iowa State University.[52] By 1890 he had migrated to the West, because he was admitted to practice law in Colorado on August 29 of that year.[53] In 1901 and 1902, Ewing practiced with Frank L. Grant under the firm name Robinson and Grant.[54]

There are several ways Helen and Ewing might have met if the story of Helen's falling off a horse is apocryphal. They both seemed to be in the second tier of the social set. In the 1899 *Social Year-Book*, Helen was in the Artists' Club, but Ewing had not yet joined.[55] By 1901–1902 both Ewing and Helen were associate members of the

Artists' Club, which may have been how they met.[56] However, Denver in those days was a small enough town that they could have met in many social settings.

When Ewing met Helen, he was probably still living with his daughter, Alcyon, and Nellie B. Graham, his first wife's sister, in a house he owned at 2535 Vine Street.[57] Alcyon, whose birthday was March 15, would have been almost six years old when Helen and Ewing were married in 1902.

The flowery articles about the February 13, 1902, wedding praised Ewing: "Mr. Robinson is a lawyer, who has been in the practice of his profession in this city for some years where he has many admirers and friends," though his role in Helen's life remains somewhat of a mystery. The description of Helen was even more embellished: "Mrs. Robinson is a woman of splendid mental achievements, a deep thinker, a profound and thoughtful student, and a companion who cannot fail to prove an inspiration along intellectual lines to the man who was fortunate enough to gain her for his bride."[58]

The marriage was consecrated by the Episcopalian Reverend Frederick W. Oakes, the director of Oakes Home for tubercular patients,[59] in the home of Owen and Eva LeFevre, who were also the witnesses on the marriage certificate. Owen Edgar LeFevre was elected district judge in 1894 with American Protective Association (APA) support. The APA was an anti-immigrant, anti-Catholic Republican group, according to Phil Goodstein and Robert Riegel.[60] The bride was given away by her brother, Mr. Judson Ring, who apparently came west for the wedding.[61] According to the newspaper, the couple "went to housekeeping" at 912 13th Avenue.

By the following year, Helen had apparently persuaded her husband to become an Episcopalian, even though Ewing's previous marriage had been presided over by a minister of Central Presbyterian Church. He was confirmed at the old St. John's Cathedral on April 5, 1903.[62]

Ewing Robinson remains something of a mystery because Helen seldom mentions him in her writing and the newspapers do not report on his activities. He had to have been a fairly progressive man to accept, some years later, the idea of his wife becoming a legislator. Ewing's daughter, Alcyon, whom Helen treated as her own, was referred to frequently in articles, and Helen dedicated her children's version of *Uncle Tom's Cabin* to her.[63] Helen's influence on her stepdaughter is clear in Alcyon's career path. She graduated from the University of Colorado with a degree in journalism. At some time she worked for her stepmother when Helen had an appointment from President Woodrow Wilson at the League of Nations. Their close relationship is also suggested by the fact that Helen went to stay with her in California during her final illness, and, when Helen died, she left most of her household goods to Alcyon.[64]

One of the few references to Ewing in the newspapers, other than his obituary, reported the unhappy news that ethics charges had been filed against him by the Colorado Bar Association.[65] What a shock it must have been to the newlyweds just a year after their marriage to have Ewing accused of taking all of a client's property and selling it. In his defense Robinson claimed he had to sell it to secure bonds for his client, Peter Johnston.[66] The attorneys for the relator were Mr. N. C. Miller, attorney general, and Mr. George L. Hodges. For the respondent Robinson they were Mr. O. E. LeFevre, Mr. H. B. Babb, and Messrs. Morrison and DeSoto. The court did not find grounds for disbarment, though it did not entirely approve of Robinson's actions. This is a summary of the findings in regard to Johnston and two other clients:

1. The fact that an attorney owes balance of account when disputed is not grounds for disbarment. (This refers to a different client, Mrs. Buffington.)

2. Failing to return an abstract of title is not grounds when evidence suggests all her papers were returned. (Mrs. Buffington.)

3. Raising the amount of a note must be clearly proven. (Client, Mr. Ames.)

4. A misstatement to a client is not grounds if the attorney is not defrauding or deceiving. (Mr. Ames.)

5. Assisting a client to avoid attachment is all right if it is reasonable to assume the client innocent. (Peter Johnston.)

6. The amount of fees is not grounds [for disbarment].

7. The fact that the attorney foreclosed on Johnston's house and furniture for professional services is not grounds for disbarment.

8. Attorney trying to establish a liability on an injunction bond four to five years ago and where, when facts brought to court and all made public and published in the press—not sufficient for disbarment after all this time (but his actions are not totally approved).

In fact, the court was quite critical of Ewing's actions in this matter. It said:

> There can be no doubt but that respondent [Ewing] was guilty of improper conduct in attempting to establish a liability on an injunction bond . . . The acts complained of occurred between four and five years before the information was filed. Respondent, when the facts in connection with the affair were brought out in court, realized he had done wrong, and promptly admitted his mistake. No one was substantially injured by his action. The whole matter was made public and published in the daily press. This publicity has, in our judgment, after the lapse of so long a period, been a sufficient punishment for respondent; and in view of the fact he has so promptly admitted his wrong and made such reparations as he could, we do not believe that any beneficial end would be accomplished by inflicting a punishment at this time, even if justified originally . . . The record with respect to some of the charges certainly discloses a state of affairs which fully warranted the relator [the Colorado Bar Association] in taking the steps it did.

The court added that it was not justified in saying the attorney was "fully exonerated." The most serious of the charges related to events that took place before Helen and Ewing were married, but these accusations probably shook Helen's faith in her husband. Fortunately for the newlyweds, Ewing was not disbarred or even censured; rather, he continued to practice law for many years.

In spite of the unpleasantness of the disbarment hearing, Helen's marriage to Ewing Robinson established her as a permanent, economically comfortable resident of Denver. While it ended her teaching career, it opened up new possibilities. Helen's newfound financial security allowed her to devote her time to writing, politics, and, eventually, public office. But first she had to be transformed from a private person into a well-known public figure.

2

Path to Victory

How did a highly qualified but very feminine schoolteacher, writer, and housewife break into the exclusive male club of the Colorado State Senate in 1912? Helen's election was even more surprising because, though women had been voting in Colorado general elections from 1894 on, the number of women elected to the Colorado House of Representatives was decreasing. The national progressive and woman suffrage movements were part of the impetus to elect more women, but they were only two of several factors that came together to propel Helen into office in 1912. In addition to these movements, there was the women's club movement, Helen's increased name recognition, the example of a few other women elected officials, her race to be the Democratic candidate for state superintendent of schools in 1910, and the new access to the primary ballot by petition. Add to those factors the 1912 split in the Democratic Party, which, ironically, helped

Helen's candidacy, and the state and national split in the Republican Party, which also boosted Helen's candidacy. As so often happens in politics, the election of the first woman senator in Colorado was a combination of multiple factors—and luck.

THE PROGRESSIVE MOVEMENT

Helen owed her election in part to the progressive movement, usually dated 1901 to the US entry into World War I in 1917.[1] The progressive parties were strongly influenced by the earlier Populists in Colorado, who won the governorship for Davis Waite and a substantial number of seats in both houses of the General Assembly in 1892. The Populist candidate for president, James B. Weaver, received more than 50 percent of the vote in Colorado that year.[2] The party wanted legislation to cure current abuses of laborers, debtors, and the poor. Specifically, to paraphrase historian Phil Goodstein's summary, the "Omaha" party platform called for government to protect ordinary people; protect public lands and resources; control or nationalize railroads; establish an eight-hour workday; and pass recall, initiative, and referendum laws. In 1892 the party was also for free silver.[3] Progressives continued to address many of these unsolved problems in the first two decades of the twentieth century.

William Chafe, professor of history at Duke University, said that almost everything admirable about the progressive movement was associated with women reformers and women's domestic concerns.[4] The growing ranks of well-educated middle-class women worked to expand what was seen as the woman's sphere: she was the moral force and protector of virtue in all things related to the home and family. Women, who were seen as "above politics," expanded this sphere into the community and the care of dependents.[5] Men, on the other hand, were to manage the more public business and political spheres.

In the late nineteenth century women began to argue for scientific, efficient motherhood and public action to solve social problems. Women, they believed, had the expertise to solve problems related to women and children anyplace in the community.[6] One contemporary woman stated the position clearly: "But Home is not contained within the four walls of an individual house. Home is the Community ... And badly do the Home and Family need their mother."[7]

Taking women further into the community, Hull House, created by Jane Addams in Chicago, and others modeled after it helped create a professional social service cadre of women who were no longer confined to the home. They were leaders in addressing the social problems that concerned the progressives.

Those who argued that women and mothers have a special understanding of many social problems have been called maternalists by scholars such as Molly Ladd-Taylor, who divides maternalists into three groups: sentimental maternalists, progressive maternalists, and progressive women reformers allied with the National Woman's Party. Helen Ring Robinson doesn't fit perfectly into any of these categories, but she is most like the progressive maternalists because she argued for an expansion of women's sphere based on the experience of the home while she carried the torch for progressive reforms in the community. She was later openly opposed to the National Woman's Party.[8] The progressives needed women like Helen in the legislature because of their unique understanding of the social problems that needed to be solved.

Because of the emphasis on women as mothers or potential mothers, the first protective legislation for workers was limited to women, while the courts struck down any protection of male workers as a violation of private contracts. Minimum wage laws for women, such as the one Helen sponsored, were enacted in fifteen states between 1912 and 1923.[9]

The related issue of child labor was one of the most distressing problems progressives wanted to address. In 1900 an estimated 2 million children were working. There were seven-year-olds working in canneries, thirteen-year-olds working eight-hour days in coal mines, twelve-year-olds working six-hour "half" days in factories. Children as young as four worked full-time in canneries and fields and suffered injuries.[10]

Progressive women in Colorado supported funding for traveling libraries, a pure-food law, a primary election law, and a minimum salary

17

of fifty dollars a month and pensions for teachers. Helen would take up some of these issues in the 1913 and 1915 legislative sessions.[11]

In addition to these issues, another strand of progressivism battled for better government. Judge Benjamin Lindsey was a leading Denver progressive who targeted the corrupt Denver city government and major business monopolies. His book *The Beast,* in which powerful corporations manipulating elected officials are compared to a beast lurking in the jungle, aroused citizens against the Denver machine. He worked closely with like-minded progressive women, including Helen.[12]

A natural consequence of the Populist movement and its heir apparent in Colorado, the progressive movement, was the demand for women's suffrage. The Populists were key to winning the vote for Colorado women in 1893, and it was fitting that a progressive such as Helen would fight to bring the vote to women in the rest of the country.

THE WOMAN SUFFRAGE MOVEMENT

Helen's writing and speeches reveal her passion for the suffrage cause, which began after she moved to Colorado in 1893, the year the extension of the vote to women was on the state ballot in the fall. The Colorado Constitution at the time of statehood in 1876 had allowed women to vote in school board elections and run for election to school boards.[13] Helen probably went to Colorado Springs in the summer of 1893 to find lodging and to prepare for her teaching job at Colorado College in the 1893–1894 school year, but there is no evidence that she participated in the suffrage campaign.[14] When the ballot issue passed that fall, Colorado men became the first voters in the country to grant women the right to vote in all elections.[15] Wyoming in 1869 and Utah in 1870 had granted women that right by votes of their territorial legislatures.[16] Helen's mentor, Sarah Platt Decker (the first president of the Woman's Club of Denver), explained how important the vote was to women and decried the idea that women must first change their communities before they should be granted that right: "The vote is an indefinable something that makes you part of the plan of the world. It means the same to women that it does to men. You never ask a boy, 'Have you closed the saloons, have you purified politics and driven all the political tricksters out of the state?' No, you put your hand on his shoulder and you say, 'To-day, my boy, you are an American citizen,' and that is what you say to your daughter."[17]

The inherent contradiction in arguing for suffrage with the maternalist reasoning and arguing for equality of the sexes eventually eliminated the maternalists' position as women took their places in the economic and political spheres. Helen saw no conflict in using both arguments.

Women did not seek the vote just to feel equal to men, though, but also to elect women to positions of power because they saw so many issues that desperately needed the benefit of the woman's point of view: determination of parental rights, economic justice for women workers, and rehabilitation for women and children who broke the law. The benefits of suffrage for women were not universally appreciated, however, as demonstrated in an essay written by Robert S. Morrison of the Colorado Bar Association for Jerome Smiley's history of Colorado in 1913. Of woman suffrage he said,

> It has been in operation sixteen years, and its effects, whether for the better or the worse, now should and fairly may be soberly considered. It has wrought no drastic changes. It has not affected the result in any contest between the larger political parties, and there is no general concession that its effects have been to the good. It has repealed no legislation inimical to women, because, with one exception there was no such legislation to repeal.[18]

The one exception Morrison was apparently referring to was the not insignificant preferential treatment of the father to rights over children, which was changed after women got the vote. Morrison continued by citing rising divorce rates, which he attributed to political differences between husband and wife. He believed that if a wife voted in a manner opposite to her husband, she simply killed her husband's vote; he seemed totally insensitive to the wife's right to equal influence in public affairs. And he groused that woman suffrage had increased the numbers in the Labor, Socialist, and Prohibition Parties—parties of which he did not approve. No doubt others shared his limited perspective. Without modern polling techniques, it would have been difficult to tell how much women influenced the outcomes of elections. Helen's entire career suggested what women could do when they had the vote and could serve as officeholders.

Denver's Roman Catholic bishop, Joseph P. Machebeuf, in fact, blamed the suffrage movement "on battalions of old maids disappointed in love" and on "women, who though married, wish to hold the reigns of family government."[19]

There was little doubt that having women in the legislature starting with the house in 1894 and having women as a major bloc of voters influenced the passage of legislation. Helen Sumner, writing in 1909, saw many important laws passed to benefit women and children in Colorado as a result of women's suffrage: that a homestead cannot be mortgaged or sold without the wife's signature, that fathers and mothers are joint guardians of children with equal powers, the eight-hour work law (declared unconstitutional in 1923), a provision for truant schools, juvenile court laws, the revision of the age of consent (to marry), and the establishment of homes for defective and delinquent children, a girls' industrial school, and a home for dependent children.[20]

Helen contended that the woman's point of view was essential to improve legislation that addressed their problems, and during her time in office she focused much of her attention on bills to improve the social and economic position of women and children.

Part of the force behind woman suffrage in this era was the changing role of women. Much of the work formerly done at home was being replaced by factories, especially the making of food products and clothing. By 1920, 28 percent of women were working outside the home. By 1900, 26 percent of American undergraduates were women, and only 60 percent of college women would marry. When they did, they had fewer children.[21] Thus the concept of separate spheres for men and women was essentially dissolving.

The first time we hear of Helen speaking on woman suffrage was in 1909 at the Convention of Women's Clubs in Leadville, where she was featured with Congressman Edward T. Taylor of Glenwood Springs.[22] Her view of woman suffrage and of women officeholders is developed in an adulatory article by Mae Bradley, a colleague at the *Rocky Mountain News,* written after Helen was elected to the senate. She describes her role in maternalist terms:

> Rather than suffrage disrupting the home, I believe it is the one solution of preservation of the home. The feminine movement is co-incident with the broadest humanitarianism.
>
> We are all on the same boat on a stormy sea; we must all do our part and take to the oars. It is that sense of personal and economic responsibility now felt as a tide all over the world, that is in a large measure due to the advance of women into public life. There never was a time when the feminine element of sympathy and motherliness was so essential to legislation as now, and the more truly feminine a woman is[,] the more truly can she bring something to legislation.[23]

Using the maternalist language and the concept that the woman's sphere provides sympathetic habits of the heart, Helen expands that sphere to the world of politics for the purpose of strengthening the home by passing legislation supportive of women and children. She gently makes the case that a woman can work outside the home or even hold public office, that women have increased the awareness that we all have responsibility for one another, and that women have important contributions to make in the legislative arena. These are themes she returned to often. In New York a few years later she stressed the need for real women officeholders, not women imitating men:

> It was the womanly woman who was needed in politics, not a creature recreated in the image of man . . .
>
> They say of a woman sometimes that "She thinks like a man" . . . They think it is a compliment, but I never could see the reason why. A woman like that is not essentially the kind of a woman needed for political work.[24]

On another occasion she added, "I have no patience with the people who say that woman's place is the home and not in politics. If you wish to conserve the family you must consider the grocers' combines. There is not a tiny arch of the home circle that is not touched with politics. To keep the home inviolate you must go into politics."[25] Though the connection was sometimes stretched, Helen understood that women's sphere had to reach beyond the home to protect the home, or more accurately, to address issues women were concerned about.

All her adult life, Helen wrote articles and gave lectures on woman suffrage. In her articles she reviews some of the peculiarities of unjust voting rights laws. For example, eight states allowed alien men to vote if they had taken out their "first papers" to become citizens. But a woman citizen who married an alien lost her citizenship under US law, whereas an alien woman who married an American man became an American citizen, apparently under the theory that a wife is a mere appendage to her husband rather than a citizen in her own right.[26]

People who opposed suffrage, she said in her old hometown of Providence, would have opposed any expansion of the right to vote: "Woman's suffrage . . . is the next step in human evolution . . . The only opposition comes from people who were left over from yesterday . . . Find an opponent of woman's suffrage and you will find a Tory, you will find someone who would have opposed Gladstone's reform innovations and all other suffrage extensions to men in the past generations."[27]

There was an economic justice agenda among the suffragettes, too. Of course, including lower-class women expanded the number of women who could prevail upon the men in their families to vote for woman suffrage. Helen shared the objectives of those who spoke for economic justice, in later years quoting with approval the views of Jane Addams: "Jane Addams and Lillian Wald are . . . defining politics as the art of relating people justly to each other . . . Though the intervention of women in public affairs has brought about improvements in civic conditions, they have not gone much deeper than wall-paper improvements after all. They have rarely even grazed the economic foundations of our House of Life."[28]

She frequently argued for economically just reforms. In the same article she cited the example of women officials who capably manage public services in some cities while in other cities they are "protected" from such cares. In the latter cities, she observed women sweeping the streets. She commented wryly that "a society that does not protect women from such sweeping should not lie awake nights planning how to protect them from bossing sweepers." In this way she criticized the doublethink required to put idealized women—potential mothers—on a pedestal while employing real women in the most physically demanding (and low-paid) work.

In talking about the suffrage efforts in factory towns and cities, she stressed the economic importance of the vote for working women to improve their situations and the growing awareness among upper- and middle-class women of the plight of poor lower-class working women:

> The greatest discovery of the nineteenth century from the stand-point of women suffragists was the discovery by woman of herself. In the twentieth century was made a still more important discovery. The "other woman" was discovered in the factory, in the steam laundry, in the sweat shop, competing with men who have a full right to the ballot. Eight million women are wage-earners. They constitute 8,000,000 reasons why the ballot should be granted to woman. And now woman, like Peter the Hermit, is seeking the Holy Sepulchre. The movement is part of the present day world-wide spiritual and democratic movement.[29]

When Helen became a state senator, she did everything she could to improve the wages of these poor working women.

Helen traveled extensively, especially after her election, promoting woman suffrage in nearly every state in the country as the states voted on the issue one by one. After a lecture trip, Helen described the mass suffrage meetings with a nearly religious fervor:

> One who has not been in the midst of it cannot realize the significance and zeal of the great woman's movement going on in the East . . .

I never realized it. The fervidness of it. The white flame that burned in its midst inspired me. I heard women preach with the same white flame with which Peter the Hermit preached his crusade. Once I wished I had lived in the stirring times; in the times when men fought with the sword for their ideals and gave their lives for causes dear to their souls. I thought of these times as I saw these women burning with the spirit of a cause to them as dear as life itself.

One of the things that impressed me was the wonderful feeling of sex loyalty and solidarity. I saw this in Baltimore, where young women with faces like opening flowers and eyes shining like the stars of Bethlehem marched together with women worn by toil; I saw it in New York; I saw it everywhere.[30]

Helen was moved to action by the fervor of these women.

THE ROLE OF WOMEN'S CLUBS

Women's clubs in Denver in the late nineteenth and early twentieth centuries not only promoted suffrage; they also prepared women for the vote, helped pass legislation important to women, and promoted the election of women candidates. This activism provided women with the skills they needed to follow politics and to participate effectively in civic life. Helen recognized the importance of the club movement to women's political success in her book *Preparing Women for Citizenship:* "Women were preparing for full citizenship through the club movement. They learned cooperation . . . [When an issue comes up] she begins to look about for her team."[31]

In the past, Helen observed, women had actually been "trained away from a sense of responsibility for civic and state and national affairs."[32] In contrast, in this era membership in women's clubs active in civic life was particularly strong in Colorado, where the proportion of club women to the general population surpassed every other state in the union. The Fortnightly Club started the Woman's Club of Denver. There was also a strong State Federation of Woman's Clubs.[33] Each of the women's clubs had legislative committees that sent representatives to the Legislative Council of the Colorado Federation of Women's Clubs. The legislators seemed to understand the importance of the women's clubs because the council met weekly during the General Assembly session in a room set aside for its use in the State Capitol. "The whole broad area of children industrially and educationally" was the focus of much of the council's activity.[34]

The organizer of the Woman's Club of Denver was Sarah Platt Decker, president from 1894 to 1899. At the end of her term the club had grown to 920 members, and it eventually exceeded 1,000 members. (By 1911 the Federation of Women's Clubs had spread to all forty-eight states and boasted over 1 million members.)[35] The club started the first traveling library, fought for equal guardianship for children, and campaigned for the creation of the State Home for Dependent and Neglected Children. From 1909 through 1913 the club's legislative committee endorsed twenty-one bills, of which eleven became law.[36] Helen joined in 1912 and continued to be a member through 1918.[37] Decker is particularly important to this story because she persuaded Helen to run for the state senate and had even promised to be her campaign manager before her sudden death.[38]

Helen was a member of several other clubs that formed an important part of her political base. She had been a member of the Wellesley Club since its founding in 1899, as was Anna Wolcott, the founder of the school where Helen taught.[39] Both Helen and Ewing Robinson were members of the Artists' Club, a predecessor of the Denver Art Museum, at least until 1908–1909. She was not listed that year as a member of the Wellesley Club, though she was listed as a member of the Monday Literary Club (Helen was president in 1911–1912) and the Writers' Club.[40] In the 1908 *Who's Who in Denver Society,* there is no indication that Ewing was a member of the Denver Club, the University Club, or the Denver Country Club, where membership was generally limited to men.[41] It appears that the Robinsons were not members of the most prestigious social circles, even though Helen was very active in several clubs.

Helen's most important club activity was the Denver Woman's Press Club (DWPC), which is particularly interesting to current members of the still flourishing club. Helen was not quite a founding member, as the club began in 1898 and she did not join until May 7, 1899,[42] but the contacts she made in the club were probably very important to her political career. Among the founding members were Minnie J. Reynolds, *Rocky Mountain News* political writer; Helen Marsh Wixson, the first woman state superintendent of public instruction; newspaper reporter Alice Polk Hill, the only woman delegate to the committee to draft a charter for the City and County of Denver in 1904; Minnie Peck Hall Krauser, reporter for the *Denver Republican* and then society editor of the *Denver Times*; and Lue Ellen Teters, later editor of the *Delineator.*[43] Membership in the DWPC was limited to thirty-five active members and fifteen associate members, at least in 1901.[44]

As long as Helen was in Denver, with the exception of the years she served in the state senate, she was active in the DWPC. In 1901 she spoke on "recent fiction" for one program, for which the announcement quoted Emerson ("Our reading is mendicant and sycophantic"). In the following club year she presented a program called "Art for Life's Sake." In 1902 she chaired the Program and Printing Committee, and in 1904 she provided a program mysteriously titled "F.W.W. on Critics."[45]

Her contributions to the club were recognized when she was elected president in 1906. In January 1907 she presented a program on George Bernard Shaw's latest work. Later that month the members of the club gave her a steamer rug before her departure for Italy. Leaving behind her husband and Alcyon, her ten-year-old stepdaughter, she was apparently gone from January to August because others presided at the meetings. Her absence created some awkwardness for the club, as she was supposed to host a reception at her home at 1222 Gaylord, though she wrote that she would not return until about the 15th or 20th of the month (unspecified). The location had to be changed. In October 1907 the club celebrated President's Day, but Mrs. Robinson was ill, so she sent a written message. More than once, in fact, she was suffering from an unspecified illness at the time of a meeting. In October 1909 flowers were sent to her when she was confined to her home because of illness.[46] As she had no natural children, we can only wonder if any of these illnesses were the result of miscarriages, though she was in her late forties by this time. In spite of her long absence in her first one-year term, she was reelected president of the DWPC twice, serving until 1909.[47]

Helen's activities in the club extended to nearly every kind of service. A January program in 1908 included her presentation of an article on Maeterlinck to be published in *The Bookman*. In March 1909 she read from one of her recently published books, which may have been her adaptation of Harriet Beecher Stowe's *Uncle Tom's Cabin*, published in 1908. She was in charge of "Newspaper Day" in January 1910 when she enlisted three women to talk about militant suffragettes and also engaged State Senator Frank G. Cannon as a speaker. In 1911, for the annual breakfast, she managed to obtain as speakers Enos Mills, US Bureau of Forestry; Hugh O'Neill, editor of the *Denver Times*; and Governor John F. Shafroth, among others. In 1912 not only was she membership chair, assisted by another woman after her election to the senate, but she also spoke at a program called "Recipes for a Happy Life." In that lecture she "emphasized the impersonal note, the sinking of one's individuality in the common interest."[48] Her own service in the legislature and in the community was certainly selfless and directed toward what she believed was the common good, right up until her death from World War I efforts. However, the fact that sinking one's individuality in the common interest was a "recipe for happiness" suggests little reliance for that happiness on her husband and stepdaughter.

Several times Helen was elected the DWPC delegate to the State Federation of Woman's Clubs and the International Press Clubs League, where she was often featured as a speaker.

In April 1908 the club's minutes reflect a dispute between the president, Helen Robinson, and a Mrs. Meyer, who was apparently denied an opportunity to speak by a motion approved by the club at a program meeting when business was not scheduled. At a subsequent business meeting on April 22, letters by Mrs. Meyer and Helen were read explaining the reasons for the meeting. "Mrs. Meyer said she had

been unjustly treated in that her right to speak had been denied her."
It isn't clear just what the dispute was about except that "the show"
the club produced was mentioned. It involved letters published in the
newspapers—some of which were anonymous, some by Mrs. Meyer,
and some by a Miss Harding, whom a handwriting expert exonerated
from having written the anonymous letters. In the end, Mrs. Meyer
was asked to resign from the club because she had insulted the president. It is difficult now to understand what this dispute was about,
but several other members of the club resigned in support of Mrs.
Meyer.[49]

Perhaps the most striking event of Helen's club presidency
occurred in 1908, when the club had to be incorporated to protect
its name, which another group had threatened to appropriate. Helen
hastily obtained a Certificate of Incorporation and filed to preserve
the name "the Denver Woman's Press Club." The minutes refer to the
"stress which existed when the Articles of Incorporation were filed."
The original club had to be dissolved, and the associate members,
who were patrons and not necessarily writers, became members of the
corporation.[50]

All of Helen's service to the club won her the support of a cadre
of influential writers who were crucial to her election. When Helen
was elected, she knew the bills the powerful Federation of Women's
Clubs supported: a workshop for the blind; an eight-hour day for
laundry workers, miners, and women; factory inspections; a free state
employment bureau; a school for the feeble-minded; laws regarding
child labor; and support for traveling libraries.[51] She would address
many of these issues.

HELEN AS WRITER

It was helpful that Helen increased her name recognition through her
writing for local newspapers during the first ten years of her marriage
(1902 to 1912). Because her features and columns were written in a
conversational tone, readers felt they knew her personally, and many of
them probably did. She was editing the book section of the *Saturday*

Magazine of the *Denver Times* by January 10, 1903.[52] In the article in that edition she reviewed more than ten books, including *A Study of Browning's Saul* by Cora Martin McDonald. Her scholarly weekly reviews, which covered nearly a page, indicated that she read a good portion of the many books she mentioned. In one review occasioned by the death of Tolstoy, she compared Tolstoy to St. Augustine. Among other parallels, she said they both declared themselves to have been great sinners, and both rejected an earlier enthusiasm—Augustine the theater, and Tolstoy the novel. Both preached that the noblest thing in life is conscious, voluntary self-sacrifice. Both disapproved of their societies and sought to bring about a better state.[53] There could be no better expression of Helen's own views, although she also suggested that the common good was the goal of the sacrificing individual. This could be a précis of the motivations for her actions.

A review of children's books the Denver librarian suggested as Christmas gifts reveals Helen's preference for imaginative, colorfully illustrated children's books. She didn't like a preachy little fairy in *The Garden of Heart's Delight* by Ida M. Huntington or the pasteurized and denatured witch in *Jackie in Rainbowland* by William L. Hill.[54] In the same article she said, "I am glad to see that stodgy stories in which commonplace little people learn their multiplication tables in an entirely commonplace manner are left as they ought to be, quite outside the pale of the collection, stewing away in their own juices."

Helen's interviews in Europe of the spouses of Maurice Maeterlinck and George Bernard Shaw, as well as of Gabriele D'Annunzio and Marion Crawford, were published in the national magazine *The Scrapbook* in 1907.[55] That was the year Helen sailed to Europe to visit the Owen LeFevres. How she gained access for these interviews is unclear, but they may be at least in part recreated by her, as some of the conversations between Helen and these women in an era before tape recorders could not have been reproduced precisely. The articles emphasized the women's role in supporting and protecting their famous husbands. The interview with Madam Maeterlinck included a discussion of her husband's *Ariane and Bluebeard*. In the story, Bluebeard holds captive a number of women who do not depart, even when they are rescued. Madam Maeterlinck explained that the women who remain behind in the dungeon, satisfied with silk and jewels, represent the old-fashioned woman, whereas Ariane, who presumably leaves, is not fascinated by such baubles. She represents the modern woman, whom Helen would have admired.

On this trip, Helen also visited Beatrice Harraden, met May Sinclair and Alice Meynell, and talked with Henrik Ibsen.[56]

Helen had a deep sympathy for the poor and oppressed, which she expressed in the dedication to her first book, an adaptation for children of *Uncle Tom's Cabin* by Harriet Beecher Stowe, which came out in 1908. She dedicated it to her stepdaughter, Alcyon, who was about twelve years old.[57] In explaining her reasons for publishing this adaptation long after slavery had ended, she argued that other forms of slavery still existed and the book was necessary to teach children to pity suffering:

> The greatest evils in our country were not swept away by the Emancipation Proclamation. Just such evils as are described in "Uncle Tom's Cabin" are, to be sure, no longer possible here. But there are even worse forms of slavery than those Mrs. Stowe tells about in her book. There are many cruel masters who still hold the lash.
>
> The boys and girls of to-day, in the South as in the North, will, as men and women, have to do their part in destroying these other forms of slavery.
>
> Every story these children read, which moves their sympathy for the poor and wretched, whether black or white, will help to fit them for the work that lies before them. Every book that teaches them to pity suffering and to hate cruelty, will bring nearer the dawn of a new Emancipation morning.
>
> Such a book, most surely, is "Uncle Tom's Cabin."[58]

In a mostly lighthearted article about the Democratic National Convention held in Denver in 1908, Helen became deadly serious when she talked about children working in sweatshops. The speaker, a Mr. Bell,

gave the Republican party full credit for its amiable plank
in regard to child labor. Then he went on to declare that the
Democratic party is not content with reforming sweat shops, but
is determined to reform the economic conditions that are sending children into the sweat shops. Whereat the big convention
went wild. And somehow it seemed to me as if that wild roar of
approval was echoed by pale baby lips in sweltering cotton mills,
that little coal-grimed hands in murky mines joined in the burst of
applause.[59]

The images of baby lips are typical of Helen's use in her writing
of references from the everyday lives of wives and mothers, but she
avoided pure sentimentality with the deadly seriousness of her message. In another article the next day Helen proudly described the
way the few women delegates led the spontaneous demonstration for
William Jennings Bryan by carrying their state flags about the auditorium and up to the platform. Again, she argued for the time when
women could ask for legislation to take children out of the mines and
factories, legislation that would succeed because women in all states
would be "sovereign"—that is, they would have the vote.[60]

Another of Helen's features, a profile of Eugene C. Stevens, headmaster of Clayton School for forty years, did approach sentimentality. The article included precious quotes from young children, such as
calling the headmaster "a big brother of the joyous heart," but it also
presented more of Helen's educational philosophy when she declared
that "what our schools cry aloud for is not a fuller development of
brains, but the currents that drive the brains. Power is not knowledge,
but cultivated emotions."[61] Helen believed that one way to develop
empathy for others was through literature (as seen in her dedication
of *Uncle Tom's Cabin* above), not through math. If children developed
sympathy for the suffering of others, she reasoned, they would do all
they could to improve the lives of the downtrodden. Later, as a legislator, she demonstrated her empathy through her bills promoting
economic justice, especially for women.

Not only was Helen a feature writer and book critic, she was also
called upon to review Sarah Bernhardt's performance when the actress

came to Denver in 1911. Helen commented in her generally favorable review that Bernhardt was getting older, but the actress chose her two plays in Denver appropriately.[62] One was *L'Aiglon, the Eaglet,* by Rostand, in which Bernhardt played Napoleon; the other was *Mdm. X,* reviewed by another writer.

The profile Helen wrote about Agnes Riddle, a member of the Colorado House of Representatives, is especially interesting because it was published in 1912, the same year Helen was elected to the state senate.[63] This amazing woman rose at 3:00 a.m. each day to get breakfast for the deliverymen of her family's dairy. Then she prepared the family breakfast for her sister's six orphaned children, whom she was raising, and finally started dinner before she rode a wagon to the nearest electric car line for the six-mile trip to the State Capitol. She was trained as a nurse and often helped her neighbors with health problems. As the secretary and organizer of the Colorado Grange, she gained a political base. Though elected as a Republican, she was not afraid to vote with the Democrats on measures she liked. She said that some of her success was the result of her not belonging to a clique and not sponsoring any bill unless she knew exactly how it mattered to her constituents.

One reason Agnes Riddle sought reelection, she said, was to establish demonstration farms where nurses could teach sanitation to farmwomen, for whom typhoid was still a threat. Mrs. Riddle said she worked with the Grange to overcome the terrible loneliness of ranch life, which drove many women into insane asylums. Though that loneliness has been somewhat alleviated today by modern communication and transportation, it is still a reality of rural life.

At the end of May 1909, Ewing and Helen made a trip to Steamboat Springs, taking advantage of the new passenger cars on the recently completed railroad built by David Moffat.[64] This trip is one of the few clues to Helen's marital situation during a period in which the couple moved frequently. After Ewing bought a house at 1441 Josephine Street in east central Denver, the couple lived there for a year. Then for some reason they moved to Hotel Metropole on Broadway for two years, although Helen is not listed there in 1905 as she was in

1904. Perhaps the move to the hotel was caused by financial difficulties related to Ewing's disbarment procedure. They returned to 1441 Josephine Street and remained there until Ewing sold the property in November 1908. From 1909 to 1919 they lived at 1222 Gaylord until Helen, who had bought the lot in 1903 before the house was built, sold the property.[65]

From 1907 to 1911–1912, Helen is listed in the *Denver Woman's Press Club Year Book* as Mrs. Ewing Robinson. Then, rather strangely, from 1912–1913 through 1920–1921, in the same publication she becomes Mrs. Helen Ring Robinson, dropping her husband's first name. That was unusual for a married woman at the time, though it may have been for political reasons.[66] In 1920 she was living at the Huntington Hotel at 1624 Grant Street. At her death in 1923, Helen was living at the Oakes Home and Ewing was living at 1035 Emerson. Helen's health, Ewing's health, or both might explain why they were living apart at the end of her life.

One possible cause of conflict between Helen and Ewing was the fact that Helen was a Democrat while Ewing was a Republican, though she said he was "indifferent to politics" and that she usually persuaded him to vote as she did on certain measures.[67]

OTHER WOMEN CANDIDATES

While Helen's name recognition was growing through her writing, others were demonstrating that women could be elected to office and could serve with distinction. A few women ran for office as soon as they could after Colorado's male voters granted them the right to vote in 1893. In 1894 Mrs. Clara Cressingham of Denver, Mrs. Frances S. Klock of Denver, and Mrs. Carrie Clyde Holley of Pueblo—all Republicans—were elected to the house in the 10th General Assembly. Progressive Frances Klock, the head of an institution called the Home for Incorrigible Girls, had worked for woman suffrage.[68] These women immediately began passing bills important to women. In the first General Assembly that had women representatives, the legislature created a state home for dependent and neglected children. Mrs. Holley passed a bill raising the age of consent to marry to eighteen years to protect girls. A very important act made married women the joint guardians of their children, with powers and duties equal to those of their husbands.[69]

Women also sponsored bills that, unfortunately, failed: civil service reform, state control of liquor traffic, indeterminate sentences, and a primary law designed to abolish the abuses of conventions.[70]

In each subsequent election, a few women followed these pioneers into the house. In 1896 Mrs. Martha B. Conine, nonpartisan; Mrs. Olive Butler, Republican; and Mrs. Evangeline Heartz, Populist, were elected. In the 1897 session the state established an industrial school for girls, prohibited the sale of cocaine, and abolished capital punishment. In 1898 three women were again elected. In the following session a compulsory-education law for all children between ages eight and fourteen was passed, and kindergartens and county high schools were created.[71] Of course, the women could not pass such legislation alone, but they were a force for these laws.

There was a woman candidate for lieutenant governor in 1894 on a minor party ticket.[72] By 1900 ten women had been elected to the house and four women had served in the statewide elected office of state superintendent of public instruction, a rather important office because the superintendent was a member of the three-person board of education, which included the secretary of state and the attorney general.[73]

After the 1898 election the number of women elected tapered off to such an extent that only one woman was elected in 1900 and in 1902 and none after that until 1908, when one was elected. Though there was only one woman in the house in the 1903 session, some major protections for women and children were passed. An act made the father and mother their children's joint and equal heirs. Employment of any child under age sixteen in any unhealthy or dangerous occupation was prohibited. In addition, women were limited to working eight hours a day in any position for which they had to stand. Also, men were compelled to support their children.[74]

The 1910 Special Session, with only one woman legislator, Alma Lafferty, referred a measure to the November ballot that was very important for women because it provided for the direct primary election. After it passed, conventions controlled by party bosses, who usually dictated a list of male candidates, were augmented by a combination of candidates selected by conventions and candidates added by petition—a strategy women could use to get on the ballot. This system remains in force in Colorado to this day. The new primary law also required parties to elect a committeeman and committeewoman in each precinct. Because the precinct committee people make up each county central committee, this resulted in many more women voting at the county assemblies, which tended to lead to the designation of more women candidates for the primary ballot.[75] (In Denver nearly 50 percent of caucus attendees and primary voters were women.)[76]

In 1910 four women were elected to the house, and in 1912, when Helen was elected to the senate, two women were elected to the house. At the end of Helen's term, in the 1916 election Agnes Riddle, who had served in the house, was elected to the senate. Then, amazingly, no woman was elected to the senate again until 1940, when Eudochia Bell Smith, Democrat, began two terms.[77] Even after Helen's election, serving in the senate was rare for Colorado women during the first half of the twentieth century.[78]

A few women won other elective offices, though, early in the century. Ellis Meredith served as vice-chair of the Democratic State Central Committee from 1904 through 1908.[79] In 1910 she was elected to the Denver Election Commission as the nominee the women's Public Service League suggested to the Citizens' Party.[80] A fighter for woman suffrage, Mary C.C. Bradford, who had taught at North High School and the Wolcott School and held a literature chair at the University of Colorado, was one of only two women delegates to the Democratic National Convention held in Denver in 1908. (The other one was from Utah.) Later, she received the Democratic designation to run for superintendent of public instruction. She was elected and served from 1913 to 1921 and 1923 to 1927.[81]

Anna Wolcott, the founder of the school where Helen last taught, was a Republican candidate for regent of the University of Colorado in 1910, an election she won. She was the sister of the late US senator Edward O. Wolcott.[82]

HELEN'S FIRST CAMPAIGNS

An important issue for progressives was the public ownership of major utilities because, they argued, the public would receive cheaper and better services. In 1906 in Denver, the gas and electric franchise was renewed in a narrow, fraudulent election.[83] To prevent another victory for a monopoly in the spring of 1910, Denver women voters formed the Public Service League, which cooperated with the Citizens' Party to oppose granting a twenty-year franchise to a streetcar company. Most meetings were secret, which frightened the machine politicians. Helen attended a mass meeting on May 3, 1910, at which Sarah Platt Decker presided.[84]

The progressive Citizens League was formed in 1910 to spur the effort to create a municipal water department.[85] In cooperation with the league, Helen spearheaded a grassroots housewives' campaign to prevent the renewal of the private franchise for water service to the city. In this, Helen's first entry into politics, the organization included neighborhood chains of communication, ballot-marking schools, and precinct captains—still the basics of grassroots political organization. The campaign was successful. Helen told the *Literary Digest* editor that it was "a question of household economies . . . and public morality, too. They wished to break the alliance between big business and crooked politics which had done so much to hurt Denver in the past."[86] In the May election voters approved municipal ownership for the water service, as well as initiative and referendum powers for the city.[87]

That same year, Helen decided to run for the office of state superintendent of public instruction, which had been designated "the woman's office" by suffrage leaders and male politicians alike.[88] It seems strange to us today that women accepted the idea that only one office should be open to them and that all the capable women would compete for that one office. Two other women also fought for the nomination: the incumbent Katherine Cook and Mary C.C. Bradford. The *Rocky Mountain News,* whose readers favored Helen (at least in the letters that were printed), sent a flood of glowing letters of support to the paper that appeared under the headline "What Women Are Saying about Mrs. Robinson."[89] Here are some samples:

> The state superintendency of public instruction is one of the most important offices in the gift of the people, and a woman thoroughly qualified by virtue of intellectual equipment and years of experience as a teacher is needed for intelligent supervision of our state's schools. Such a woman is Mrs. Helen Ring Robinson, and women should rally to her support independently of the party standard they customarily raise.
>
> —ELSIE SEELYE PRATT

> With all her brains she is pre-eminently a tactful, womanly woman, and it is this unusual combination of talent and culture with sweet womanliness that commands the admiration and love of all who come in contact with her. Of her talents as a writer and public speaker, I say nothing; they are admitted by all to be of a high order . . . In all the relations of life, as teacher, wife, mother, clubwoman and housekeeper she is the model woman who will, as you say "reflect distinction upon the office and honor upon the womanhood of Colorado."
>
> —MRS. EDWARD F. HERMANNS

One woman complained that the men had not learned anything from the example of the Citizens' Party, which allowed women to pick their own candidate. But just as all offices should have been open to women, all voters—including the men—should have had a role in selecting the candidates. This focus on one office, however, did guarantee the election of at least one woman.

Carrie Ward wrote:

> We hoped it would be a lesson to the other parties, but it seems as if they are going to try and do things the same old way, and a bunch of men get together somewhere and decide what offices they will let the women have, and then choose the women to fill

them, regardless whether they suit the women or not. We've had just about enough of it, and we're about ready to stand with a party that treats us with some respect.

There are a lot of women, Democrats and Independents and some Republicans, that would like to vote for Helen Ring Robinson, but they tell me the women won't have any say about the nomination for state superintendent . . . It's a great help to a ticket to have women on it that women like to work for, feel will represent them, and do the state credit . . . When one like Mrs. Robinson is in the field the men ought to quit and let the women nominate somebody that will represent them.[90]

The incumbent Katherine Cook had the support of the teachers' association leader, while Helen received continued favorable comments from the *Rocky Mountain News*. A *News* reporter said of Helen, "The conduct of Colorado woman politicians has been a subject for deep study for the Eastern writer. Mrs. Helen Ring Robinson, a woman of superior education and experience in instruction, brilliant, cultured, quiet, reserved, bears no resemblance to the stereotyped idea of the woman politician."[91] Unfortunately for Helen, at the Democratic Convention in September, Cook won the nomination. (This was just before passage of the law allowing a candidate to put his or her name on the ballot by petition.) Afterward, the reporter again commented on Robinson's candidacy: "Mrs. Helen Ring Robinson, a woman whose culture and experience in the profession of instruction places her at the head of brilliantly educated women in Colorado, was pushed aside by the machine."[92]

Such "earned press," as opposed to paid advertising, could only help Helen's political career. It added to the reputation she had already gained as a lecturer and writer.

In the 1910 general election, Democratic women who were offended by the way the Democratic candidate for superintendent of instruction had been chosen bolted the party to support the Republican candidate, Helen Marsh Wixson. Following a bipartisan campaign led by Helen Ring Robinson's ally Helen Loring Grenfell, Wixson won the general election.[93] The fact that Wixson also had been president of the Denver Woman's Press Club from 1899 to 1904 no doubt helped her campaign.

Helen referred to this disappointing and very public defeat in a November column when she said she had given up politics two months before "aided and abetted by my fellow Democrats in convention assembled."[94] She went on to talk about a need to fill that void in her life and then turned to reviewing books. Helen did not give up her political activity for long. Actually, this first run for office probably helped build her name recognition and the widespread support she needed for her state senate race two years later.

FRACTURED PARTIES OF 1912

By August 1912 Helen's pride had recovered sufficiently for her to announce that she was a candidate for the Democratic nomination for state senate.[95] According to her later comments to the *Rocky Mountain News,* Sarah Platt Decker encouraged her to run by promising to be her campaign manager, before Decker's untimely death.[96] As the short campaign unfolded in the late summer and fall of 1912, the nomination process was confused by deep divisions in both parties. Amazingly, the divisions improved Helen's chances at the polls.

The machine, which the *Rocky Mountain News* called the "Evans-Speer Gang," still smarting from the defeat in the municipal election that spring, did its best to control the regular Democratic Denver county convention on August 8. It succeeded, with the notable exceptions of the nominations of Judge Ben Lindsey for the Juvenile Court and Helen Ring Robinson for the state senate. A candidate needed 10 percent of the delegates to make the ballot; with 180 votes, Helen was the fifth-highest vote getter of ten senatorial candidates, which won her a place on the Democratic ticket in the September primary. Three of these candidates would be selected in the primary to run at large from Denver in the November general election. One of the ten candidates was another woman, Representative Alma Lafferty, who had received just two more votes than Helen.[97]

As Robyn Muncy has pointed out, the women thought of them-selves as running only against the other women, and in a sense they were because voters were possibly willing to elect one woman to the senate as a kind of experiment but not many women.[98] Of course, in the at-large primary and general elections for the Denver seats, they were running against men and women alike. Dora Phelps Buell, an influential woman leader, supported Harriet Wright for that slot. Consequently, she wrote arguments against the nominations of Lafferty and Robinson, even though, technically, all three could have been selected for the three Denver slots.[99]

The day after the Democratic convention, Helen also became the only woman senate candidate on the Progressive Democrats' ticket. This Democratic splinter group, which met from 10:00 in the morning until 5:30 in the evening, bolted the Democratic machine convention but nevertheless nominated some of the same candidates. Helen's nomination was not without opposition, however. A. J. Woodruff opposed her on the grounds that she was not a progressive, which suggests that she did not attend this rump session of the Progressive Democrats. John I. Tierney, C. J. Pitschke (possibly C. G. Pitschke, according to the 1912 *Denver City Directory*), and John Rush defended her. The positions on issues that Helen expressed later as a senator certainly qualified her as a progressive.

The general election ballot shows that the Progressive Democrats also nominated Reuben J. Morris. Morris and Helen have "Democratic Citizens" after their names, apparently to indicate they were placed on the ballot both by the Democratic Party and by petition (Citizens). The Progressive Democrats also granted five places on their slate to women candidates for representative. Because the deadline for filing the petitions was the same day as the Progressive Democrats' convention, the secretary of state kindly stayed open until midnight to accommodate these filings.[100] If the Progressive Democrats had actually formed a separate party, they would have split the Democratic votes.

Alice Rohe of the *Rocky Mountain News* asked Helen just before the primary election why she was running. Her response reflected a great deal of thought and idealism about what women could contribute to the legislative process:

> It is not because I feel that it is merely my right or because there are so many women to be represented, because I am cleverer than a man or because I can do the same thing in the senate as a man, that I desire to be a state senator . . . It is because I am different—that is the keynote. If I could not bring something new to the legislature I would not want to be sent there. I would regard my destiny as remaining at home and devoting myself to Irish crochet.[101]

A "collective motherliness" is what Helen sought to bring to the General Assembly. Rohe continued with praise for Helen, which could not have hurt her chances in the election: "For of all the women who have ever entered the political field in Colorado, none more thoroughly typifies the feminine than Mrs. Robinson. Feminine she is in the finer sensibilities, the quick intuitive understanding, the broad sympathies of life, the knowledge of the application of economic principles to women and to the home."[102]

In the same interview, though, Helen blamed the people who underpay women for the "social evil," the polite term for prostitution, letting voters know she would be a tough fighter for justice for all women.

A Woman's Senatorial League was formed specifically to elect Helen.[103] This was a forerunner of the political committees created today to elect candidates. Rohe of the *Rocky Mountain News* said Helen was conducting her campaign nearly single-handedly except for this organization composed of prominent women. We know, at least, that the committee had stationery printed, as Helen used some of it for a letter to the Hon. Ben Lindsey in December of that year. At the top of the page was a list of women on her campaign committee, including Helen Grenfell, and an endorsement quote from Ellis Meredith of the *Rocky Mountain News:* "Mrs. Robinson has the larger vision and the broader view of affairs so much needed in legislative halls." The reason for organizing the Woman's Senatorial League is clear on the stationery. Under the heading "Woman's Senatorial League" is its purpose:

"The League supports Helen Ring Robinson for State Senator."[104] We don't know whether this league was limited to the women listed or what role it played in Helen's winning the election.

The next unusual activity in the election saga before the primary was a secret meeting of the "Evans-Speer Gang" to endorse the machine candidates on the Democratic primary ballot. The *Rocky Mountain News* raged against a Democratic Party Executive Committee that, it said, was required by law to oversee a fair process for all Democratic candidates—an ideal for the behavior of party officers that many still hold today. "Not without open treachery and grossest violation of its powers can it take sides or express preferences," the angry front-page article shouted in a fever pitch that would not be found even on editorial pages today. The paper listed all the machine-endorsed candidates and urged voters not to vote for them.[105] One of these candidates was the other Democratic woman candidate, Representative Alma Lafferty, while Helen mercifully escaped endorsement by the machine. Some of the "endorsed" candidates were scrambling desperately to keep their names off the list or to keep it secret because they knew it would hurt more than it would help. This endorsement was to be printed on "tickets," what we would now call sample ballots, and distributed to Democrats by machine workers. To counter this move the *Rocky Mountain News* printed a ballot for the primary indicating its endorsed Democratic and Republican candidates. Helen made the "good" *Rocky Mountain News* endorsement list along with Reuben J. Morris and Harry Risley.[106]

After all these machinations, Helen won a great victory in the primary election, the consequence in part of the divisions in the Democratic Party because she received the designation of both the regular party assembly and the rump Progressive Democrats. In addition, she had escaped the kiss-of-death endorsement of the Evans-Speer machine and received the "good guys" endorsement of the *Rocky Mountain News*. The fact that she was one of only two candidates for three slots endorsed by the Progressive Democrats and one of only three candidates endorsed by the *Rocky Mountain News* also helped because for those who were influenced by these organizations, the votes were not split into a larger field of candidates. For those who perceived that a woman candidate was running only against the other woman candidate, Helen, with all these endorsements, was clearly the person most likely to win that seat for women.

In the results of the September primary, the top three Democrats in the Denver contest for the three at-large seats for state senate were Joseph Berry with 4,677 votes, Helen Robinson with just slightly fewer votes at 4,665, and Reuben J. Morris with 4,110 votes.[107]

In the 1912 campaign the Republicans were more divided than the Democrats, both at the national and state levels. Progressive Republicans had hoped the national convention would nominate Teddy Roosevelt for president; they were disappointed when the party went for the incumbent William Howard Taft. After Roosevelt left the party and formed the Bull Moose Progressive Party, Colorado progressives (Republicans) similarly organized a completely separate party.[108] The race for the Colorado governorship illustrates the cost of these divisions to the Republican Party. There were six candidates: a Democrat (Elias Ammons), a Progressive Bull Moose Republican candidate (Edward Costigan), a regular Republican (Clifford Parks), a Socialist (Charles Ahlstrom), a Socialist Labor candidate (Jonathan Billings), and a Prohibition Party candidate (John Ketchum).[109] Just as the split in the national Republican Party elected the Democrat Woodrow Wilson president, the split in the state Republican Party elected the only Democrat on the ballot, Elias Ammons, governor.[110] Because the Colorado Bull Moose Republicans had formally established a new and separate party, their candidates did not run against the "regular" Republican candidates in the primary, which would have pared down the field to one Republican candidate. Even in the state senate races in the general election, there was a regular Republican slate and a Progressive Republican slate.

As a result of that division, the November election was a Democratic landslide. Helen won! The other two Democratic candidates for state senator from Denver also beat the Republican candidates with overwhelming numbers. Helen, in fact, ran first, ahead of all the others. She received 24,836 votes; Joseph S. Berry, 24,282; and Reuben J.

Morris, 24,261, so those three Democrats were elected from Denver. The next-highest, but unsuccessful, candidates were all Progressive Bull Moose Party members: Gail Laughlin, 21,044; J. Irving Carper, 20,065; and Don F. Cowell, 19,948.[111] The Democratic sweep was decisive statewide, giving the Democrats control of the senate 24 to 11, of the house by an overwhelming 52 to 13, and of the governor's office.[112]

There were thirty-two measures on the ballot in the same election, several drafted by progressives Ben Lindsey and Edward Costigan using the newly won power of the initiative. Among those that passed were the women's eight-hour day, mothers' compensation, miners' eight-hour day, a headless ballot (making it harder to vote a straight party ticket), a civil service system, recall of elected officials, and referral of some Colorado Supreme Court decisions to the voters. The laws protecting workers were passed by a coalition of women and labor.[113]

Helen gave credit for her election to the recently deceased Sarah Platt Decker, who had encouraged her to run for office. Decker, Helen commented mysteriously, "kept her promise . . . Somehow, in ways I cannot fathom, by means I may not know, she indeed sent me help." Helen fervently hoped she would prove worthy of that help.[114]

The day after the election, much of the political world was in shock. Progressive Democratic control swept the state all at once, and much to everyone's surprise, for the first time a woman had been elected to the Colorado State Senate, establishing Colorado as a leader in American politics and, indeed, in the world. Many newspaper articles claimed Helen Ring Robinson was the first woman elected to any senate in the country. However, there was an earlier state senator, Martha Maria Hughes Cannon (1857–1932), a Democrat, first elected in Utah in November 1896. She served from 1897 to 1905. She was the fourth of the plural wives of Angus M. Cannon, who ran the same year as his wife for an at-large seat as a Republican but was defeated.[115] Helen, then, was the second woman in the world to be seated as a member of a state senate when she took office in 1913. At that time she was the only woman serving in any state senate. The first woman to serve in the US Congress, Jeanette Rankin, was not elected until 1916, after women in Montana were granted the vote in 1914. (Before 1918 she was gerrymandered out of a seat, an experience with which I am very familiar.)[116] Even the English Parliament did not have a woman member until Countess Constance Markiewicz, who did not actually take her seat, was elected in 1918. Viscountess Nancy Astor was the first woman to take her seat in Parliament after the 1919 election.[117]

Every new legislator learns that the period between the election in November and the beginning of the session, January 2 in 1913, is way too short to prepare all the bills she would like to introduce. Helen, though, managed to introduce many important bills in her first session and quickly became a very effective senator.

3

"The Housewife of the Senate"

Change was in the air when Helen Robinson was elected to the Colorado senate in November 1912. In that same election, reform-minded voters amended the constitution to provide home rule for cities, recall of elected public officers, recall of judicial decisions, prevention of forced political contributions from civil servants, and elimination of straight party-line voting. They also passed statutes limiting miners to six hours of labor per day and limiting women to seven hours per day in manufacturing, mechanical, and mercantile establishments as well as laundries, hotels, and restaurants. They passed the Mothers' Compensation Act to support dependent and neglected children either in the state home or in their own homes. This act provided that a child in the state home who was not adopted within six months should be boarded out to a suitable family, a provision recognizing the greater benefit of home placement over institutional life.[1]

ENTER: A WOMAN SENATOR

Helen's agenda was congruent with the progressive 1912 ballot issues. Just what she had in mind for her four-year term of office was described in maternalist terms in an interview three days after the election. Helen's announced objective was to be "the housewife of the senate"; she was rightfully proud of the competence of most housewives. She said:

> I am going to be the housewife of the senate . . . There will be so many men there that I shall let them look after themselves and I shall take it upon myself to look after the women and children. I wish to be a spokeswoman of the women and children in Colorado in the legislature, and I shall feel honored to introduce any laws drawn up for their welfare and protection . . . I believe a woman who has qualified as a capable mother and housewife can qualify as a capable legislator. I hold my new responsibilities to the people of the state as sacred as I hold my responsibilities to my husband and my daughter.[2]

Her interests, in fact, were broader than the welfare and protection of women and children, but she always felt particularly responsible to them.

When Helen entered the senate, her colleagues had to adjust to the idea of a woman in their midst. The senate chamber remains much the same today as it was then. It is a very intimate marble and wood chamber with only thirty-five small desks arranged in a semicircle facing a raised dais where the president presides. Over the dais is a bank of stained glass windows commemorating pioneer Colorado leaders, all men at the time. As the senators had no other office, much of their work had to be done in the smoky chamber at the same time members of the press, the lobbying corps, and the public circulated on the floor. Over the floor on three sides is a balcony with rows of seats for spectators behind a meticulously polished brass rail. Like the United States Senate, often called the most elite club in the world, it was until that day an exclusively male domain.

Helen later described how the men received her: "At first they were conscious of the fact that one of their members was a woman.

But in a short time they forgot all about that and treated me as one of themselves, which I considered a compliment. The only difference I remarked was that they did remove their hats and cigars when speaking to me."[3]

Helen's election led to an extensive interview by *Rocky Mountain News* reporter Mae Bradley.[4] Senator Robinson, she said, "is a woman who crimps her hair and wears soft, trailing dresses in the house; she believes in fairies, is a good deal of a mystic, who quotes poetry and is an authority on Maeterlinck." Several years earlier, Bradley said, Helen went on a literary trip of European cities where she "mingled" with Henrik Ibsen, Alice Meynell, Elinor Glyn, Beatrice Harraden, May Sinclair, Marion Crawford, and Maeterlinck. (Helen wrote articles on the spouses of several famous men after this trip.)

Helen, Bradley continued, directed the studies of her stepdaughter, Alcyon, now in high school, who was "very proud of her mother's senatorial honors." According to Bradley, Helen loved gardening and would have liked being a farmer. One of her first summers in Colorado, perhaps during her first visit in 1892, she rode and mastered an unmanageable horse at Wagon Wheel Gap. Presumably, Helen herself told the reporter this story.

As for issues the new woman senator would take on, Bradley found her "a sincere champion for all that will protect or preserve the home, the mother, the child or the school." Helen hoped to introduce a minimum wage bill for county schoolteachers because "teaching is the most sacred vocation next to motherhood," she declared. She told Bradley she had also been studying the causes of "the social evil," a euphemism for prostitution, which she believed was the result of the poor wages paid to many women. If society tolerates such low wages, it shares the blame for prostitution, she argued. Her solution was a minimum wage law for women. On this subject Helen told Bradley, "The social evil lies at the door of all of us who consent to women being paid less than they can decently live on. Any industry that doesn't pay women a living wage is a parasitical industry on the social body, and the social evil can never be eradicated by stoning or segregation, but through the paying of a living wage." Helen had been meeting with business girls and women at the YMCA, working on a bill that stipulated that wages would be regulated in different industries by a commission.[5]

When the General Assembly convened on January 1, 1913, the eyes of the nation were on the pioneering woman in the Colorado senate. Even the *Washington Post* covered the event, erroneously calling Helen the first woman senator in the United States. The paper said Helen wore "a fetching dull primrose gown," an example of the longstanding press habit of focusing on what women office holders wear rather than on what they say or do. The other senators "bowed profoundly when they addressed her" as "Mrs. Senator Robinson" to distinguish her from the other (male) Senator Robinson. The men feared they would not be able to smoke in the senate because of her presence, but they were relieved when she said "she would not have the sacred custom broken."[6]

The senate's first task was to elect a president pro tem, who would preside in the absence of the president of the senate, who was at that time the lieutenant governor. Some articles say women and radical Democratic senators promoted Helen for this role. Helen, though, declared "with true senatorial courtesy that the office belonged to a veteran 'holdover' senator, and not to a newcomer."[7] The Democratic anti-machine faction did not want William Adams to be president pro tem, but he was finally elected on the eighteenth ballot after gaining Republican support in exchange for promising he would allow Casimiro Barela to be seated in spite of an unsavory disputed election.[8] Helen received only one vote on the eighteenth and final ballot. One paper declared that the age of chivalry had passed because, "after eloquent nominating speeches by the gallant few," the Democratic senators did not elect Helen Robinson president pro tem.[9]

The president, rather than the senate majority leader as is current practice, probably determined the chairmanships and committee assignments of all members.[10] All the chairs were, like Helen, members of the majority Democratic Party. Helen was appointed chair of the Committee on Education and Educational Institutions, a plum appointment. She also served on the State Institutions and Public

Buildings Committee, the Privileges and Elections Committee, the City and County of Denver Committee, the Judiciary Committee, and, between sessions, on the Special Committee on Institutions.[11]

GOVERNOR'S AGENDA

One of the first events of the General Assembly, as in all sessions, was the January 14 address by the newly elected governor, Elias M. Ammons, who laid out his view of the major issues facing the legislature. Ammons came out against conservation because of its "definition of preserving things in their natural state undeveloped for future generations."[12] He also objected to a scheme to tax federal lands and send the money to the federal government. In contrast, in modern times the federal government sends money to the states, known as Payments in Lieu of Taxes (PILTs), to make up for the taxes states cannot collect on federal lands.

Ammons knew the coal fields were a hotbed of conflict, but perhaps he did not understand how violent it would become the following year when his indecisiveness added to the chaos in the coal fields. He suggested "effective legislation enacted for the preservation of the lives and health of the workers in the coal mines, and the best conservation of coal," which were important issues, but he ignored entirely the need for a better process to settle strikes. The strike in the northern coal fields proved to be one of the major issues of the session.

Ammons had several recommendations for election reforms. Limiting the governor, who was then elected to two-year terms, to one four-year term was one of his progressive ideas. (Colorado now limits the governor to two four-year terms.) Ammons wanted to hold the gubernatorial election in a year when there was no presidential election, which is when that election is scheduled now. Because he believed conventions were still controlled by political trading, he wanted to eliminate the convention piece of the nomination process. Presumably, then, all candidates would gain access to the ballot by petition. Since the legislature had not reapportioned the congressional seats, Colorado had two members of the US Congress elected by districts and two elected at large. Ammons urged the legislature to create four separate districts, which it did.[13] Shortly after his inaugural address, Ammons announced economy moves and cuts in state personnel.[14]

Helen was one of the spokespersons for 200 Democratic women who met with the governor-elect before he was sworn in to urge him to appoint women to high positions. He promised that women would have a fair share of opportunity. Senator Robinson and Representative Frances Lee spoke of the need for unity among Democratic women and promised to look after the interests of the fair sex.[15]

IN DEFENSE OF COLORADO WOMEN

Early in her first session, Helen established herself as a force to be reckoned with. A Colorado senator, John Hecker, had slurred Denver women; specifically he contended that "women in Denver drink more highballs than men," according to a report in a Washington paper.[16] He repeated the calumny in the state senate on February 5 by saying, "Twenty women to one man in Denver drink intoxicating liquor, and they drink more than men." The second statement followed a "vigorous attack by Mrs. Helen Ring Robinson."[17]

Senator Hecker tried to explain that the press had misquoted him. He had been quoting a Washington paper and speaking of the women of Washington, but he didn't have the good judgment to stop there. He added that "while he had not made any such statement heretofore, he was willing to father it and would bring proof if any one wished." Helen's riposte on personal privilege was devastating and bordered on personal attack—not ordinarily allowed in the senate, not even on personal privilege:

> Mrs. Robinson rose to a question of personal privilege this morning and leveled her oratorical guns against Senator Hecker . . . "Mr. President: When I hear a person with vain mouthings multiplying zero by zero I pay no attention to his babblings . . . And as I turn away from such futilities, Mr. President, without hearing them, so

even more surely do I close my ears to all disagreeable, discordant noises of life when their hearing can do me or others no possible good . . .

I say this in explanation of the fact, Mr. President, that ever since my first week in this Senate chamber I have heard practically no single syllable of all the various noises which have been hurtled from desk 31 where sits the senator from the first [Hecker]. When he has begun to speak, Mr. President, I have discussed parliamentary procedure with my native to the right, or I have answered the letter of a constituent—read a bill that was on the calendar—or indulged in some other profitable business.

I take the first opportunity which presents itself . . . to denounce it publicly as a reckless and infamous statement, made in utter disregard of the truth and common decency . . . It may indeed be that in the Street of Forbidden Things, in the red purlieus of lost souls and ruined bodies . . . that here prostitute women do indeed drink more cocktails and highballs than even the prostitute men, their companions . . . If the senator . . . garners his information from the murk and slime of such places, he has no right to spread such information over the records of this honorable body . . . [It is] a means of libelling [*sic*] my sisters and your wives and daughters.[18]

In concluding Helen said "the women of Colorado need no defenses from me . . . And I protest that the women of Colorado are surpassed by none in all true womanly qualities—and that many of them have in addition a breadth of vision, a range of sympathies, far less general among their sisters of Europe or their sisters of the East. The result, I believe, Mr. President, of that equality of citizenship which has been theirs for nearly twenty years."[19]

Helen threatened "to move the expulsion of Hecker from the Senate if it [such a charge] should be repeated." Actually, he did repeat it. There is no record of Helen's motion, so perhaps cooler heads prevailed upon both of them. Such a motion, if she even made it, would probably have been ruled out of order. The next day the staff of the state house sent Helen flowers for her defense of Denver women against Senator Hecker's drinking charge, and a resolution praising her response was passed by the Woman's Senatorial League.[20] She had given notice that insults or even slights against the fairer sex would not go unanswered as long as Mrs. Robinson was in the senate.

One indication of the respect the other senators had for Senator Robinson was her selection to read the Gettysburg Address, the only senate activity on Lincoln's birthday.[21] Presenting the address is a special honor. In the 1990s, when I was in the senate, the Lincoln's birthday memorial address was presented by the senior member, President Pro Tem Harold McCormick, while the senate recessed from its regular business. Then the speech would be "spread upon the journal" for the day. Helen also chaired the Committee of the Whole (the entire senate) on March 17, 1913, and signed the committee's report. This role is sometimes passed among all members and sometimes rotated only among members of the majority party.

Some explanation of legislative procedure might be helpful here. All bills must go through three steps on the floor of each house in addition to passing out of any committees to which they are assigned. These steps are First Reading (or introduction), when the bill is assigned to a committee; Second Reading (or Committee of the Whole), after the bill passes out of committee, which is when most of the floor debate takes place; and, if the bill passes on Second Reading, Third Reading (final passage), which must take place at least one day after Second Reading. In Third Reading a majority of all members elected (not just members present) is required for passage. This takes eighteen votes in the senate and thirty-three votes in the house. The votes of all members are recorded on Third Reading in the journals of each house. If the bill originates in the house, it goes through the process there first and then moves to the senate, and vice versa.

As Helen had promised, she sponsored many bills to improve the lives of women, but she also fought to improve education, to pay men minimum wages, to protect neglected children, and to obtain better care for the mentally ill.

BILLS FOR WOMEN

During the two months between the election and the convening of the session in January, Helen faced the task all new legislators face: determining what bills she would introduce in her first year congruent with the issues she had talked about in her campaign. She had several suggestions from her progressive allies. Two sources of bill proposals were the Woman's Club of Denver and the joint legislative council of the women's clubs, which worked for legislation on issues that affected women and children such as playgrounds, children's gardens, a system of civil service, minimum wage for women, Juvenile Court, traveling libraries, and an industrial home for women.[22]

One source of proposals for bills was Judge Ben Lindsey, who proposed twelve progressive bills for women that inspired several of Helen's bills in this session and in the next regular session in 1915. Among them were bills permitting women to sit on juries, permitting women associate judges in juvenile courts, forbidding the publishing of pictures of young girls charged as delinquents or being held as witnesses against men, supporting the codification of laws pertaining to women and children, creating a state board for child and animal protection, raising the age of majority for girls to twenty-one, and establishing a system of adult probation.[23] He was helpful in writing Helen's bill for a minimum wage for women set for each industry by a commission. He wrote Helen on January 2, 1913, indicating his general interest in legislation for children and his desire that she recommend some of his ideas. He wanted to meet with her at lunch or some evening.[24] A letter he wrote to her a few weeks later made it clear that he was the major architect of her bill on a minimum wage for women. He had studied the Wisconsin and Massachusetts laws and determined that the Massachusetts version was "just about as good a law as we can well propose at this time." He discussed the possible elimination of a separate commission but the absolute necessity of having the State Bureau of Labor Statistics involved with clerical help that would require $1,500 a year. He concluded that "I think you are safe in introducing the bill at once."[25]

The bill inspired by Judge Lindsey (SB 147) provided for a wage commission of three, including at least one woman, with full powers to investigate working conditions and to determine minimum wages for women and minor employees in a wide range of industries. The bill sat so long on the calendar, even though it was a "platform bill," that Helen said she was growing weary of further postponement. Women anxious for its passage were crowding the senate every day.[26] It passed out of the senate on March 6,[27] but it gained the opposition of at least five of Denver's department stores that wanted one statewide minimum wage, which they assumed would be lower than a wage set just for Denver. Helen said that many women and girls in Denver were paid less than a living wage, as low as four dollars a week. When the girls protested, their employers made insulting innuendos that "good looking girls ought to get extra money from gentlemen friends."[28]

Progressives recognized that the low wages paid to women contributed to the rise of prostitution. However, Denver mayor Henry J. Arnold's solution to the problem of prostitution was to suddenly announce that all the women would be driven from Market Street; they all departed. When he was asked what would become of them, he replied, "I don't know; they will have to take care of themselves." Denver's first policewoman, Josephine Roche, wrote that her survey showed that 50 percent of the girls who turned to prostitution were driven by economic necessity, though some were just worn out and weary. She urged the Woman's Club of Denver to oppose legislation creating a segregated district for prostitutes. Under public pressure, Governor Ammons promised to investigate the working and living conditions of working girls in Colorado right after the session ended.[29]

Because Helen's minimum wage bill appeared to be in danger in the house, Representative Agnes Riddle called for a legislative investigation. The house sponsor, Representative Frances Lee, did not think Helen's bill would accomplish enough or that the title was broad enough to allow the amendments the house wanted to add.[30] The opposition to the bill was denounced by Representatives Lee and Riddle and Senator Robinson, as was the merchants' plea for a six-dollar-per-week wage for eighteen- to twenty-year-olds. There was friction between the two houses over the bill, even between the women members in the house. Representative Lee also charged that the senate was liable to let partisan prejudice and interhouse jealousy tie up the bill. Senate Democrats objected to the sponsorship in the house of an outstanding representative, Agnes Riddle, because she was a Republican, so Representative Riddle withdrew her name from the bill.[31]

Helen's bill on minimum wages finally passed the house and senate on April 14, 1913, the day before adjournment.[32] As he considered whether to sign the bill, Governor Ammons met with representatives of the big department stores, promising to meet with representatives of working women and minors as well. He signed the bill on May 14, just within the thirty days allowed.[33]

When the wage-setting process Helen put in place in 1913 is compared to the very modest minimum wage law now in effect, the broad sweep of its provisions is striking. The bill created the State Wage Board, a three-person board appointed by the governor to investigate industries in which wages were believed inadequate "to supply the necessary cost of living, maintain them [women employees] in health, and supply the necessary comforts of life." The board was to propose a minimum wage for women and minors in that industry in specific geographic areas. Hearings were then to be held on the proposed wage. An employer could appeal the wage determination to the district court. Employers who violated the minimum wage law could be fined up to $100 and spend up to three months in jail. A smaller fine prevented the discharge of employees who testified, an early whistle-blower protection provision. Special minimum wages were set for women who were "physically defective."[34]

A later Robinson bill, SB 471, would have provided for a minimum wage for women in industrial occupations, but it did not pass. Perhaps a second bill was introduced because the first bill was held up by an unfriendly committee chairman.[35]

Though there was a national campaign for a minimum wage for women, starting with a 1910 speech by Florence Kelly to the National Conference of Charities and Corrections, such bills were harder to pass than working-hour limitations. In fact, no such laws were passed until the Massachusetts law in 1912. In 1913 eight states passed minimum wage laws, and fifteen states eventually did so. In most areas labor opposed these laws because it preferred strikes as the tool to increase wages, but in Colorado representatives of women laborers worked with women's club members to pass the women's minimum wage bill. In any event, the passage of this bill was an amazing achievement. A state American Federation of Labor press release praised the women's clubs and women members of the state legislature for their support of labor bills. (The effort ended in 1923 because the Colorado Supreme Court ruled by a vote of five to three that a minimum wage for women was unconstitutional.)[36]

Several of the bills Helen sponsored or cosponsored were of special interest to housewives. On SB 84, which entitled the state to acquire smelters, sugar factories, flour and feed mills, and canning factories with $4 million in bonds, Helen was only a cosponsor—the seventh senator to sign on to the bill. The unsuccessful bill was sponsored by Senator B. F. Carver.[37] This bill may have been a threat to food monopolies that Helen did not expect to pass, but it was consistent with her earlier campaign against the renewal of another monopoly—a water company's Denver franchise.

The idea of the bill was that the state would acquire at least one each of the named entities (smelter, sugar mill, and so on) and "protect and develop them." The state would also insist on railroad transportation rates that were no more than reasonable compensation and on abattoirs (slaughterhouses) placed at various points around the state to save the added cost of shipping livestock to Chicago to be slaughtered and then shipping the meat back to Colorado.

Housewives would also have appreciated two of Helen's bills on pure food, SB 111 and SB 112, though they did not pass. The first prohibited the manufacture, sale, storage, or transportation of adulterated or misbranded foods and drugs and provided for a food and drug commission. The second bill provided for the sanitation of bakeries, canneries, packing houses, and so on, wherever food was prepared.[38] Helen voted for another successful bill on a similar topic, SB 210, by Senator Sherman S. Bellesfield.[39] The fact that such bills were needed suggests the questionable purity of many foods offered for sale. Although a federal law on pure food and drugs had passed, it only applied to food in interstate commerce.

Helen believed that justice required that women be allowed to serve on juries. She was encouraged in this effort by Judge Lindsey. In a letter to Representative Agnes Riddell [*sic*] early in the session, Judge Lindsey revealed that he was promoting five bills. Among them was the provision that women should be allowed to serve on juries, which he said Helen would sponsor in the senate, and he urged Representative Riddell [*sic*] to sponsor the bill in the house.[40] Juries made up entirely of men regularly determined the guilt or innocence of both men and women. A Juvenile Court judge, Lindsey probably also believed women would be more understanding of children's problems and be less likely to send them to detention facilities. Helen's bills on this subject—all unsuccessful—were SB 52, Constitutional Amendment to Section 23 of Article II of the Constitution; SB 482, Fixing Qualification of Jurors; and SB 483, Amendment to the Constitution, Article XI, Concerning Right of Trial by Jury.

SB 52 would have permitted three-fourths, as opposed to all, of a jury to find a verdict in civil cases, and it proposed a very modern view of the criminally insane, who were not to be tried unless and until they regained their sanity. It also provided for a thirteenth, alternate juror. After an amendment, women were to be allowed to sit on juries unless they asked to be excused on the plea of sex. On January 31 the first vote on the constitutional amendment lost by one vote, 23 to 11.[41] As a constitutional amendment, SB 52 needed a two-thirds vote, or twenty-four votes, but it died on Third Reading—even after reconsideration—on a vote of 21 to 12 with two absent.[42] Helen, as always, was ahead of her time. Modern women are surprised to learn that the Colorado constitutional amendment to allow women to sit on juries did not pass until 1944.[43]

When SB 52 was defeated on the first senate vote, Helen gave notice of a motion to reconsider.[44] Her vote was changed to a "nay" vote in the *Senate Journal,* leading to a two-hour debate the next day because she was upset that her "nay" vote would make it look as if she had changed her mind about her own bill. Her charge that the *Journal* record was false was denied by President Stephen R. Fitzgarrald.[45] Perhaps she did not understand that ordinarily one must be on the prevailing side—in this case the negative side—to move to reconsider, as those familiar with parliamentary procedure would know. Thus her initial "yea" vote needed to be changed to a "nay" vote and recorded that way in the *Journal*. Helen even tried for a second reconsideration of the bill, but that was properly ruled out of order as reconsideration is only allowed once. At least one paper believed the provision in the same bill to allow three-fourths of the jury to rule in civil cases was defeated "by the corporations which bitterly feared any changes in the laws on juries that would wipe out the practice of preventing verdicts for damages [against corporations] by 'getting' one juror [on the side of the corporation] and putting the victims to the expense of long litigation." A bill for a constitutional amendment to permit women to serve as jurors, HB 708 by Representatives Lee and Riddle, was killed in the house by the adoption of an adverse Constitutional Amendments Committee report on February 27.[46]

Helen's SB 482 would not only have permitted women to sit on juries but would also have prevented discrimination against any person who spoke "Spanish or Mexican," based on the claim that they could not understand the English language. On March 1 the Judiciary Committee referred SB 482 to the floor, which is the last reference to it in the *Journal*.[47]

Helen's SB 483 closely resembled SB 52 in that it allowed women to serve as jurors and provided that nine of the twelve members of a grand jury could find an indictment. On February 18 the Committee on Constitutional Amendments referred the bill to the floor without recommendation, suggesting a lack of support in the committee.[48] After that, the bill isn't mentioned again.

BILLS TO IMPROVE EDUCATION

In this era, many rural Colorado schools met for very short sessions because school ended when the county ran out of money to pay the teachers, who were usually women. Setting a minimum number of months for schools to be open was essential because some districts had shortened the school year to as little as two or three months. In addition, teachers needed more adequate pay to be attracted to, and remain in, rural schools. In response to these problems, Helen proposed a minimum salary of $500 a year for public school teachers. When Helen mentioned such a bill to Mae Bradley, she told her that "the teacher molds the thoughts, aspirations and ideals of the pupil much as the potter molds the clay."[49] Her SB 83 also established county boards of education. Both provisions were Democratic platform bills, suggesting that Helen was attuned to the major issues articulated by her party and that the party members trusted her to carry major bills.[50]

When the Committee of the Whole reported on this bill, Helen moved to divide and defeat SB 83[51] as recommended in the April 1 Committee of the Whole report, separating SB 83 from HB 262—a motion she offered because the committee had already considered and passed HB 262, by Messrs. Phelp and Skinner and Mrs. Lee, on the same subject, which had the advantage of having already passed in the house. Apparently the senate—and even Helen—preferred this house version.[52] Helen was more successful as the senate sponsor of this house bill, which corrected the problem of small rural districts being unable to raise enough money to pay teachers for a full school term. The bill's solution was to set aside a certain amount of money from the school lands fund for these poor districts before distributing the rest across the state, while setting a minimum teachers' salary of fifty dollars a month and a minimum length of six months for the school term. Communities at higher altitudes—over 8,000 feet—had to hold school for only four months, a solution that reflects the common legislative practice of exempting or reducing requirements for rural or small counties to gain the votes needed for passage.

The bill also allowed county commissioners to levy a property tax for schools of up to 10 mills, or $10 per $1,000 assessed value.[53] By April 4 the bill had passed the senate and needed to return to the house for approval of changes. After HB 262 passed, Helen moved to adopt the other half of the Committee of the Whole report, which killed her SB 83 by removing the enacting clause.[54]

The new bill closely resembled Helen's original effort. Under this bill teachers were to be paid a minimum of fifty dollars a month for six months or fifty dollars a month for four months in schools at altitudes over 8,000 feet. Helen cited this bill in a later magazine article to illustrate the difference between women senators and men senators, the women being protective of children and the men protective of property. While she and the other women legislators saw the bill as a benefit to the children of the semiarid plains counties, the men legislators saw it as a blow to their districts' property interests because money would have been taken off the top of the statewide school fund to assist poor districts before the pro rata distribution to the counties, taking money from all districts to give it to the poorer districts (see SB 178 further on).[55] When Helen saw that the bill was about to fail, she delayed consideration until she could quietly persuade more senators to support it. She managed to pass the bill when it came up again, and it did become law.[56]

The rural accommodation was also evident in Helen's SB 313, which set compensation of county superintendents and assistant superintendents of schools. Counties were divided into four classes based on population with different levels of salary, from $1,000 to $2,800 a year.[57] The Judiciary Committee referred the bill to the County Affairs Committee, which amended it slightly and referred it to the floor on February 25 with a positive recommendation.[58] The bill apparently died because it is not mentioned in the *Senate Journal* after that.

As with HB 262, which she shepherded through the senate, Helen had earlier sponsored SB 178, Apportionment of the Public School Fund—an amazing early attempt at equalization in school finance that would have allocated some money according to the wealth of the district. It would have distributed four-fifths of the money in the public school income fund—the money derived from the school lands Colorado had acquired from the federal government at statehood—on a per-pupil basis throughout the state. One-fifth of the money would have been distributed to poor districts that could not raise enough property tax to pay teachers the minimum salary Helen had proposed in her SB 83. The Judiciary Committee referred it favorably to the Committee of the Whole on February 11,[59] but that is the last reference to SB 178. Helen also tried to create a school law commission in SB 199 to look at the laws of other states and recommend changes to Colorado's school finance laws. The bill passed out of the senate but failed on Third Reading in the house.[60]

Her SB 192, Appropriations for Colorado Traveling Library Commission, was postponed indefinitely on the last day of the session.[61] This bill and SB 418, Appropriations for Traveling Libraries of Colorado, were meant to benefit a program that sent trunks of books traveling throughout the state, some of them sponsored in honor of members of the Denver Woman's Press Club.[62] The latter bill provided for payment of the expenses of maintaining the free traveling libraries. Though the long appropriation bill already had $1,500 for this purpose, Helen's bill appropriated $1,546.84 for the indebtedness of the free traveling libraries. The bill passed both houses but was vetoed by the governor, perhaps because it was a duplicate appropriation.[63]

In another case in which Helen was ahead of her time, she passed Senate Joint Resolution (SJR) 14, National Aid for Vocational and Industrial Training, sponsored by Mrs. Lee and Mrs. Riddle in the house. The resolution called for per-capita support from the federal government for vocational training in grammar, secondary, and technical schools. Helen may have been inspired to sponsor the resolution by the memory of her many siblings who, lacking education, had worked in cotton mills in Rhode Island. Another provision of the resolution proposed a national university in Washington, DC, to head up the educational system of the union and called for a cabinet-level secretary of education, an idea that wasn't implemented until 1980.[64]

A BILL FOR MINIMUM WAGES FOR MEN

In a departure from bills concerning women or education, Helen cosponsored SB 179 by Senator Harvey E. Garman, regulating wages and hours for men in any public service corporation—whether providing light, heat, power, water, transportation, or telephone service. The work hours were not, except in emergencies, to exceed eight hours in a twenty-four-hour period. These employments were also declared to be injurious to health and dangerous to life and limb. The bill was referred to the Labor Committee,[65] which on the last day of the session recommended that the bill be postponed indefinitely (killed) on the pretext that the matter was covered in house bills.[66] But no minimum wage law for men passed in this session.[67] Considering the powerful interests this bill was taking on, the outcome was not surprising.

BILLS TO PROTECT CHILDREN

Judge Lindsey perhaps suggested Helen's successful bill to protect children, SB 390, Protection of Abused, Neglected, and Dependent Children, cosponsored by Messrs. W. L. Philbin and J. C. Cantu. It provided that when a child is committed to the State Home for Dependent and Neglected Children by any county or juvenile court, the home's board of control would not be subject to any order of the court. If the board—which included women—determined that it was in the best interest of the child, he or she could be kept in the home, placed in a permanent family home, or returned to the child's parents subject to conditions for the child's welfare.[68] The concept of the best interest of the child and even the same language of "abuse and neglect" is still prominent in Colorado law regarding out-of-home placement of children. One newspaper described the bill as a measure "to prevent using the state home for neglected children as a detention home," a practice that commingled abused and neglected children with juvenile delinquents.[69]

Helen tried in SB 40 to get a two-year appropriation of $17,000 for the state home for maintenance and improvement.[70] This bill passed initially. Two bills on the same subject, HB 84 and HB 157, the latter of which refers to the $17,000 already approved in Helen's bill and subtracts that amount from the total appropriation, also passed.[71] For some reason, on February 14 Helen moved for the adoption of an adverse Finance Committee report on her own SB 40, thereby killing the bill. The motion passed.[72] Another one of her bills on the same subject, SB 110, passed, which might explain why she killed SB 40. The second bill was vetoed by the governor, probably as part of his economy moves.[73]

Judge Lindsey was also the instigator of SB 128, to regulate the age of employment of minors in messenger services and businesses on streets in cities and counties with populations over 10,000. Helen voted for the bill, which passed Third Reading on February 11, 30 to 0.[74] The minimum age was sixteen years for messengers and twelve years for newspaper peddlers and other street employment.[75]

BILLS FOR THE MENTALLY ILL

Looking beyond her focus on women and children, early in the session Helen introduced Senate Concurrent Resolution (SCR) 2 to appoint a committee to investigate the state insane asylums. One of her whereas clauses observed that "there is a belief current in all parts of Colorado that the State Asylum for the Insane at Pueblo, Colorado, and the State Home for Mental Defectives at Arvada, Colorado, are not conducted according to the most modern and effective methods."[76]

The resolution was held up in committee for two weeks until the Democratic caucus decided to pursue it without further delay.[77] Then it was adopted in the senate, 31 to 2 with two absent.[78] The *Denver Express* called it "a personal victory for Mrs. Robinson, who broke down every barrier of delay and obstruction which parliamentary tactics could devise." Helen demonstrated a clear understanding of the history of treatment of mental illness. With that understanding, she had found conditions in the institutions deplorable. She complained that

> Colorado has not progressed very far in its attitude toward these
> unfortunates. Society first regarded the insane as possessed of dev
> ils and used beatings to drive out these evil spirits. Then human
> ity suggested that they should simply be confined, not for their
> good but for the protection of society. Colorado has stopped at

this stage while the modern thought has demanded that they be treated as the sick and remedies given to restore reason.

The Colorado asylum still treats the insane as prisoners and the asylum is regarded as a jail, rather than a hospital.[79]

Helen's comments were especially poignant in light of the later nervous breakdown of her stepdaughter, Alcyon.

When Helen's SCR 2 got to the house, however, the representatives voted to lay it on the table because the Pueblo representative, naturally protective of the mental institution in his district, thought the resolution was a reflection on the institution's manager.[80] Wisely, in her House Joint Resolution (HJR) 11, which was nearly identical to Helen's, Mrs. Lee accepted an amendment to expand the investigation to all such institutions, so that it no longer pointed directly to the Pueblo director.[81] Subsequently, Helen supported Mrs. Lee's resolution in the senate.

One of the charges against the care in the institutions was that those who did not die of acute mania died of tuberculosis or other diseases spread within the institution. The issue was so sensitive that the investigation in response to Mrs. Lee's successful resolution was conducted in secret. The committee included both the house sponsor, Mrs. Lee, and Senator Robinson.[82] As the committee was being organized, there was apparently a contest for the chairmanship between Representative Kennedy and Helen.[83] Mrs. Lee ultimately became the chair.[84]

Another bill by Helen, SB 367, was also related to mentally incompetent persons. It provided that if those close to the person in question agreed, the court could proceed to an immediate hearing. The last action on the bill, which apparently died, was the Judiciary Committee referral of it to the Committee of the Whole on March 1.[85]

A RESOLUTION TO SURVEY ALL STATE INSTITUTIONS

Helen sponsored an important Senate Joint Resolution (SJR 21), which charged a special committee with a great responsibility: visit all the state institutions and report their needs for the next twenty years. This special committee was to report to the Twentieth General Assembly in 1915.[86] The committee initially was to consist of five senate holdover members and five house members elected in 1914, but this composition was a bone of contention. The resolution was laid on the table on a 17 to 15 vote, with Helen voting against.[87] An effort to change the number of committee members failed on a 15 to 15 vote.[88]

On the last day of the session, Helen moved to take SJR 21 off the table and then to change the committee membership to two holdover senators and three representatives to be elected in 1914, a proposal that passed 17 to 15.[89] This amendment may have been required for passage in the house, whose members still argue today that joint committees should have more house members than senate members because there are more total members in the house (sixty-five compared to thirty-five). The committee's charge was to collect statistics and information; investigate the cost of improvements, building, and equipment the institutions would require for the next twenty years; and consider amending the constitution to permit selling bonds to build improvements at the institutions. The resolution did ultimately pass, and Helen was elected or appointed chair of the committee.[90]

OTHER BILLS BY HELEN RING ROBINSON

In the era before the current five-bill limit, Helen introduced many other bills in 1913, according to the *List of Bills,* because she was a proactive legislator who tried to solve nearly every important problem that interested her.[91] Helen's SB 368 was an effort to regulate transportation by fixing a penalty for delay by carriers. If carriers delayed delivery, they would be fined at the same daily rate they charged for storage. The bill was postponed indefinitely on the last day of the session. It apparently never passed out of the senate Judiciary Committee.

In SB 258, on burial places for the United Spanish War and Grand Army veterans, Helen tried to create community committees to buy cemetery sections for veterans. The bill came out of the senate Military Affairs Committee on March 11 with a favorable recommendation and was added to the General Orders (Committee of the Whole) calendar.[92] But no further action was recorded. In another bill for veterans, SB 389, Helen wanted to establish a committee to govern the Soldiers' and Sailors' Home. The Committee on Military Affairs referred it to the Committee of the Whole without recommendation, which was the last reference to it in the *Journal*.[93]

A few bills may have been suggested by her lawyer husband. SB 320 would have amended the statutes relating to homesteads. This bill, which increased the amount of the homestead exemption from debt collection to $3,000, passed on Second Reading[94] but was defeated 17 to 15 on Third Reading in the senate,[95] one vote short of the eighteen necessary for passage on Third Reading.

SB 373 and SB 374, Helen's other technical legal bills, sought to amend statutes relating to bonds of executors, administrators, guardians, and conservators. These bills may have arisen out of the problem Ewing had with his bond as executor of his first wife's estate (see chapter 1). The bills failed, but HB 475 by Mr. Smedley, which dealt at length with the settling of estates, did pass.[96]

BILLS SPONSORED BY OTHER LEGISLATORS

One bill Helen supported, SB 76, failed on a 17 to 17 vote in the senate, which was probably for the best. A constitutional amendment on the ballot allowing recall of judicial decisions had passed on the November 1912 state ballot, and this bill by Senator Affolter provided procedures for its implementation.[97] The amendment provided that, for a brief period, a supreme court decision about the constitutionality of a law could be referred to a vote of the people, who could overturn that decision. It also provided for the referral of laws passed by the legislature to a vote of the people. The bill was supported by Judge Ben Lindsey and by the Direct Legislation League of Colorado. If it had passed, it would have extended the uncertainty about the constitutionality of a law beyond a Colorado Supreme Court decision. Only the supreme court could hear cases about constitutionality, and then it had to remand them back to a lower court for decisions on other matters. Before the lower court acted, the issue could be referred to the people for a vote. It is not difficult to imagine the delay and legal uncertainty such a provision would have created.[98]

Helen supported several funding bills. SB 350, by her former adversary Senator Hecker, was an appropriation to the Colorado Publicity League, an early attempt at state promotion of tourism. Helen was the eighth named sponsor on the bill, which was postponed indefinitely on the last day of the session by the Finance Committee. Helen tried unsuccessfully to fund state highways in SB 429 with an appropriation of $10,000, none of which could be spent within cities. This bill was also postponed indefinitely on the last day of the session in the Finance Committee.[99]

In an article published in February, Helen was said to be considering a bill to require health certificates for marriage, a proposal she claimed had the backing of physicians, women's clubs, ministers, and the Society for the Prevention and Control of Tuberculosis because it had the potential of slowing the spread of tuberculosis. There was, however, no record of her introducing such a bill.[100] She did, though, support a bill that required the health board to keep records of tuberculosis patients. Initially she was opposed, but she said "a personal investigation had convinced her that the bill would not work any undue hardship upon the average person affected, and that the greater good for the greater number caused her to withdraw her former opposition and support the bill." The bill became law.[101]

Helen voted to kill a bill on boxing, although she said she was not opposed to boxing as a manly art. "The bill was full of jokers," she said. It would even have "permitted fist fights in any arena when the boxing commission might give a permit for them."[102]

Helen's role as a newspaper journalist made her the natural champion for freedom of the press against Senator Hecker. The maverick senator tried twice to pass bills one paper called "press-muzzling." SB 331, Concerning Vicious Journalism and Prescribing Penalties Therefor, passed 20 to 14 on Third Reading in the senate[103] on April 3

and moved to the house, where it was postponed indefinitely in committee.[104] This version said it was unlawful for a newspaper to publish
"indecent or disgusting details, whether true or not, of any crime, vice,
scandal or other matter which publication shall have a tendency to
corrupt private morals or to offend common decency, or to make vice
or crime seem attractive." The penalties could be as high as a $1,000
fine and one year in jail.[105]

Senator Hecker had a second bill restricting freedom of the press.
SB 332 provided that civil actions could be brought against any
newspaper by any person who has been injured by the publication of
false or defamatory information or "indecent or disgusting details,"
whether true or not. Some animosity may have remained between
Senator Hecker and Senator Robinson after her biting defense of
Denver women against his charge about their drinking more than
men. Helen, who had regularly written articles for the *Rocky Mountain
News,* argued strongly against the anti-press bill on the floor of the
senate:

> This bill was introduced on behalf of the Citizens' Protective
> league [*sic*]. If you look at the list of names in this league you will
> see that the real movers, those who are paying for its advertise-
> ments, are not mentioned in its membership. The men who are
> backing this movement are those who have fattened on special
> privilege, who have sought to crush the people by the aid of their
> subsidized newspapers and are now trying, through this bill, to
> crowd back into privilege again . . .
>
> This measure provides the means for putting out of business
> the newspapers that have the courage to speak the truth about
> men and measures.[106]

This anti–free press bill was defeated on Third Reading in the senate on March 13 on a 15 to 18 vote.[107] One Colorado out-state paper
called it a "freak libel bill," which was killed as a result of the efforts of
Helen Ring Robinson. The paper added, "That worthy lady has shown
remarkably good sense and judgement since entering the legislative
hall as one of its honored members."[108]

BILLS REGULATING PUBLIC UTILITIES

Regulation of public utilities, including railroads, was the session's hottest issue, but Helen did not seem to be greatly involved in this issue, perhaps because she and the other progressive Democratic senators became a small minority faction when the other Democrats allied themselves with the Republicans on the issue. Both political parties had promised an honest public utilities law in their platforms before the election.[109] The lobbyist for the phone company, a Mr. Field, attempted to influence legislators by offering free long-distance service from the State Capitol for members of the General Assembly. According to the *Denver Express,* he wanted a "false" public utilities bill. The gas and electric power interests supported the bill, the paper claimed, because they could "thrive under a Public Utilities Commission they help name."[110]

The major bill to create a public utilities commission, SB 1 by Senators Burris and Van Tilborg, originally allowed cities to run their own utility companies and also provided that home rule cities could select their own franchise providers—a provision the utility companies wanted and one that would also have been supported by Denver, a home rule city since 1902.[111] After coming out of committee on January 28, it was stripped of the home rule provision. At least one Denver newspaper writer was outraged, accusing the senators who voted for this amendment of being "spineless" and "tools of Special Privilege" because they didn't allow cities to determine by a vote of the people which companies could use their streets.[112] Helen was not one of those excoriated.

Business interests were so concerned about the bill that they met en masse with all the members of the senate to tell them about provisions they felt would hinder the state's development.[113] The utility bill, which applied to railroads, was attacked by former Senator Patterson and even by Governor Ammons when Newman Erb threatened to stop building the Moffat Tunnel (to provide railroad service through the central mountains) if it passed.[114] Senator Hiram Hilts tried to amend the bill to exempt [rail] roads not organized under the laws of the state of Colorado, especially in respect to sections of the bill that required Public Utilities Commission approval to mortgage property, issue stocks, and raise rates.[115]

Helen and six other Democratic senators became an isolated faction when the rest of the Democrats and the machine Republicans voted to make William Adams president of the senate. None of their bills were scheduled on Special Orders (which are often the agenda every day); they were not recognized by the president when they tried to have their bills heard. Nevertheless, they consistently voted for bills pledged in their party platform, and they fought the assault on the utilities bill.[116] The Burris–Van Tilborg bill passed Third Reading in the senate on February 27 with thirty-four votes, apparently satisfying most of the senators.[117]

In the house, the utility bill passed with railroads included and the right of the new Public Utilities Commission to prevent ownership of parallel lines, mergers, and interlocking directorates. Home rule was restored to cities.[118] However, the latter provision was lost in the conference committee. The bill also exempted regulation of new railroad construction.[119] After some consideration and under pressure for and against the bill, the governor signed this legislation.

THE BILL ON THE NORTHERN COLORADO COAL STRIKE

HJR (House Joint Resolution) 9 on the northern Colorado coal strike by four representatives from the affected district called for an investigation in Boulder and Weld Counties[120]—an investigation that was necessary, the resolution argued, because of claims that the coal operators refused to arbitrate with the miners as provided by law and assertions that some companies had reduced the price of their coal in an effort to break the companies paying higher wages for union labor. The resolution granted subpoena power to a committee and called for a report on the evils, if they existed; the causes of the strike; and measures needed to end the strife.[121] Helen voted for the resolution when it passed on Third Reading by a 29 to 2 vote.[122]

When the committee established by HJR 9 reported to the senate, Helen moved that both the majority and minority reports be postponed indefinitely, but the motion failed.[123] Perhaps she thought the report was not critical enough of the mine owners. Rocky Mountain Fuel Company, which had purchased the northern mines, had never recognized unions in its southern Colorado fields and announced that it did not intend to do so in the northern ones.[124] The report also said that the union needed to carry out its contracts with employers more faithfully.[125]

In general, the legislative session was considered beneficial for the labor causes Helen supported. An eight-hour day for miners was passed to replace the "fake" eight-hour-day law passed by voters in November 1912.[126] Workmen were no longer forced to assume risk, which had barred them from recovery for injuries sustained on the job. A bill ended the theory of contributory negligence. Helen was responsible for some of labor's successes, having passed her bill establishing a minimum wage commission for women and children and supporting another sponsor's bill establishing minimum wages for teachers after her version of a teachers' salary bill died. There were other successful labor-backed bills on mine inspection and public utilities regulation.[127]

When the session began, US senators were still elected by the state legislature. Senator Hecker, true to form, was the only Democrat in the senate who did not vote for the people's choices at the preferential vote in 1912, Senators John F. Shafroth and Charles S. Thomas. In April Helen supported and the legislature ratified SCR 1, the US constitutional amendment allowing for the direct election of senators.[128] There were no votes against it.[129]

Other noteworthy bills in this session included a memorial to the US Congress urging the establishment of Rocky Mountain National Park, which passed through the house but did not make it through the senate.[130] The Democratic caucuses in each house endorsed a bill to establish a highway commission to approve all highway construction, removing individual road bills and all lobbying for them from consideration by the legislature.[131]

Of the ambitious twenty-seven bills and resolutions Helen sponsored, five passed but two, both related to appropriations, were vetoed—one for the State Home for Dependent and Neglected Children and the other for traveling libraries. Helen's resolution for National Aid for Vocational Training also passed. She could be pleased that, as she had promised, she had effectively worked for a great many measures benefiting women and children. By comparison, other sponsors in 1915, when such data were available, introduced between two and thirty-one bills. Leaders introduced as many as sixty-eight. Evangeline Heartz, the only woman representative in 1915, only introduced two bills, one for the relief of a specific individual.[132]

Helen's most important achievement, though, was changing the image of a state senator. *The Independent,* a national magazine, asked her to write an article about her experiences as the second woman senator in the country. She began with an anecdote about a telegram addressed to Senator H. R. Robinson delivered under her hotel room door in New York. The bellhop had written on it "paged in bar and barber-shop," but, of course, he did not find her in those places. Helen noted that he had a conventional view of what a senator would look like.[133]

Just as other senators represented special interests, Helen also represented a special interest, as she proudly proclaimed:

> I also represented a special interest, just as surely as did the railroad men. I represented a special industry, just as truly as did the Denver grocer. I represented the interest of the wife and mother. I represented the industry of the housewife. And when the other housewives of Colorado realized that, in these days of the high cost of living, the so called "Grocers' Trust" had their man in the state senate, they were very glad that they had their woman there to watch him.[134]

Helen made a distinction between men and women in general. Men, she believed, were more inclined to protect property, and women were more likely to conserve human life. She said that when she spoke about matters of "social motherliness," she was more influential with the men. When she was asked how the other senators treated her, she always replied, "My colleagues treated me exactly as if I were a gentleman—and I was proud of them." She attributed this to their twenty years of experience with woman suffrage in Colorado.[135]

On the whole, Helen's first session was a great success for her and, through her leadership, for all women aspiring to hold public office. Her impact was summarized in a *Denver Republican* article taken from the *St. Louis Star* in March 1913, which attempted to stress traditional feminine values rather than Helen's very apparent success as a capable lawmaker:

> She is a brilliant and witty speaker and her bon mots are expected to give zest to the legislative session. Her wit, however, is never acid. It is quaint and subtle and if one word should be chosen to describe this first woman state senator, this adroit woman politician, it would be, not "brilliant" or "brainy" or "accomplished"— though she is all of these—but the good old word "lovable." She has the greatest of all womanly gifts, the gift of charm. No Denver woman is more popular socially. No one has more devoted friends. Denver has no more notable housewife, no more devoted wife and mother.[136]

Helen was more than "lovable"; she was amazingly effective in her first year. Being in the majority party helped her pass her bills, a position she would not enjoy in the next regular session. She would need all the skills she could muster in the crisis the following year when violence erupted in Colorado's southern coal fields. After just one year in the senate, she would be a spokesperson for women in the state's response to the 1914 Ludlow Massacre.

4

THE LUDLOW MASSACRE AND SPECIAL SESSION

THE FIGHT FOR WOMAN SUFFRAGE

In the interim between the 1913 legislative session and the eruption of violence in the southern coal fields the following spring, Helen again turned her attention to the cause of woman suffrage. Other states were slowly adopting such provisions: eight between 1910 and 1915 and fifteen more between 1915 and 1919.[1] The unions had joined the fight by 1910, and there was a convergence of diverse groups in the suffrage cause between those who argued from the maternalist point of view and those who stood for equal rights for women.[2]

As the only woman state senator at that time, Helen was sought after as a speaker by many suffrage organizations across the country and even in Canada.[3] Shortly after the conclusion of the session, she traveled to the East Coast for a speaking tour of five states—including New York, New Jersey, Pennsylvania, and Maryland—a tour in which

---

she presented more than sixty addresses.[4] She was in the East by May 10 and did not return to Denver until July 9.

In October she planned to tour and lecture in Ohio and Michigan.[5] At the end of 1913 Helen had returned to the East again, according to the *Wellesley College News,* where she spoke to a large audience at Unity Church in Pittsfield, Massachusetts, under the auspices of the Pittsfield Equal Franchise League in a lecture titled "The Relations Existing between the Home and the Ballot Box." She demonstrated how politics have come from outside the home to inside, requiring the attention of women.[6] She also spoke at a meeting of the Massachusetts Woman Suffrage Association.[7] She was on her way to a meeting of the National American Woman Suffrage Association in Washington, DC, which she addressed along with Dr. Anna Howard Shaw, the group's longtime president; Jane Addams; and three low-wage women workers. About that speech, Elizabeth Cady Stanton said, "Senator Robinson gave a keen and comprehensive account of women as legislators."[8] At that meeting Helen also introduced a set of resolutions asking President Woodrow Wilson to support the woman suffrage amendment to the US Constitution in his upcoming message to the US Congress, which represented a shift in her advocacy of the state-by-state strategy.[9] This also represented a shift to a national strategy in one wing of the movement. A new party, the Congressional Union for Woman Suffrage (CU), led by Alice Paul, had been formed in early 1913 under the sponsorship of the National American Woman Suffrage Association to concentrate on passing a federal constitutional amendment.[10] The campaign was formally launched in 1914.[11]

Also in December, Helen spoke to the Portsmouth Equal Suffrage League in Portsmouth, New Hampshire, where the local paper reported her speech at length. She described a woman who opposed woman suffrage as one of those people "with hard-boiled minds." Such people believe women are not half of the human race "but a subspecies . . . for purposes of reproduction solely." Then she disposed of the argument that many women do not want the vote. She categorized all women into two groups, one active in improving their community and one sitting lazily at home. She argued that everyone in the first group supported woman suffrage. The best argument in favor of woman suffrage, she said, was the "good old argument of democracy": "Believe in democracy and you must believe in equal suffrage." If the vote is withheld from women "there is a subject class, politically." She called the vote the "badge of equality." In concluding she said, "Its [the vote's] possession by women will gradually sweep away the lingering tradition of woman inferiority—to the benefit of men just as surely as to the benefit of women."[12] Most of these arguments depart from the maternalist position.

In January 1914 Helen debated the suffrage issue in Symphony Hall in Boston at a meeting sponsored by the Economic Club of Boston. The opposing position was presented by another Wellesley alumna. Eleven hundred people listened to her speech at the Hotel Astor in New York. So enthused were they that Helen "frequently had to ask for silence when the points she scored on the anti-suffragists were applauded."[13]

In February we find her speaking in Colorado Springs on religion outside a church and then to the New York State Senate, the first time a woman had addressed that body since Elizabeth Cady Stanton spoke to the senators in 1848; though sixty-six years had passed, the speeches were no doubt similar.[14]

Her appearance alone was living proof that a woman politician could be feminine and stylish, as evidenced by the newspaper articles describing her gowns—one of them blue with a matching blue hat. Helen's speeches sounded familiar themes. Refuting popular stereotypes, she said that suffragettes did not have faces like vinegar jugs or cropped hair. They did not consume large quantities of alcohol. She stressed the need for real women in legislatures with the typical views of mothers and housewives because she thought a woman legislator's positions should be different from those of the man sitting next to her. She argued against leaving everything related to the home to men "who have always been proverbially careless housekeepers."[15] And she emphasized how important it was to include women's sympathies and points of view in shaping legislation. The grocery combine was her favorite example of an interest group that needed to be countered by the interests of housewife-legislators.[16]

One man in the Hartford audience argued that the fact that women had never served in state senates and that there was only one woman senator in the United States at the time proved that women should not be there. She asked what inference he would draw about women's fitness from the fact that the Colorado penitentiary incarcerated 803 men and only 87 women.[17]

In an interview for the newspaper in Providence, her former hometown, she added that woman suffrage was the next step in the evolutionary expansion of the number of persons entitled to vote. She argued, too, for an end to the double standard of morality for men and women.[18] Initially, the suffrage movement had been led by society women who had the leisure to attend meetings.[19] But Helen observed that in the twentieth century the "other woman" was discovered in the factory, the steam laundry, and the sweatshop, competing with men in the workforce. Recruiting these "discovered" women added to the political base of those advocating suffrage.[20]

Though the tour may have succeeded in raising support for woman suffrage, one Colorado newspaper called her lecture tour of New York State "a dismal financial failure," adding that "Helen takes herself too seriously."[21] It is unclear whether Helen charged a fee for her lectures for herself or whether the meetings were intended to raise money for the cause of woman suffrage. In spite of this comment, Helen continued to lecture, speaking on an unspecified subject in March at a Unitarian church in Colorado Springs.[22] (For more on Helen's views on woman suffrage, see chapter 2.)

In February 1914 one New York paper gave the impression that Mrs. James J. Brown, the "Unsinkable Molly Brown" of *Titanic* fame, was running for the Colorado State Senate against Helen "at the coming election." This is an error on the part of the reporter because Helen's term did not end for two more years, and that same day a story appeared saying that Mrs. Brown was entertaining Senator Helen Ring Robinson of Colorado in Newport, indicating that the two were friends.[23] Other articles make it clear that Mrs. Brown was running for the US Congress or the US Senate, as she had in 1909 and 1911, not the state legislature. By June the suffragists were urging Mrs. Brown to make the race for the US Congress. Her alliance with Helen was indicated in a July article that said that Mrs. Brown's attorney, Helen, and Judge Lindsey all believed "conditions are ripe for her [Brown] to begin her campaign for the nomination to succeed Senator Charles S. Thomas, whose term expires next year."[24]

COAL MINERS' STRIKE

By 1902, 35 percent of the Colorado workforce belonged to unions.[25] Yet there was no law adequately addressing strikes. The most significant event in Colorado in late 1913 and 1914 was the United Mine Workers' strike in the southern part of the state. The union planned a convention in Trinidad on September 15, 1913, and made the mistake of inviting the mine operators to attend, which only served to mobilize their forces against the miners. Barron Beshoar describes the response.

> The only effect [of the invitation] was an increase in the number of guards at the various camps. Spies, camp marshals, and gunmen swarmed through the company towns and into Trinidad. Miners knew they would be discharged if they left camp to attend the Trinidad convention. Beatings and black listings would follow. Sheriff Jefferson Farr, flanked by 326 deputies, many of whom were imported from other states, swore that not a miner from his district would get to the convention. His deputies, employed, armed, and paid by the Colorado Fuel and Iron Company (CF&I), were scattered about Walsenburg and along the roads to watch for delegates.[26]

Before the strike even began on September 23, 1913, it was clear that law enforcement was merely a tool of the mine owners. In an effort to maintain order, Governor Elias Ammons called out the National Guard, which arrived at a train siding near Ludlow on October 31.[27] The strikers had few problems with the National Guard at first, but then a number of the professional men in that force asked to be relieved and were replaced with mine guards.[28]

The main union demand was that it be recognized by company management as the bargaining agent for the miners. The miners also wanted to select the weighmen, receive a 10 percent wage increase, and have safety laws enforced. In addition, they were seeking the right to trade at any store, to choose their living facilities, and to choose their own doctors.[29]

On December 2 a local grand jury under the mine operators' control reported with indictments of twenty-five union miners, but the Justice Department quashed the indictments before any arrests were made.[30] Also, in the early months of 1914 a congressional committee convened in Trinidad to hear testimony from the combatants.[31]

In April Helen Ring Robinson was commissioned by the *New York American* to investigate the coal fields owned by CF&I and to write an article about her observations; the article was published just nine days before the Ludlow Massacre. The corruption of government in the area was startling, Helen observed:

> In the city of Trinidad the Rockefeller interests are all powerful. The officials of the company control the courts, control the sheriff's office, control the County Commissioners. A word from these officials in the past had served to close a public road or to open one. It has caused licenses to be revoked from men believed to be unfriendly to the Colorado Fuel and Iron Company. And another word has opened the doors of jails to freedom for notorious thugs and outlaws.[32]

Helen complained in the same article about the open, most notorious red light district in the country in Trinidad while, ironically, mine owner John D. Rockefeller was investigating the white slave traffic elsewhere. She complained that Rockefeller money had not built one institution for social uplift in Huerfano or Las Animas Counties, and she implied that Rockefeller had no conscience.

The conditions in the coal fields continued to deteriorate because both civil law enforcement and the National Guard were controlled by the mine owners, resulting in the total absence of an impartial agency for law and order. A CF&I manager admitted to Helen that the company's mine guards were also acting as members of the Colorado National Guard paid by Colorado taxpayers. The mine operators refused to meet with strike leaders to discuss certain matters in regard to wages and to the miners' right to trade at non-company stores simply because the union officials were from out of state. Helen found this position ridiculous. She later wrote, "Perhaps all the wasted millions and the wasted lives of the past red weeks might have been saved if at that juncture the people of Colorado had realized that it was the time and place to . . . burst into universal echoing peals of mocking laughter at the idea of absentee mine owners refusing to treat with absentee labor leaders because of their absenteeism."[33]

The Rockefeller interests also consistently refused to recognize that a union could speak for the workers. One major grievance miners had was their belief that the managers robbed them every working day by underweighing their coal, a problem that could have been eased with union check weighmen. A strategy that weakened labor organizing efforts was the mine owners' importation of wave after wave of European immigrants who spoke thirty-two languages other than English. By constantly replacing the workers, the operators could more easily exploit them, Helen said. There was also an element of racial and class hatred between mine owners and mine workers, Helen recognized in another article.[34]

In spite of all she saw during this investigation, Helen was convinced that "the coal operators do not really mean badly. Most of the time they do not mean anything." She found that the problem was that the strike zone "is controlled by capitalists without vision." Helen concluded the *New York American* article by recommending that CF&I owner John D. Rockefeller spend a week in Las Animas and Huerfano. Five months later, after the massacre, John D. Rockefeller Jr. did tour the southern coal fields.

Senator Robinson was harsher in a 1915 assessment of the elder Rockefeller: "Our recent disastrous coal strike in Southern Colorado could undoubtedly have been averted if a certain man at No. 26 Broadway had not gone into a twilight sleep and brought forth the monstrous doctrine that there was 'nothing to arbitrate' in a matter that concerned directly 12,000 men engaged in the most hazardous occupation known in industry."[35]

In the report of the United States Industrial Relations Commission the following August, Rockefeller was blamed for the strike violence and the incidents at Ludlow. Rockefeller was chided for his antisocial spirit, "the perversion of and contempt for government, the disregard of public welfare, and the defiance of public opinion during the Colorado strike." The report said that Helen, as a member of the Committee of Privileges and Elections, had investigated conditions in Las Animas County. She had "listened for three weeks to the story of political conditions there . . . Long before the strike was ordered she realized that the industrial situation was hopeless because the political situation appeared hopeless." Helen testified as follows:

> I found during those two days of investigation in Trinidad, I found a vortex of mad, swirling hate that I did not know existed in the world until I went down there . . .
>
> I found that while the counties of Las Animas and Huerfano are geographically a part of Colorado, yet industrially and politically they are a barony or a principality of the Colorado Fuel and Iron Co. Such situations, of course, must mean a knitting together of the industrial and political situation, and I don't wish to say that the Colorado Fuel and Iron Co. have limited their efforts to Las Animas and Huerfano Counties. If that were so the situation in the State itself would not be so seriously affected by them; but they have in time past reached out beyond the boundaries of their principality and made and unmade governors.[36]

A University of Colorado professor, James H. Brewster, who had had the courage to testify before the federal commission, wrote to Helen to protest criticism he had received for speaking in defense of the miners. He was fired as a consequence of his courageous act.[37]

Helen's trip to the coal fields affected her deeply: "I was feeling horribly depressed after viewing the terrible conditions in the southern part of the state. When I read of the action that *The News* had taken in the matter it gave a lift to my heart that was wonderful." [The

Rocky Mountain News had apparently called for the intervention of President Wilson.][38]

The governor removed most of the National Guard on April 14, 1914, but two companies remained: Company A, a cavalry outfit made up of mine guards, pit bosses, mine superintendents, and mine clerks; and Company B, composed of mine guards, professional soldiers, and adventurers. Both were under the control of the county sheriff and economically dependent on CF&I.[39]

A full-scale battle broke out on April 20, 1914. Helen conceded that the strikers may have fired first,[40] but it was undisputed that a Gatling gun (an early form of machine gun) was fired into the tent city of Ludlow. Women and children fled or hid in cellars excavated under the tents. When the tents were set on fire by the militia, who were probably unaware of the people hiding in the cellars, two women and eleven children who had huddled in one of these pits died. Beyond the deaths, Helen described what the torching meant to these impoverished people: "It must not be forgotten that these tents were the strikers' homes; that what little they possessed of earthly goods was gathered under those tent roofs. A cooking stove, a table, some wooden chairs and stools, a bedstead or two with shabby bedding, bright calico curtains for tent partitions and family photographs, at least one of them the picture of a bridal couple in distinctive wedding finery—that was all."[41]

By the end of the battle Louis Tikas, the union strike leader, had also been killed, and an eleven-year-old boy was dead.[42] Several parties including local ministers attempted to search the camp to recover any bodies that had been missed, but they were twice turned back by General John Chase, who commanded the National Guard.[43] In fact, the *Denver Express* reporter was turned away Wednesday morning and reported that General Chase approved the order to fire when relatives tried to recover bodies. The reporter said that Mrs. Frank Snyder, whose eleven-year-old son had been killed, was allowed to drag his body and take her other four children out of the tent before gunmen burned it. After the reporter was able to sneak into the camp in disguise on Wednesday afternoon, he described the horror of the burned women and children he found there.[44] At some point a committee of women was organized to go to Trinidad to investigate and search the field for bodies.[45]

Strikers responded by attacking mines, blowing up mining equipment, and dynamiting mines where families of officials had gone for protection. Civil war had come to the southern coal fields.[46]

Soon after the massacre, Helen called for a special session of the legislature so she could tell the truth about the way the state militia had been used.[47] Of course, only the governor or two-thirds of the legislators acting together could call a special session.[48]

THE WOMEN'S DEMANDS

The women of Denver, particularly members of the Woman's Peace Association, were horrified by the bloodshed of men, women, and children continuing in the coal fields. They published notices on the front pages of the *Denver Post* and the *Rocky Mountain News* calling for a mass demonstration of women at the State Capitol. The text read:

> Women of Colorado—For the sake of your slain sisters and their murdered children, for the sake of your sisters whose humble homes have been ruthlessly destroyed, for the sake of the earnest men who are being wounded and killed every hour because they tried to better their conditions of life, we summon you to a meeting at the capitol at 10 o'clock Saturday morning.
>
> In the name of the womanhood of Colorado we will demand that these infamies cease; we will demand that another hideous holocaust be prevented by the intervention of federal troops; we will demand the establishment of law, and we will take steps to initiate the repeal of the infamous decision by which Mother Jones was imprisoned shamelessly.
>
> Your help is needed.
>
> The Woman's Peace Association[49]

Mother Jones was a labor sympathizer who frequently spoke at rallies and demonstrated with strikers around the country in spite of her advanced age. She spent twenty-six days in the Walsenburg County Courthouse jail for her "incendiary speeches" on behalf of miners.[50]

In a meeting of 200 leading Denver women on April 23, Helen Robinson spoke passionately about the conditions in the southern coal fields, which she had just visited. She asserted that it was ignorance of conditions among the women that had led to the Ludlow Massacre. "We are to blame," she declared, "because we have allowed to pass unchallenged the conditions which have resulted in this terrible warfare." She cited the fact that thirty-six nationalities were herded together at the mines because they were thus easier to handle. The mine operators had made no effort to help the foreigners.[51] According to the *Denver Express,* Helen was "choked with sobs" as she spoke. She called Rockefeller "smug" for his investigation of white slavery in Europe and his testimony to the congressional committee that his conscience was free of responsibility in Colorado. She cried out, "My God, where will it end?"[52]

On Saturday, April 25, 1,000 women did indeed gather in the rotunda of the State Capitol. The speakers mounted the stairs to the second floor to address the crowd. When the crowd moved toward the governor's office, a messenger for the governor convinced them that if they went to the House of Representatives' chamber, the governor would come to address them. Several speeches were given there, including one by Senator Robinson. At the meeting, the body of women passed a resolution to put on the ballot a constitutional amendment to allow the state to seize and operate mines. They also started a collection to aid the victims in the strike district and sent a telegram to President Wilson urging immediate federal aid. To pass the time, they sang "America" and "The Battle Hymn of the Republic."[53]

After some time, when the governor did not appear in the house chamber, the chair, Alma Lafferty, named a committee of three to go to the governor's office: Mrs. Stuart D. Walling, Representative Evangeline Heartz, and Senator Helen Ring Robinson.[54] Because the governor kept the women waiting for half an hour while he admitted law officers, Helen demanded to know why they were kept waiting while the gentlemen were admitted. "They are officers of the law," the messenger replied. According to Beshoar, Helen replied, "And we are citizens . . . You tell that governor we want to see him and we want to see him now."[55] The *Denver Post* account gives Helen a smaller role, yet the women are portrayed in every account as absolutely determined to force the governor to ask the president for aid.

Shortly thereafter, the ladies were admitted to the governor's office. Here is Beshoar's report of that conversation:

> "Governor Ammons," Mrs. Robinson said, "we are here simply to escort you to the house chamber above and to ask your immediate presence there. The women wish to present some resolutions to you" . . .
>
> "Can't you present the resolutions now?" he asked. "I have important matters to attend to, ladies. I have just received word that there is fighting going on at three mines in the strike district. The attorney for the mine workers is waiting to confer with me. There are steps which must be taken immediately to prevent loss of life. I have no time to listen to resolutions."
>
> "We, too, represent those who are desirous of preventing loss of life," Mrs. Robinson replied sharply. "Governor Ammons, as the state's chief executive you owe it to the women of Colorado to appear before them. We were assured before we retired upstairs that you would come up."[56]

Governor Ammons and Lieutenant Governor Stephen R. Fitzgarrald tried to put the women off until noon because of the shooting going on in the coal fields. Helen replied, "We'll give you just five minutes." Reluctantly, the governor finally consented to go to the second-floor house chamber to talk with the women. In the house, Mrs. Lafferty introduced Mrs. Anna Steele, widow of former Supreme Court Chief Justice Robert W. Steele. She demanded the immediate intervention of federal troops and the withdrawal of state troops and the arrests of their leaders. She accused Representative Taylor of putting out a "cooked up" version of a telegram saying the congressional delegation had asked President Wilson for troops and been told that sending troops to Colorado was not possible. She further asserted that the real telegram in reply said that nothing could be done about sending help until Governor Ammons asked for federal troops. She demanded that the governor send a telegram at once asking for aid.[57]

The governor replied that he had received a telegram saying there was no hope of help, but he would like to check it to be sure it was the actual reply. Again he tried to delay his answer to the women until the next day, but they were insistent that he should send a telegram at once asking for aid.

The governor's response was pathetic:

> I was assured when I came up here that you were going to help me. God knows I need help. I don't need anything else. I have used up what little ability I have to serve this state and to bring about an adjustment in this matter. I have had only a few hours to get in touch with the situation. I am trying to organize a committee to go down south and make an investigation to get the facts . . .
>
> I didn't go to bed last night until two o'clock, when I tried to get a little sleep . . . And I am willing to spend every hour of every day of the coming weeks in an effort to adjust this matter without further bloodshed. Will you give me a chance? I ask you as good citizens, to give me your help and support. Give me an opportunity, an opportunity. I can't do anything unless I have public sentiment back of me.[58]

The governor slipped out of the chamber, but Helen and the rest of the special committee followed him right back to his office on the first floor. They told his staff that they intended to camp in the governor's office until the telegram was sent. Helen said they were willing to remain in session forty-eight or seventy-two hours if necessary, making them one of the earliest sit-ins for peace in US political history.[59] Finally, the governor dictated a tentative telegram to President Wilson asking for federal troops if he could not control the situation in the southern Colorado coal fields. Mrs. Steele and Mrs. Lafferty announced that they would wait in the governor's office for a reply. The crowd of women waited in the house chambers, too.

When the reply came, Wilson was noncommittal about sending federal troops. At 9:15 p.m., when the women had been waiting for more than ten hours, the governor finally asked the president for the help the women demanded.[60] The telegram read,

> The situation has passed beyond the ability of the state to control. This domestic violence is the result of an industrial controversy between interstate organizations with headquarters outside the State of Colorado. I therefore, urgently request that you send forthwith to Ludlow, Colorado, and to such other portions of the state as the commanding officer may deem necessary, not less than one battalion of infantry and one troop of cavalry.[61]

A few minutes later Governor Ammons issued a call to the legislature to convene May 4 in a special session, specifying the topics it could consider: paying for the National Guard obligations, addressing the labor problems, and other related issues. He told the newspapers, "Nothing except the payment of the troops and other matters pertaining to the strike and its possible settlement will go into the call."[62]

In a letter written after the session ended, Helen proudly described the role of the women in forcing the governor to call upon the president for federal assistance:

> Certainly I know of no other state in the Union where, against the protests of all the "big interests" of the state a governor could have been forced to send a call for federal troops to stop the bloodshed that both of the leading parties in the contest wished to continue shedding—could have been forced, I repeat, by the women of the capital city. Of course you have read the story of how Gov. Ammons responded to the demands of "the women of Denver."[63]

Before the special session began, Helen wanted to visit Ludlow and see the scene of the massacre for herself. She telegraphed Major W. A. Holbrook, in charge of the federal troops, asking for permission to visit Ludlow that Saturday. He let her know it would be safe for her to do so.[64] After her trip to the battleground, Helen blamed Colorado Fuel and Iron "for the murder of men, women, and children at Ludlow." She said there was "no doubt that the outrage at Ludlow is the result of a deliberate attempt by the coal operators and their plug-uglies in the militia to destroy the Ludlow tent colony."[65]

Helen and Representative Lafferty led a relief effort for the miners and their families that resulted in some conflict, at least as reported in the press. Molly Brown apparently gave $1,000 to relieve the "women and children coal strike sufferers," but she was quoted as saying that Senator Robinson and Representative Lafferty spent the money on railroad trips and hotel bills. Both legislators denied the accusation, and Mrs. Brown also denied having made the statement. All this came out in a story the following year when the garment workers union denied that the union ever received any money from Mrs. Brown.[66]

After President Wilson sent in the federal troops, temporary peace came at last to the coal fields of Colorado. Helen believed the next task was to "establish industrial peace on foundations of industrial justice."[67]

THE SPECIAL SESSION OF 1914

Though during that era the General Assembly ordinarily met only in odd-numbered years, the constitution allows the governor or two-thirds of the legislators to call an Extraordinary Session at other times and to limit the subjects of the legislation that can be considered. Governor Ammons's most pressing need was some means of paying the National Guard he had deployed. Six items appeared on the governor's call:

> First—To provide for paying . . . the expenses which have been or shall be incurred in restoring and preserving peace . . . during the coal miners' strike of 1913 and 1914 . . .
>
> Second—To enact a law submitting to the people of the State an amendment to the Constitution to empower the Legislature to enact laws for arbitration in all labor disputes . . .
>
> Third—To enact a law establishing a State Constabulary or State peace officers . . .
>
> Fourth—To enact a law or laws authorizing the Governor and other proper officers in times of internal disorder, to close saloons

and otherwise to regulate or prohibit the sale, gift, purchase and use of intoxicating liquors . . .

Fifth—To enact a law or laws authorizing the Governor, in times of internal disorder, to regulate or prohibit the sale, gift and purchase of firearms and ammunition, and the carrying thereof, except by authorized persons.

Sixth—To appropriate the sum necessary to defray the expenses of the special session hereby called.[68]

In debate during the Extraordinary Session, Senator Arthur Cornforth of Colorado Springs declared "that the women had forced the call from him [the governor] in the first place." The senator wanted the women to convince the governor to expand the subjects in the call.[69] The movement to expand the subjects was necessitated by the ruling of Attorney General Farrar that under the limited subjects in the governor's call, the legislature could not pass any laws directly relative to the current strike.[70] Representative Warren Persons's resolution, HJR 4, calling on Ammons to enlarge the call, passed in the house. The General Assembly wanted to be able to consider "constructive laws which will prevent industrial conflicts."[71] The resolution contained a letter to Governor Ammons which reasoned that since the state owned and leased all the coal mines, it should be able to set standards and prices and wages or reclaim the land from companies that violated the laws.[72] Also, legislators thought the General Assembly should have the power to provide for immediate arbitration and that any violation of the rules should lead to forfeiture. In the senate Helen moved that HJR 4 be adopted; at first it passed 18 to 14, though Senator Casimiro Barela gave notice that he would move to reconsider.[73] In a surprising series of events the resolution was adopted, reconsidered, and defeated—all within a twenty-four-hour period.[74] When Senator Barela switched to opposition, Helen lost that critical eighteenth vote.

Similarly, HJR 7 said the legislature could provide for the purchase, lease, development, and operation of coal lands and mines. The supreme court was asked to determine the constitutionality of such a proposal.[75] The senate withdrew its request,[76] and the bill disappeared.

Helen was one of those who argued fervently for greater scope of action when the senate debated whether to ask the governor to enlarge the call. "The counties of Las Animas and Huerfano are a vortex of hate," she cried. She continued:

> Coal operators hate the strikers bitterly, and the strikers hate their former employers just as intensely. Little children whose words should be only of love, have vile, obscene epithets for state militiamen and company officials. This hate is a heritage from the strike of 1903, because we temporized instead of settling it once [and] for all. Now we must act . . . Are you going to leave another heritage of bitterness for your sons to deal with? Are you going to kill more women and children to write shame across the name of the state? Or are you going to be men and settle this business right?[77]

When Senator Van Tilborg proposed a resolution (SJR 3) calling for a joint committee to recommend arbitration laws, Helen offered an amendment that would allow the legislature to adjourn and then reconvene with a broader call from the governor that would allow the General Assembly to consider the committee's recommendation.[78] She later withdrew the amendment, but Senator Affolter managed to add a similar one. SJR 3 passed in the senate 15 to 13,[79] which appears to be an error in the *Journal* because eighteen votes are required for passage. The house laid the resolution on the table.[80]

Call Item 1: Paying the Expenses of the National Guard

As to the first item on the call, HB 1, providing for the bonding necessary to pay the men of the National Guard for restoring peace during the coal strikes, did become law. Helen, who believed the $1 million appropriation would foster another Ludlow because it gave the governor control over $300,000 beyond the debt already incurred, denounced the proposal. She feared the governor would use the additional money to employ the discredited National Guard. She voted against the bill in that form on Third Reading, when it passed 23 to

10.[81] Because the bill still appropriated $1 million, she voted against the Conference Committee report, too.[82]

One bill proposed by progressive Democrat Warren Persons in the house would have created a graduated income tax ranging from 1 percent to 5 percent, but it did not pass. Ironically, it would have required the mining companies themselves to pay for much of the debt incurred to protect their property.[83] A similar bill died earlier in the senate.

Helen was denied the unanimous consent senators needed at that time to offer a Third Reading amendment that would prevent payment to agents of the coal mining companies. The amendment, which closely paralleled a house amendment that had been stricken in the senate,[84] read as follows:

> Provided, that no part of the bonds hereunder authorized to be issued shall be used to pay men or exchanged for certificates of indebtedness for such pay, who shall be found to have enlisted in the National Guard of Colorado, or in the service of the National Guard without formal enlistment and who were at the time of such enlistment, or in such service, acting as mine guards, or were employed by any detective agency at any time during the strike in Colorado during the year of 1914.[85]

Helen objected to the bill in the strongest terms. She commented bitterly that to pass this bill, "to pay for the gunmen, thugs and penitentiary sweepings enlisted as militiamen at the dictates of the richest Sunday school teacher in the world," would be a degradation for the state. In speaking of the governor, the senator said that to be governor of Colorado required "brains, courage, force and fairness, and on these charges the present governor can prove an alibi."[86] It is no surprise that she voted against the bill after her amendment failed.[87]

The *Rocky Mountain News* noted that the vote to pay the militia may have been influenced by the fact that CF&I agents were present at the legislature. After Adams was elected senate president, the entire session was controlled by machine Democrats and Republicans, putting Helen, a progressive Democrat, in the minority.[88]

Some senators wanted to pass a bill to pay the National Guard and go home, but Helen told them "there is important work to be done before this special session ends." In the Democratic caucus she scolded them: "If you gentleman think you can pass the appropriation bill and quickly adjourn without hearing from the people later . . . you have as much perspicuity as little black kittens. Wake up, gentlemen, wake up!"[89]

Call Item 2: Referring Constitutional Amendment on Arbitration to the People

The special session did not pass a bill relating to the second item on the call—to refer a constitutional amendment to the people empowering the legislature to enact laws establishing arbitration in labor disputes. Arbitration of labor disputes was the subject many legislators wanted to address, yet they were limited by the governor's call to referring a constitutional amendment to the people that, if it passed, would then enable a future General Assembly to pass such an arbitration measure. Many argued that this was an unnecessary step, that they already had such power.

One of the three arbitration proposals introduced, SB 5, was sponsored by Helen and Senator Edward Affolter and drafted by former US senator Thomas M. Patterson at Helen's request. Like the governor's proposal, it was a constitutional amendment giving the legislature the power to pass laws related to compulsory arbitration of labor disputes, but, more than that, it added enforcement through court decrees.[90] SB 5 was referred to the Committee of the Whole by the Constitutional Amendments Committee without recommendation on May 8,[91] but it then disappeared from the *Journal*. The bill itself is missing from the State Archives.

SB 4 by Senator Pearson was a bill on arbitration, which Helen attempted to make a mirror image of her bill. The section she wished to add said:

> The General Assembly shall provide by law for the arbitration of all or any controversies between employers and their employes

[*sic*], touching wages, hours of labor and condition of labor; and such laws shall provide for the appearance of employers for themselves or by attorneys and of employes either for themselves or through such labor unions as they may be associated with and by attorneys; and such laws may provide for such arbitration to be conducted by boards, committees, commissions, or otherwise, as the legislature may decide; and the legislature may confer on such arbitration bodies, power, and authority to issue subpoenas for witnesses and the productions of documents and papers, and to otherwise compel the giving and production of testimony as same may be done by courts of record in this state.

And the legislature shall also provide for the full enforcement of any decree made by any such arbitration body or individuals; and there shall be no appeal from any such decree in arbitration proceedings.

Helen's amendment to the Committee of the Whole report failed on a vote of 9 to 19, with the progressives voting for and the machine members against. Without her amendment the bill drew a "nay" vote from her. It failed on a 13 to 15 vote.[92]

On this topic, however, the General Assembly did pass SJR 6, Investigation of the Persons Concerned in the Coal Strike of 1913–1914, by voice vote.[93] This study required research into all the circumstances of mining and into the violence during the strikes by a committee, which was to report to the next regular session in 1915; amazingly, state officials were expected to effect a settlement.[94] In HJR 6, also passed in the senate by voice vote, the house gave further directions hostile to the miners. It asked the investigators to find out who the leaders of the strike were, their nationalities and former occupations, how many spoke English, and whether they had taken part "in insurrections, war, lawlessness or violence in this country or elsewhere." It passed by voice vote.[95]

Call Item 3: Establishing a State Constabulary

In response to the third item on the call—to establish a state constabulary—the legislature merely passed a resolution, HJR 3, saying that the people of Colorado "recognize that the first and highest duty of citizens is to respect and render obedience to the law."[96] Helen voted against this fairly innocuous resolution, perhaps because of the travesty of the National Guard's enforcement of the law at Ludlow. More significant was SB 3, the administration bill on establishing a state police force. Helen voted for a motion to strike the enacting clause on the Committee of the Whole report, and the bill died 7 to 21.[97] There was a general fear that a state constabulary would be controlled by industry forces and would be as lawless as the National Guard had been at Ludlow.

Call Items 4 and 5: Controlling Saloons and Guns

The fourth and fifth items on the governor's call—saloon closures and gun sales—led to legislation (SB 2) allowing the governor to close saloons and end the sale of liquor whenever he perceived a condition of "riot, insurrection or invasion." Helen voted for this measure, which had overwhelming support, passing on the Third Reading 28 to 2.[98] Similarly, HB 4 on firearms and ammunition passed, even though the Senate Judiciary Committee had recommended postponing it indefinitely.[99] Thus began the continuing legislative debate on gun control. The bill allowed the governor to declare a condition of riot or insurrection and prohibit the sale, carrying, or use of firearms in any area of the state, except that the governor or his representative could give a permit to someone to defend his home, person, or property.[100]

Item 6: Paying the Expenses of the Session

The routine last item on the call, paying for the expenses of the Extraordinary Session, also passed.[101]

HELEN'S MEMORIAL TO PRESIDENT WILSON

Helen introduced Senate Joint Memorial (SJM) 1 addressed to President Woodrow Wilson asserting that the federal troops had established a truce in the strike fields and that their continued presence was essential until the existing controversy was settled.[102] The memorial was considered on May 15 and adopted 18 to 12, at least in the senate.[103] Helen and the other progressives were able to pass this memorial in the senate because the controlling machine wanted in exchange a two-thirds vote to adopt the emergency clause on the militia appropriations bill, an apparent case of unconstitutional vote trading.[104]

On May 8 Helen supported Senator John I. Tierney's extraordinary resolution, SJR 4, denouncing the governor, but it lost on a 7 to 22 vote, as the administration's machine controlled the senate.[105] The language of the resolution shows just how vituperative the session had become. The resolve clause said, in part,

> While we stand unalterably in support of law and order, it is
> anarchy to condone the lawlessness of officials sworn to enforce
> the law, and that while we hold all due respect for an office, it is
> unrighteous to make use of that sentiment in an attempt to pre-
> vent condemnation of the weak, corrupt or incompetent man in
> the office, since to do so is to transfer to an individual the love
> and the loyalty that is the sole due of the state and the sovereign
> people.[106]

The resolution was defeated 7 to 22.[107] A few days later Senator W. C. Robinson introduced a resolution calling on the governor to resign because of his incompetency.[108] Helen and others joined in the attack.[109] Apparently, she had second thoughts later because she voted against the resolution, which failed 3 to 26.[110]

When the session ended without a satisfactory solution to the violence in southern Colorado, President Wilson sent a telegram of reprimand to Governor Ammons, accusing him of forfeiting the sovereignty of the state because of his dependence on federal army forces. The text of the telegram was on the front page of the *Denver Express*:

> Am disturbed to hear the probability of the adjournment of your
> legislature and feel bound to remind you that my constitutional
> obligations with regard to the maintenance of order in Colorado
> are not to be indefinitely continued by the inaction of the state

legislature. The federal forces are there only until the state of Colorado has time and opportunity to resume complete sovereignty and control in the matter. I cannot conceive that the state is willing to forego her sovereignty or to throw herself entirely on the government of the United States and I am quite clear that she has no constitutional right to do so when it is within the power of her legislature to take effective action.

WOODROW WILSON[111]

Governor Ammons replied in a telegram, claiming that the appropriation of funds to pay the National Guard would allow him to control the situation. He also claimed that "a committee on mediation on the present strike has been provided for and appointed," when, in truth, the legislative committee was authorized only to investigate the causes of the strike.[112] Once again the governor, under the influence of the coal operators, was not totally honest in his representation. A senator tried to have the telegrams from and to the president read in the senate, but that was prohibited by rules. Helen managed to get the last, untruthful line about mediation into the explanation of her vote, which all senators are allowed at the time of announcing their "yea" or "nay." She read the last sentence of the telegram and declared, "I know of no such committee which has been appointed by this assembly."[113]

That night the muckraking author Upton Sinclair and Helen were guests at a dinner party at the home of Mrs. Steele, widow of Robert W. Steele, the late chief justice of the Colorado Supreme Court. Helen urged Sinclair to find out if the Associated Press (AP) was going to accurately report the facts about the communications with the president. Sinclair called the AP editor, who forced Sinclair to back down, in part because Sinclair could not believe the governor of the state would lie to the president. After further investigation he realized that everyone understood the committee's real purpose: "The purpose of this new legislative committee was to collect a lot of facts prejudicial to the strikers. Its members were all machine politicians of the very worst type. The idea of such a committee attempting to 'mediate,' or to 'settle the strike,' would have been regarded as a joke by the whole State."[114]

As a result of Sinclair's vigorous efforts with the papers and the AP service, the *Rocky Mountain News* finally printed the truth in an editorial headed "To the Patriots of Colorado": "Not one word about mediation is contained in the entire resolution. The committee is given no power to mediate. They may investigate, examine and report, and that is all . . . A committee on mediation has not been provided for; and none has been appointed. Think of the inutterable weakness of such conduct! Think of its stupidity!"[115]

The governor wasn't through with his lies. He told the *Denver Post* that a reading of the resolution would reveal that the committee had the power to "assist in settling the strike," which was just another falsehood.[116]

In one of two extant letters written by Helen Ring Robinson, she summarized her experience of the session: "The stress of our industrial situation here in Colorado with the extra session of the General Assembly which it entailed has required during the past month every moment of my time and every energy of my soul and body."[117]

There is no doubt that Helen was a major player in the exposure of the mine owners' actions before the session and in the debate and legislation passed in the special session. The major problem—how to settle strikes—remained unresolved. Action was called for in the next regular session of the legislature in 1915. Helen's role received a glowing report in *Harper's Weekly*:

> The only woman senator in the United States already fully tested and a proved honor to her state, still further established her statesmanship during the Colorado civil war. Several times she sought her information at the seat of battle. She talked with the militia and their wives as well as with the strikers and leaders. Where so many were blinded by hate, she was tolerant. Even when her heart suffered, she was calm. When she sympathized most, she had the needed scepticism [*sic*] of the investigator, and she knew that many of the women who poured out their sufferings to her were impetuous, gifted and inevitable liars. She sought also not the easiest temporary escape but permanent solutions. She is an example of the undoubted truth that politics is one of

the occupations in which a number of women are needed; and one of the occupations in which the first-class female intellect shows at its best.[118]

Helen testified about the Ludlow strike before the United States Industrial Relations Commission. She said she had studied the Canadian compulsory investigation law designed to prevent strikes.[119]

SUFFRAGISTS' NEW STRATEGY

After the special session ended, Helen continued her advocacy for woman suffrage. That summer Mrs. Chapman Catt, president of the International Suffrage Alliance, announced that women were to be admitted to the International Parliamentary Union to be held in Stockholm. Helen was to attend with women of the Finnish Parliament and other members of world legislative bodies who believed in peace and arbitration.[120]

In 1914 Helen also attended the great Marble House Conference at the mansion built by Alva Vanderbilt in Newport, Rhode Island, where she was a featured speaker. She was on the platform July 8 with Chicago Juvenile Court judge Mary M. Bartelme, education leader Ella Flagg Young, philanthropist Maud Billington Booth of the Volunteers of America, reformist Florence Kelly of the National Consumers League, and—most important because of the political force she represented—Rose Schneiderman of the National Women's Trade Union League.[121] She may have been at Marble House again at the end of August when the Congressional Union met. The union adopted the strategy that it would hold the party in power responsible for not giving women the right to vote. That bridge-burning policy meant holding President Wilson and the Democrats responsible, even though many of them had supported woman suffrage. By 1916 the Congressional Union, which became the Woman's Party, was urging women in the states where they could vote to cast that vote against candidates of any party that did not support suffrage or office holders who had been unsuccessful in passing suffrage legislation.[122] Helen did not support that strategy in the 1916 election because she thought it would hurt Woodrow Wilson's reelection campaign.

Helen undoubtedly prepared her bills in anticipation of the 1915 General Assembly, where she would have a reduced role after the Democrats lost control of both houses in the November election.

This is the first picture available of Helen Ring Robinson, taken around 1907 when she was president of the Denver Woman's Press Club. It appeared many times in the *Denver Post,* first on August 28, 1906. Courtesy, Denver Woman's Press Club from *Yearbook, 1907–1908,* frontispiece.

Helen King Robinson

PRESIDENT DENVER WOMAN'S PRESS CLUB

Helen served three years as president of the Denver Woman's Press Club in the time she was writing for the *Rocky Mountain News* and other periodicals. Date: 1908 or before. Courtesy, Denver Woman's Press Club from *Yearbook, 1908–1909,* frontispiece.

Views and Reviews
By Helen Ring Robinson

DURING the past week I have received two letters asking me to discuss the Patterson murder trial—though the place of the discussion was not plainly specified as these book columns.

In any case you need not be alarmed, Friendly Reader. For I would not give space here to a stench, even if there were not several other topics inviting attention.

There is hate, for example—a word, by the way, that should replace in murder trials the nauseating use of the word "love," which now so frequently prevails on such occasions.

And while on the subject of hate I feel impelled to chronicle the fact that Miranda tells me a certain woman tells her that she "hates" me because of something I once wrote or said or because of the way I wear my laugh—or

MRS. HELEN RING ROBINSON.

for some equally unreasonable reason. I feel very sorry and I wish the woman in question would come some day and have a cup of tea with me. It is really pretty good tea, and there is always plenty of cream and sugar.

I feel especially disposed to extend this cordial invitation because of recalling my Sydney Smith. "Don't introduce me to that man," said the witty canon on one occasion, "for I feel it my duty to hate him, and you can't hate a man when you know him."

In any case I would gladly do everything in my power to turn the mind of anyone from hate; for there is such hideous wastefulness in that emotion. And its by-product, as all are now agreed, is a kind of dirt-colored poisonous exhalation that is absorbed again into the system of the hater.

So I repeat here my invitation to the woman who "hates" me because of the way I wear my laugh. If she will only drink a cup or two of tea with me, with plenty of cream and sugar, we may, perhaps, become boons and laugh at each other—the very truest test of friendliness.

And here, to "clinch" the things I might say about laughter, permit me to quote from Chesterton:

"Laughter and love are everywhere. The cathedrals, built in the age that loved God, are full of blasphemous grotesques. The mother laughs continually at the child, the lover laughs continu-

Lane Co., New York) criticism grows respectful.

This legend of King Alfred beset by Danes, this poem "telescoping history" with faith and fervor is a remarkable achievement. It shows that the "Real Gilbert Chesterton" is a poet first and only a novelist and essayist afterwards. It shows him master of the phrase—that glows in a verse like this:

"Her face was like an open word
When brave men speak and choose,
The very colors of her coat
Were better than good news."

It shows him master of the ringing ballad measure of the poetic fires that burn in a stanza like this:

"To grow old cowed in a conquered land,
With the sun itself discrowned,
To see trees crouch and cattle slink—
Death is a better ale to drink
And by high Death on the fell brink,
That flagon shall go round."

It shows many other things. Not the least of them that Mr. Chesterton's day is still before him. (He is only 37). A man who can write both "Heretics" and "The Ballad of the

side my desk, clamoring for notice, I observe that there are an unusually large number of fairy stories in this collection also, though only one of them, if my memory serves me, has found a place in the "golden index" of Mr. Hadley's choosing.

In at least two cases I must add—the worse for the library list!

There is Selma Lagerlof's "Further Adventures of Nils," for example (Doubleday, Page & Co., New York). And even as I write this sentence I realize that an author who has achieved the distinction of winning a Nobel literary prize of $40,000 must, perforce, exert something of a hypnotic influence upon mere book reviewers. But when I turn again to this new book by the Swedish novelist, and read how Grayskin, the elk, meets with a "happy end;" how Karr, the terrier, faces his fate like a brave warrior; when I learn what the wild geese say to one another as they fly northward—then, indeed, I know that hypnotism has nothing at all to do with it. Enchantment is the only proper word. The enchantment of the art of this Swedish schoolmistress, who can travel blithely in Hans Christian Anderson land and discover new secrets for her telling. It is a quaintly delightful book; a volume to make youngsters recognize something of the feel of forests on their souls.

And here is another of the great names of contemporary European literature—even the name of Anatole France—linked with a story of childhood, of dwarfs and fairies and enchantments. "Honey-Bee" is the blessed yarn, and Mrs. John Lane is its translator from the French (John Lane Co., New York). "Honey-Bee," let it be known, was a darling golden-haired little princess, who lived in a land far off and a time dim and distant, while George of Blanchlande, who was reared with her as her foster brother, was a prince, "young, handsome, faithful and brave." And the very first lesson these children learned was "noblesse oblige." So it is not at all strange that when they went faring among nixies that lived under the water and gnomes that dwelt under the earth they still found pleasant places.

On general principles I believe the boys and girls of this democracy of ours have been overfed on princes and princesses; but if they must have them in their stories, then certainly I vote for the "Honey-Bee" and George of Blancheland sort.

But the story is not for every child. France distinctly warns some little folks away from it. This he declares

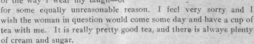

This picture appeared above Helen's regular newspaper columns on books and current events. "Views and Reviews," *Rocky Mountain News*, November 27, 1911, p. 10. Courtesy, Western History Collection, Denver Public Library.

Helen was interviewed extensively shortly after her election because she was a novelty—the first woman state senator in Colorado and the second in the country to serve in such a body. *Denver Republican*, November 8, 1912, p. 10. Courtesy, Western History Collection, Denver Public Library; also available from the Library of Congress.

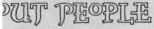

Women have been elected to other political offices, but Helen Ring Robinson of Colorado, teacher and writer, is the first of her sex to have been chosen a State Senator

Carrel, who by his marvelous discoveries won a Nobel prize as a notable benefactor y, although born in France, has achieved triumphs in America, his adopted country

in certain surgical operations was the difficulty of sewing together several veins or arteries. Doctor Carrel introduced a novel method of sewing that made possible feats of arterial surgery that could not otherwise be attempted. More recently his achievements in the surgical grafting of limbs, the transplanting of organs such as the kidneys without ill effect, and the maintaining of life, function and growth for protracted periods in organs and tissues apart from the body, have been the talk of the medical world. One of his latest and most directly practical discoveries, the result of five years of experimentation, indicates that by the use of a stimulating medium the growth of tissues necessary for the healing of wounds and the knitting of broken bones may be wonderfully accelerated. It is believed by surgeons to be quite possible that when the new method is perfected a broken bone may be mended within a week, a flesh wound healed within a day, and that large areas of skin removed by accidental burning or scalding may be rapidly replaced without the long and uncertain process of grafting. Doctor Carrel is rather short in stature, with a finely rounded head, a ready smile and the most perfect manners in the world.

the expedi-
dge of the
en carried
rt at least,
d the nine
during the
l job—that
ight lasted
or listened
ll-throated
: "We get
o eat it at
fast—eight
vs how to
an houses.

HELEN RING ROBINSON, *State Senator*—This year, in which for the first time a woman cast an electoral vote for a Presidential candidate (even though for a losing one), has also been signalized by the first appearance of a woman as a member of the Senate of one of these United States. We have had several woman mayors and woman members of the lower houses of state legislatures, but Mrs. Helen Ring Robinson has the distinction of being the first State Senator of her sex in this country. Colorado has had equal suffrage for nineteen years, and the lower branch of the Legislature that met two years ago had four woman members. These women conscientiously championed measures emanating from women's clubs and similar organizations, especially such measures as were framed to better the condition of working women and to safeguard the morals of the young; but at the end

This photo accompanied one of the many articles about Helen that appeared in national women's periodicals after her election. A. Guiterman, *Woman's Home Companion*, April 1913, p. 5. Courtesy, Denver Public Library.

Taken when Helen was a senator, this frequently reproduced picture conveys some of her confidence and good nature. Published in James Semple, *Representative Women of Colorado* (Denver: by the author, 1914), p.67. Date: ca. 1910. Courtesy, Bain Collection, Library of Congress.

Helen Ring Robinson

After one regular session and one special session in the Colorado State Senate, Helen remained a force to be reckoned with in 1915, though she decided not to run for a second term. Pictorial Roster Twentieth General Assembly, 1915 (Denver: Pictorial Roster Publishing, 1915). Courtesy, Stephen H. Hart Library, History Colorado, F-6558, Denver.

5

THE "SILLY" TWENTIETH GENERAL ASSEMBLY

The political winds turned decidedly conservative in Colorado at the November 1914 election. Voters passed the prohibition of the sale of intoxicating liquors as of January 1916, 129,589 to 118,017. Control of the next regular General Assembly shifted back to the "law and order" Republicans in a landslide victory.[1] Of the seventeen senators elected, only five were Democrats.[2] The control in the senate was then a tight 18 to 17 for the Republicans; all but one of the committee chairs and leaders of the senate were Republicans, including the president of the senate, Lieutenant Governor Moses Lewis, who was elected for the 1915–1916 term. Which party is in charge can determine where a senator sits, and in later years it came to determine how desirable his or her office space is. While I was in office, the majority Republicans officed one Democratic senator in a windowless broom closet, which he claimed to like.

The sole Democratic committee chair during this session was Barney Napier, who had run for governor.[3] Helen, a holdover senator, lost the chairmanship of the Committee on Education and Educational Institutions. She served as a member of that committee and of two others, the City and County of Denver Committee and the Revision and Engrossment Committee.[4] Helen was still the only woman in the senate; there was also only one woman in the house, Representative Evangeline Heartz.[5]

With a one-vote margin, every member of the majority party had to "stick" to the party position or party bills would lose. Further, only one defection from the Republican majority was needed for the minority party to succeed in passing its bills. The Democrats did succeed in forcing approval of former Governor Ammons's recess appointments.[6] Later in the session the conversion of one Republican on the workers' compensation issue did allow the Democrats to take over. Even then, the Republicans still had the veto power of the new Republican governor, George A. Carlson.

TRANSITION FROM AMMONS TO CARLSON

Though the governorship changed from Democratic to Republican hands, we saw in the 1914 special session (see chapter 4) that Helen often opposed Democratic governor Elias Ammons, so a Republican governor was not a major change for her.

Shortly after the General Assembly convened on January 6, retiring Governor Ammons addressed a joint session on many of the same themes he had put forth in the special session. He wanted stronger penalties "for treason, sedition and armed resistance of the militia or civil officers of the state and the several counties." He pretended not to understand the public distrust of the National Guard, infamous for its actions in the Ludlow Massacre. He decried the lack of an existing law on industrial disputes to help him address the recent coal strike. In addition, he talked about the civil service initiative passed in the 1912 election and the prohibition initiative; he suggested forbidding the collection of petition signatures for pay, which is now permitted;

and he reported that the new Public Utilities Commission had been organized.[7]

In his first speech to the legislators on January 12, the new governor Carlson glorified the state with comments that sounded not just conservative but faintly suggestive of fascism:

> Our schools should give more serious attention to the development of the sense of civic obligation. They should instill into every student the conviction that his or her first duty is loyalty to the state. The strong individualist is not only of no value to the state but he is a man of arrested and contracted development. The sense of loyalty to the state should be developed until it becomes like the devotion to family. This is true education . . . If all native or adopted sons and daughters of the Centennial state will have riveted in their minds the consciousness . . . that they are mutually related to one great, real living and throbbing entity—their state—which they are ready to serve and willing to defend, then internal dissension will be impossible and peace, good will and justice will become a reality.[8]

Public lands and all the state's natural resources, Carlson believed, should be open for development. Higher education institutions should be given generous state support, he said.[9]

On the unfinished business of the 1914 Extraordinary Session, Governor Carlson wanted to put through pro-employer workers' compensation, which would prohibit workers from filing lawsuits against employers. To end labor strife he called for the establishment of an industrial commission to administer laws concerning the relationship between employer and employee, with no mention of a constitutional amendment, which Governor Ammons had argued had to come first. The industrial commission would regulate safety and health and provide arbitration and mediation. In addition, it would run a system of workers' compensation.[10] This became the key issue of the session, one that led to the Democratic takeover of the senate, at least temporarily. Because this issue dominated legislative discussion for two years, it is worth examining more closely.

BATTLE OVER WORKERS' COMPENSATION

The drive for a Colorado industrial commission was a consequence of the progressive movement and its faith in experts to solve problems. Teddy Roosevelt had proposed such a commission at the federal level in 1906. Unions would be prohibited from striking while the dispute was being investigated.[11]

Republican senator William Eaton introduced SB 99, the bill Carlson supported, on January 25, but many legislators believed it was fatally flawed because it covered two subjects: an industrial commission and a workers' compensation system. Embracing two subjects violated the constitutional rule, which is still in force, that each bill can contain only one subject. Further, all amendments must "fit under the title"; that is, they may not expand the subject beyond that title (though the scope of a bill may be narrowed by amendment), and all amendments must be germane to that title. In addition to establishing the Industrial Commission, the Eaton bill would have provided compensation to employees for accidental injury or death out of an insurance plan it created for that compensation, an attempt to design Colorado's first workers' compensation plan.[12] Senate Democrats opposed the bill because it provided workers' compensation through private insurance and eliminated the state labor department, supporter of workers' rights.[13]

After a motion passed to print 1,000 copies of SB 99, Helen moved to print 200 more copies, suggesting her assessment that this was an important piece of legislation that should be broadly distributed.[14] (In those days bills were printed only if a committee felt they were worthy of further consideration.)

Senate Democrats, including Helen, were determined to fight the first version of SB 99, and they received help from an unexpected quarter. On February 26 they staged a coup, defeating SB 99 in the Committee of the Whole, 19 to 15, because the seventeen Democrats were joined by Republican senator William J. Candlish of Leadville.[15] They sent the bill for further amendment to a Special Committee consisting of Senator Candlish and Senator George Lewis, with the plan of modeling the new bill after an Ohio law already approved by the US Supreme Court (see Committee of the Whole report).[16] The other Republican voting to kill the bill was Senator Francis J. Knauss, who intended to move for reconsideration the following Monday. (He voted "nay" because the person making the motion for reconsideration has to have voted with the prevailing side.)[17]

In the committee the Democrats and Candlish planned to substitute SB 461, Senator Lewis and Senator Edward Affolter's bill on workers' compensation introduced February 4, for SB 99. The Finance Committee was expected to report out both bills in order to have two titles, one for the Industrial Commission and one for workers' compensation, which would be amended to provide higher payments to injured workers than the governor's bill allowed.[18] The Special Committee struck the entire bill and wrote a new one that created an industrial commission that promoted voluntary arbitration or mediation.

When the new version of SB 99 came to the floor, Senator Eaton tried a strike-below amendment on Third Reading, which would have wiped out the committee version and replaced it with his, but this effort was defeated again by the same 18 to 17 Democratic majority with the help of Senator Candlish. Helen, of course, voted with the Democrats.[19] SB 99 finally passed 18 to 16 on Third Reading with Helen's support,[20] suggesting that, with amendments, it had become acceptable to some Democrats.

The bill, after much amendment, passed 35 to 20 in the house.[21] On March 30, when house members learned that the senate did not concur in their amendments, the house voted to adhere to its own version and requested a conference committee. Responding angrily in the kind of dispute that frequently breaks out between the house and the senate, the senate considered reorganizing all senate committees in retaliation for the Republican-controlled house having killed its workers' compensation bill. With Candlish's vote, the Democrats had become the majority party by the margin of one and thus had the power to appoint all new (Democratic) committee chairs and make all committee assignments.[22]

It is difficult, if not impossible, to know how many changes were made to the bill before its final passage, but the Democratic control of the senate very likely forced the Republican house and governor to make some concessions. Though the workers' compensation plan was voluntary, there would be stringent penalties for companies that did not participate. Because the plan was to be administered by the insurance commissioner, no new staff was needed.[23]

The final version of SB 99 set up a new system of compensating workers for accidental injury or death, to be administered by the Industrial Commission. Every employer of four or more workers was required to insure his employees.

The Colorado Industrial Commission was created separately in HB 177. With this law Colorado became the first state in the nation to implement a proposal President Theodore Roosevelt had presented to the US Congress in 1906. It provided a way for government to investigate labor disputes before allowing workers to strike.[24] Colorado's Industrial Commission consisted of three state officials: the governor, the attorney general, and the secretary of state.[25]

When the governor's industrial bill passed the house, a conference committee was needed to settle the differences between the two houses. There are always three conference committee members from each house, two from the majority party and one from the minority party. The Democrats successfully maneuvered to put Candlish on the committee as one of the Republicans, though he was voting with the Democrats on this issue.[26] Thus two of the three senate members would take the Democratic position, even though by party numbers the Republicans controlled the senate. According to one Denver paper, HB 177, the Drake bill, which began in the house, was originally identical to SB 99, the Eaton bill in the senate.[27] But the bill was changed. The bill shows a lengthy amendment to be inserted "after striking all following enabling clause."[28]

HB 177 charged the Industrial Commission with overseeing worker safety and the insurance plan to pay the compensation. It covered all workers except domestic workers, farmhands, and those in businesses with fewer than four employees. Persons seeking employment in the mines were to be examined ahead of time by county boards to be sure they were competent. The arbitration the bill provided was not binding unless both parties agreed ahead of time that it should be. Lockouts and strikes were prohibited unless preceded by arbitration.[29] Another bill, HB 604, permitted the formation of mutual liability insurance companies to provide the workers' compensation insurance for employees.[30]

When the administration's weak workers' compensation bill, SB 99, and the Industrial Commission bill, HB 177, passed, it was better than nothing, according to the *Denver Express*.[31] In the early years of the commission it protected consumers rather than workers and settled most disputes in favor of management.[32]

CIRCUS IN THE HOUSE—AND THE SENATE

Passing significant legislation was made more difficult for Helen by the tone of the session in the house. The events that occurred on the floor of the house during this session were shocking by modern standards. The behavior of this General Assembly was so juvenile that the liberal *Denver Express* labeled it "the Silly Twentieth."[33] Lobbyists and visitors usually mobbed the floors of both houses, but, at the beginning of this year, visitors on the floor were limited to newspaper reporters and staff. Even reporters could make it difficult for legislators to follow what was happening. (Today, reporters are limited to a table at the front of the chamber and benches around the perimeter of the floor.) Removing lobbyists from the floor permanently would have allowed legislators to vote more independently. However, before long they were right back at the legislators' elbows, pleading for votes that favored their interest groups.[34] Practically nothing was accomplished in the first few weeks of the session, which some blamed not on the lobbyists but on a split in the majority Republican Party.[35]

A court case "uncovered" paid lobbyists, which was considered shocking at the time. S. A. Coston testified that he was given $100 by James Quigg Newton to travel with Governor Carlson to Madison, Wisconsin. Coston was employed by three coal companies to pass SB 321, SB 330, and SB 430 to pay for the companies' losses during the coal strike. Coston, as well as Newton, later denied having lobbied

Carlson. In response to this story, the legislature passed a resolution to investigate lobbying.[36] At the present time the noise and importunities of lobbyists, who are now openly paid to try to influence legislators, are confined to the lobby area outside the arched glass windows in the rear of the chamber, where they are reduced to sending notes by way of the sergeants-at-arms begging legislators to come off the floor to talk to them. If the president of the senate is annoyed by the number of members who have been called to the lobby, he or she will not allow the lobbyists to send in any more notes.

In party caucuses during this session there was frequent unconstitutional vote trading, according to the *Denver Express*.[37] Vote trading is defined as an agreement by legislator A to support the bill of legislator B in exchange for legislator B's agreement to support the bill of legislator A. This was and is explicitly prohibited in the Colorado Constitution.

An example of the shocking behavior on the floor of the house was the case of Representative W. W. Howland. The Denver political machine, what Judge Ben Lindsey called "the Beast" in his book by that name, delivered a wad of money to Representative Howland on the floor of the house. Under investigation, Howland said the money was to be given to a woman detective whose job was to "get something" on Judge Lindsey. Judge Lindsey was accused of certain immoral acts on a particular night, but at the time of the alleged impropriety he was in the East at the home of none other than Teddy Roosevelt, who vouched for him. Howland had given an entirely different story about the money to a grand jury investigating the situation.[38] Howland was arrested for perjury on March 15 and expelled by a vote of the house the next day.[39] Eventually, Howland was acquitted of the charge of bribery because, though he had lied under oath, that was not material to the charge of bribery.[40]

Not even the rules of procedure were followed in this unruly session. Though most of the disturbances took place in the house, long considered—at least by the senate—to have a lower standard of decorum than the senate, irregularities also occurred in the senate. (The house generally accuses the members of the senate of being senile, causing them to nod off.) On March 30 the president of the senate refused to "put" (take a vote on) a motion of Senator Burris to go into the Committee of the Whole to vote on Representative Edward Sabin's utility bill. He probably feared that in the Committee of the Whole the utility bill would lose, but such a violation of the rules was shocking. With majority control of the senate, the president should have been able to lead his party to vote as he wished rather than blatantly violating procedure by refusing to take a vote.[41] Again, in the house, by simply reversing the "yeas" and "nays," a winning vote to strike the entire Sabin utility bill (HB 287) below the enabling clause was fraudulently called a losing vote. Had the chair ruled correctly, the bill would have died.[42] Perhaps because of the public opprobrium attached to HB 287 by these incidents, the Committee of the Whole recommended that SB 229 be substituted for HB 287. This substitute bill passed both houses but was vetoed by the governor[43] (see the section Bills Threatening Home Rule below).

The most flagrant violation of decorum was an eruption of fisticuffs between a representative and the editor of the *Denver Express*. The trouble began on the house floor when editor Charles Newell, who was interviewing a representative, casually sat down in Representative Schmidt's unoccupied chair. He exchanged some banter with Representative Alphonse Ardourel, who then angrily followed Newell to the back of the chamber and socked him with a glancing blow. (The feisty Ardourel had fought the lightweight champion of the world at the Press Club during the previous session.)[44] The speaker of the house called everyone to order and demanded that Newell, who had received the blow, appear the next day "before the bar of the House." When Newell appeared the next day, he was accused not of disorderly conduct but of sitting in a member's chair. There was and is a rule against anyone but the assigned member sitting in his or her chair, as if the power of the office resided in the chair rather than in the person elected.[45]

Newell filed a charge of assault against Ardourel, who was arrested in the house chamber. Ardourel was later found guilty of assault without provocation and fined $10 and costs. The judge declared that a member of the house "is obliged to conform to the laws of the state." Ardourel appealed his conviction but later dropped the appeal and paid his fine, which the newspaper said was his admission of guilt. Newell sued Ardourel for $10,000 for assault and Speaker Steward for $50,000 for false arrest.[46]

In another example of threatened violence, one representative, Robert Harris, received a death threat over his bill to prohibit giving or receiving tips. We can only wonder why that aroused such passion.[47]

ANTI-PROGRESSIVES ATTACK

Members of the new conservative Republican majority led by Representatives Sabin and Ardourel quickly introduced bills to reverse the progressive changes passed at the polls and in the General Assembly over the previous five years. A conservative Democrat, Senator George West, introduced bills to repeal the direct primary, recall of officials, and recall of judges' decisions. He wanted to force the Republicans to either kill or endorse these progressive measures.[48] Representative Ardourel targeted free speech (four bills); others were aimed at Judge Lindsey and the Juvenile Court (four bills) and the initiative and referendum powers.[49] Finally, the conservatives tried to emasculate the new civil service system.

Three of Representative Sabin's bills were attacks on Helen's legislation of the previous session. Two were HB 292 and HB 390, both to repeal the minimum wage bill for women and minors. His third attack on earlier bills was SB 584, which would have given parents the right to reclaim their children from the State Home for Dependent and Neglected Children in certain cases of dependency. It is perhaps a tribute to Helen that none of these bills passed.

Ardourel's first bill attacking free speech (HB 1) was extraordinary in that it proposed the death penalty for speech it considered treason, a penalty that was soon amended to imprisonment. The crime would have included anyone who took up arms to defend his or her family against a government force (such as the National Guard at Ludlow). The second made it a crime of sedition to defy civil officers of the state or the militia or to make a public speech or publish anything inflammatory in character and having a tendency to incite public disorder.[50] These bills are particularly objectionable when one remembers the National Guard's unjustified attacks on civilians in the southern Colorado mining fields the previous year.

Representative Edward Sabin and his friends were out to kill any bill proposed by Judge Ben Lindsey, Helen's progressive ally.[51] In a direct attack on Lindsey, who had just been elected judge of the Juvenile Court, Sabin attempted to eliminate the Juvenile Court by introducing four anti-Lindsey bills on February 2—House Bills 346, 347, 348, and 349. HB 346 would have created new courts and judges. Helen pointed out that the new judges would provide no relief because they were to be given additional duties. This bill initially passed but ultimately died on Third Reading on a vote of 17 to 18, with Helen voting against.[52] HB 347 removed juveniles from the jurisdiction of the Juvenile Court and placed them in the newly created courts. This passed 19 to 15,[53] with Helen opposing.[54] HB 348 repealed the law establishing juvenile courts in the larger counties. When the bill was heard in the senate, Helen moved to amend the Committee of the Whole report by striking the enacting clause ("be it enacted that . . ."), which would have killed the bill.[55] The motion was not voted on, however. The bill passed Third Reading on an 18 to 16 vote; Helen voted against it. HB 349, like 347, gave divorce and juvenile matters to the district court. It passed Second Reading on a 20 to 14 vote.[56]

The "bitter fight" against these bills in the senate was led by Senators Tierney, Affolter, and Helen. One newspaper called the bills "a vicious menace to child welfare."[57] Eventually, the governor vetoed SB 348 (repealing juvenile courts in large counties) and SB 349, giving divorce and juvenile matters to other courts,[58] so this attempt to reverse some of the progressive agenda was defeated.

The recently created civil service was also on the chopping block. In a proposed return to the spoils system in HB 173, every governor would have been empowered to appoint a new three-person civil service commission. Then the governor could have replaced all current state employees with his own people. There were more breeches of decorum in the house during the deliberation of this bill on March 24. During Second Reading the Committee of the Whole chairman, Representative Schmidt, got into a tussle over a pitcher of ice water a Democrat was kindly bringing him because he had complained of thirst. Both men were drenched as a result. After the house Democrats filibustered all afternoon, the speaker imposed a gag rule. A request to read the bill at length—a request that is always honored in some form—was refused.[59] The bill finally passed on Third Reading in the house on March 29, even though the Democrats complained that the rules had been violated when the chair had refused the request to read it at length.[60] In the senate Helen voted against the bill, but it passed 18 to 17 on April 10, the last day of the session.[61]

THE REPORT ON ALL STATE INSTITUTIONS

In this circus atmosphere, Helen, who was so passionate about improving the lives of women and children, must have been something of a misfit. She was still given responsibilities, as represented by her serving on the three-person ceremonial committee to notify the house that the senate was organized and ready for business[62] and her chairing the Committee of the Whole, a job the president can assign temporarily to any member.[63] Her most significant assignment came out of a resolution of the previous regular session, SJR 21—the joint committee to visit all state institutions and report to the General Assembly on their needs for the next twenty years. She chaired the committee, which was not fully appointed until after the house members were elected in November 1914. It had a tight schedule and the enormous task of visiting all the institutions before January, when it was to report to the General Assembly. The committee flatly refused to take on the impossible task of forecasting expenses for twenty years but did propose the institutions' priorities and financial needs for the next two years, particularly in capital and maintenance—performing much like the current Joint Budget Committee and Capital Development Committee combined. The two-year period was the minimum it could address because the General Assembly would not meet again in regular session until 1917.

The report of this special committee, printed in full in the *Senate Journal*,[64] throws some light on the early years of many Colorado institutions that still exist today. The problems are similar to those the state faces now, just on a smaller scale. Here are a few of the comments.

The report divided institutions into four types: Educational, Dependent (the State Home for Dependent and Neglected Children and the Soldiers' and Sailors' Home), Penal (Colorado State Penitentiary, Colorado State Reformatory, State Industrial Schools for Boys, and State Industrial School for Girls), and Defective (Colorado Insane Asylum and the State Home for Mental Defectives).

Interestingly, each educational institution received support from a property tax mill levy. At the University of Colorado, enrollment over the past ten years had increased 254 percent, while the revenue from the mill levy had only increased 15 percent. The university was praised for its high quality, but it was also overcrowded. The greatest need cited by the committee was for a women's dormitory, the lack of which caused careful parents to enroll their daughters in eastern colleges. The second building needed was a medical school building.[65]

The State Agricultural College (Colorado State University) in Fort Collins received $85,000 per year from the mill levy. It needed a new heating plant, and its administrators wanted to receive the interest on the State Land Board funds to which they believed they were entitled. The Veterinary Department also needed $10,000.[66]

At Fort Lewis College in Durango, the new school had an enrollment of only 37 in the current year but reached 5,000 students through its extension courses. The committee recommended a $2,000 purchase of livestock to be run on the land, which its members believed would make the school nearly self-sustaining.[67]

The Colorado School of Mines in Golden, which had an experimental and research department, was in excellent financial condition. The committee recommended releasing $25,000 of the $60,000 of its balance accumulated from both student fees and its mill levy.[68]

Enrollment at the State Teachers' College (University of Northern Colorado) in Greeley was 1,850. Its one-fifth mill levy raised $86,000 a year. The committee recommended $102,000 for construction and maintenance, though the president wanted a larger appropriation.[69]

The Gunnison State Normal School (Western State College) and the Colorado School for the Deaf and Blind in Colorado Springs were also reviewed.[70]

In the institutions classified as "Dependent," the committee remarked on the high quality of the buildings at the State Home for Dependent and Neglected Children (Denver) and the reasonable cost—$12,000 to $18,000 per building. The committee subsequently reduced the appropriations for buildings at other institutions after learning that buildings could be constructed for so little.[71]

At the major penal institution, Colorado State Penitentiary in Cañon City, the report said, the warden put the prisoners to work on highways, three farms, and a garden tract. The prisoners also constructed all the new buildings. The profit from these endeavors was $55,412. Nevertheless, then, as now, the prison needed one of the largest appropriations—$272,000. In the last biennial period 1,004 men had been confined there, and there had been twenty-six escapes.[72]

In commenting on the Colorado State Reformatory, the committee lamented the fact that residents were not sentenced there for a long enough period of time, suggesting great confidence in the salutary effect of incarceration on juveniles. "The institution can never be of any real benefit to the state until at least a minimum period of one year is spent there by the prisoners," the report opined. Most of the 149 inmates were out on their honor working on ranches.[73]

The committee wanted to draw attention to the fact that the State Industrial School for Girls and the State Home for Dependent and Neglected Children, the two institutions whose boards were composed chiefly of women, were managed with surpassing efficiency and economy. As the only woman on this committee, Helen probably made this observation. She later commented that women have more time to devote to boards and for cultivating social understanding.[74] At the Industrial School for Girls, the residents went to school but also made and repaired their own clothes and were trained in domestic and industrial work. The girls' home counties paid the school fifty cents per girl per day.

Among the institutions for the "defectives" was the Colorado State Insane Asylum, with 1,190 inmates. In this era before the establishment of the Fort Logan Mental Health Center, the asylum needed more room, since its several hundred overflow patients were housed in the Denver city hospital and various county jails and poor farms around the state. Among the many needs was a new kitchen for the male department, where the kitchen was "unsanitary and disgraceful." The water supply was also "unsatisfactory."[75] The committee recommended a Denver branch for the Pueblo asylum, perhaps at the Ridge home location. In total it asked for $452,000 for the State Insane Asylum at Pueblo and $200,000 to build a Denver branch.[76]

About 80 "mental defectives" between ages five and twenty were cared for at the State Home and Training School for Mental Defectives at Ridge, but another 100 children around the state "should be in this institution."[77] The committee recommended building another cottage.

In its conclusion, the committee observed that it was impossible to collect reliable information on which to plan for the next twenty years: "The figures necessary as the basis of such recommendations would at best be only approximate and must depend upon the unknowable future growth of the state."[78] The committee recommended that the state pay as it goes, rather than amend the constitution to allow for more extensive bonding for construction. The Insane Asylum needs were so great that the members initially thought more bonding might be necessary; however, the constitution allowed for fifteen-year bonds, which they thought would be adequate. A central board of supervision for all institutions was recommended, one that could keep records at a central office of lands platted to show all improvements. The committee also recommended a central insurance adviser and consideration of the state carrying its own insurance.[79]

The legislature passed a bill for a similar survey before the next regular session in 1917 on a 26 to 7 vote. Helen was absent for the vote.[80]

Other than chairing this major committee, Helen was less successful in the Twentieth General Assembly than she had been in the Nineteenth because she was in the minority party. Consequently, she passed just two of the nine bills she introduced.

HELEN'S BILLS ON WOMEN'S ISSUES

Helen continued to be an advocate for women, as she had been in the two previous sessions. She acted on the recommendation of her interim committee that a women's residence hall be constructed at the University of Colorado by cosponsoring SB 407 with Senator Elliot. She had observed that many families sent their daughters east to school because of the lack of appropriate housing for them on the Boulder campus. Unfortunately, the bill in the Colorado Archives does not have a dollar amount in the appropriations blank, probably because it did not get as far as the Appropriations Committee. The bill was referred to the Finance Committee, where it disappeared.[81]

Except for two bills addressing the evils of prostitution, Helen lacked the critical mass of women legislators and progressive men to pass bills that would improve the lot of women. Nevertheless, she put forth the ideas she believed in. First, as she had done in 1913, she sponsored a minimum wage bill to see that working single women earned enough to support themselves without having to resort to prostitution.[82] This bill closely resembled one Helen had passed in the 1913 session, but apparently she felt that law needed some amendment. In the second bill she went after the owners or renters of brothels.

SB 48, on the determination of minimum wages for women and minors, created a board of three commissioners to inquire into the wages of women and girls. The bill made it "unlawful to employ women in any occupation within the State of Colorado for wages which are inadequate to supply the necessary cost of living and to maintain them in health." It also made it unlawful to employ minors "for unreasonably low wages." The board was to set minimum wages after investigating various occupations. When the board found that

---

some women were underpaid, it could appoint a "conference," which resembled a mediation panel. The conference would report its recommendation to the commission.[83]

The minimum wage bill moved through both houses with overwhelming support, having been introduced in the senate on January 15 and sent to the Committee on Labor.[84] It passed Third Reading in the house 48 to 2, with 14 absent.[85] In spite of this strong support, Governor Carlson vetoed the bill on April 7.[86] He may have thought the 1913 law was enough, though he cut the funding for the commission set up to carry out that law from $1,770.80 plus $480 to just $100 (HB 551). This partial veto was not recorded as are other cuts in appropriations.[87]

Helen's other successful bill, one to fight prostitution, was SB 88, concerning nuisances and providing penalties. The text declared, "Every building or place used in whole or in part for the purpose of lewdness, assignation or prostitution is a nuisance, whether the same be a public or private nuisance, and every building or place, or the ground itself, in or upon which such acts of lewdness, assignation or prostitution is [sic] conducted, permitted or carried on, and the furniture, fixtures, musical instruments and contents are also declared a nuisance, and shall be enjoined and abated as hereinafter provided." The district attorney or any resident could maintain an action in equity. The property could be sold and the building closed for a year. The abatement could be canceled if the owner ceased the activity, paid costs, and posted a bond. If there was no reasonable ground for the action, the citizen who brought it could be assessed costs, an effort to avoid frivolous lawsuits.[88] Helen tried an amendment to the Committee of the Whole report to shift costs and damages to a plaintiff who brought a false suit. She withdrew it before the Second Reading vote. Disobeying a court injunction could lead to a fine of $200 to $1,000, jail for one month to life, or both. SB 88 passed Third Reading without debate, possibly because the men were too embarrassed to discuss prostitution with the woman senator, on a 26 to 7 vote on March 3 after Helen demanded a call of the senate.[89] SB 88 passed, and it was not vetoed.[90]

Helen also tried to improve divorce law for women, though today we would find her proposal one-sided as it allowed women a new cause for divorce that was not granted to men—probably because in that era men were by law the family providers.[91] SB 152 provided that if a husband "shall have been adjudged insane or mentally incompetent by a court of competent jurisdiction and shall have remained incurably insane or mentally incompetent for a period of five years or more prior to the beginning of the action for divorce," a divorce was justified.[92] We can only speculate that Helen had personal experience with mental illness, but she certainly had empathy for the families in such cases. Though we don't know if her husband, Ewing, had any mental illness, his daughter had a breakdown in early adulthood, indicating the possibility of such illness in Ewing's family.[93] Because Helen sensed that this bill would never come out of the Judiciary Committee, she tried to attach her bill as an amendment to Senator William Robinson's divorce bill (SB 9) shortening the qualifying period of mental illness to two years. This led to heated discussion in the senate, where Helen declared that "a woman with an insane husband and with little children to care for should not be permanently prohibited from remarrying."[94] Helen's amendment failed and William Robinson's bill passed 20 to 14, with Helen voting against.[95] Helen's bill died in the Judiciary Committee on the last day of the session.[96]

SB 584 by Representative Sabin was an effort to reverse a law Helen had passed in 1913. The new bill would have allowed parents to reclaim their children within a year of having given them up to a children's home, which was often done for reasons of poverty. Their inability to reclaim their children was the consequence of Helen's bill giving the decision about releasing children to a board at the State Home for Dependent and Neglected Children. In perhaps the only newspaper article ever printed in that paper that was critical of her, the *Denver Express* devoted an entire front-page editorial to attacking Helen and her continued support for her earlier legislation, contrasting the children with hogs taken to satisfy a debt that, unlike the children, could always be reclaimed.[97] She defended the bill strongly:

"My bill passed two years ago made the board of trustees of the State Home for Dependent Children the sole judge of whether their parents are capable of redeeming them," said Mrs. Robinson. "I thought then, and I still think, that women members of the board are better qualified to judge of a mother's fitness to care for children once turned over to the state than is a jury of men in court.

"Poverty is not the only reason mothers are adjudged unfit to care for their children."

"Do you think any appointive board which people have no voice in electing and which the people can not recall should be clothed with judicial powers from which there is no appeal?" she was asked.

"Yes," she replied. "And I know the women are better able to judge such cases."[98]

Perhaps Helen and the *Denver Express* would have had less divergent views if they had made distinctions about the causes of the state home placement. If a child was placed only because of his or her parents' poverty, the parents should have had the ability to reclaim the child when their situation improved. However, if the parents had been guilty of abuse or neglect, then a board might have been the best place for that decision. Judges and members of juries, of course, were all men. Sabin's bill made it to the senate, where it was sent to the Judiciary Committee, which referred it to the Committee of the Whole without recommendation. There is no record of the bill after that, and Helen's law remained in force, suggesting that Helen was able to sway her colleagues to support her position and suppress this bill.[99]

Helen's SB 391, making it unlawful to destroy food products in restraint of trade, was part of her effort to look out for the economic interests of housewives, the "special interest" she had promised to represent. It would have made destroying food for the purpose of establishing higher prices a misdemeanor punishable by a $100 to $500 fine and up to six months in jail. Such tricks were apparently a problem at the time. The bill was introduced on February 4 and sent to the Committee on Horticulture, which referred it favorably to the

Committee of the Whole.[100] There is no record of Second or Third Reading.

Another food-related bill, SB 458, sponsored by Senator Hamilton and Helen, concerned cold storage. Facilities for storing fresh meat products, fish, game, poultry, eggs, and butter were to be licensed by the state. A commission would establish basic sanitary rules. The cold storage facility had to be cooled to at most 45 degrees, and it was not allowed to keep food that was tainted, diseased, or otherwise unfit for human consumption. No food could be held longer than one year. The fact that the only woman in the senate considered such a bill necessary suggests that there were many problems with food quality in this era of uncertain or nonexistent refrigeration. SB 458 was postponed indefinitely in the State Affairs Committee.[101]

PROPOSED CHANGES IN THE JUSTICE SYSTEM

As with her bills in the previous regular session to allow women to sit on juries, Helen continued to take an interest in the justice system. She sponsored SB 310 to permit adult probation. An adult probation bill had been suggested by Judge Ben Lindsey to the Colorado Social Services League in April 1914, so perhaps he was the source of this idea. The bill extended the possibility of up to four years of probation for all persons charged with misdemeanors and felonies except those punishable by death or life imprisonment or persons who committed violent rape. It also provided for the deduction of child support from wages. The bill passed in the senate 32 to 1 but died in the house. Today, it is hard to imagine a legal system without adult probation.[102]

In early January Helen talked about a bill to create a reformatory for adult women offenders who were at that time housed at the men's penitentiary in Cañon City. However, there is no record of her actually introducing such a bill.[103]

Helen was apparently the deciding vote in defeating a bill that would have eliminated the right of the supreme court to make its own rules. She had been undecided about how to vote and suddenly decided to vote "no" in an important vote for maintaining the independence of the judiciary.[104] Perhaps her hesitation was influenced by Ewing's earlier disbarment case before the supreme court.

BILLS THREATENING HOME RULE

Helen helped protect the home rule provision in the Colorado Constitution, which gave special powers to larger cities. Two bills in particular threatened this power and, if passed, would have led to lengthy lawsuits over the constitutionality of the laws. For the private Denver Union Water Company, Representative Sabin introduced HB 287 to prohibit local governments from owning any utility if a private company was already providing the service. This would have forever prohibited Denver from forming the Denver Water Board. When asked, Attorney General Fred Farrar opined that the bill would not apply to Denver because of the constitutional home rule provision. Also, he said, the bill would not apply to current contracts but would subject future contracts to the newly established Public Utilities Commission. The bill's effect would have been a period of protracted lawsuits, during which time private companies could continue their monopolies.[105]

It was on the utility bill that the chair of the Committee of the Whole falsely announced a vote, reversing the "yea" and "nay" votes. Reporter Edward T. Leech said, "I saw [Representative] Seivers Fincher, who was in the chair, deliberately report falsely the vote on the amendment in order to show that the amendment had lost, when in fact, it had carried." The amendment, to strike the enacting clause, would have killed the bill if it had been declared passed.[106] On March 22 the Committee of the Whole recommended that SB 229 by Senator Leroy J. Williams be substituted for Sabin's HB 287, after which HB 287 conveniently disappeared. (In the senate Helen had voted against SB 229, but it had passed 21 to 11.)[107] The Williams utility bill passed the house on April 3,[108] but it was ultimately vetoed by the governor.

Helen and Representative Evangeline Heartz, the only two women in the legislature, were praised for fighting against the Sabin bill. Until the governor vetoed it, the *Denver Express* planned to lead a petition drive to try to kill the law at the polls.[109] The bill was only designed "to give the Water Company a court standing for a long fight to prevent Denver's owning its own water system," the paper asserted.[110] Earlier, the *Express* had concluded that the senate passage of the bill showed that the senate was still "owned by corporations."[111]

The other home rule issue related to the regulation of taxis, which Denver jealously guarded as a city prerogative. Senator Charles Hamilton's SB 219 provided for the licensing of operators and the regulation of taxis by the state. Helen attempted to amend the bill to prohibit licensees from carrying passengers for hire and to maintain the right of cities to regulate taxis through past and future ordinances. Her amendment to the Committee of the Whole report lost by voice vote, and the bill passed Second Reading.[112] Interestingly, the bill set a speed limit in town of one mile in three minutes, or twenty miles an hour. The taxi regulation bill passed 28 to 7, with Helen among the 7 votes against.[113] It was also vetoed by the governor. Thus the home rule power of larger cities was maintained.

MISCELLANEOUS BILLS BY HELEN AND OTHERS

Helen opposed SB 10 by Senator Casimiro Barela, a bill to allow counties to buy land for fairs and horse racing and to manage and operate them, in part because Denver's Overland Park had become "a hell hole," she said, since the racing commission was organized.[114] After Senator Lewis's failing motion to except the bill from the Committee of the Whole report,[115] she sought unanimous consent to offer an amendment on Third Reading. She wanted to insert that "nothing in this act shall be construed as permitting racetrack or any other form of gambling." Consent to offer an amendment was not granted, and the bill passed on Third Reading.[116] Helen was one of ten votes against, while twenty-two senators voted for the bill.

SB 163, on railroad cars, which Helen sponsored, limited the number of freight cars on a grade to thirty and freight cars on the flat to fifty. Also, there could be no more than twelve passenger cars in one train. This was one of four bills supported by railway men, so her introduction of this bill pleased her allies in labor. The committee on railroads reported SB 163 without recommendation to the Committee of the Whole.[117] It was not considered further.[118] (Though this bill is perfectly serious, it is reminiscent of the silly amendment a member of the "Cowboy Caucus" tried to add to my bill when I was a greenhorn in the senate. It required that freight trains had to have—every ten cars—a high coupling and a low cut-out opening so drivers tired of waiting in their cars at train crossings could dash through! Needless to say, the amendment was withdrawn before a vote.)

Helen cosponsored SB 405 by Senator Barela to pay an assistant sergeant-at-arms of the senate for the first month of 1895. This interesting alliance of the long-serving Republican and Senator Robinson was designed to redress a twenty-year oversight. It involved a payment of $291 with interest. The bill passed both houses, but the parsimonious governor vetoed it, as he did every other bill for the relief of an individual.[119]

The State Historical and Natural History Society, incorporated and approved by the Second General Assembly in 1879, was further defined in SB 316 by Senator Eaton. The society was made the trustee of the state collections and of reports then owned by the society. Helen tried to amend the bill with a Committee of the Whole amendment to strike section 7, but her amendment failed 13 to 21.[120] She may have been trying to allow the public to vote on the bill by striking the emergency clause, section 6 in the final bill. The emergency clause prevented reference of the bill to the people for a vote. In the house the enacting clause had been stricken, and then that action was reconsidered, so there was some controversy over the bill.

House Joint Memorial (HJM) 1 was a memorial addressed to the US Congress endorsing the idea of the creation of Rocky Mountain National Park. Helen voted "yea," along with the twenty-six other senators present.[121] A bill to establish the park had passed the US Senate and was pending in the US House. The memorial asked that the bill be favorably acted upon and approved by the president. It enumerated the beauties of the park, including Longs Peak. The resolution claimed, "The proposed park is unsurpassed in beauty by any other National Park."[122] Not everyone appreciated the federal lands in Colorado, though. Two years earlier, Democratic governor Ammons had ranted against federal government control of land in the state. He had said, "It is damnable . . . the way the federal government has held back, has retarded our growth, not only the growth of Colorado, but the growth of other Western states." Senator Shafroth seemed equally unhappy with the situation.[123]

HB 229, relating to qualifications of school superintendents, passed the house on March 2, 1915.[124] It divided the counties into seven classes to set the level of salaries proportional to county population, a technique still used for county salaries. The bill passed Third Reading in the senate 34 to 1 with Helen's support,[125] but the governor vetoed the bill—probably because it raised the salaries of some superintendents, even though this would have required local, rather than state, money.

In summing up the session, the *Denver Express* commented that the Colorado Insane Asylum had been given badly needed money, which may have been the result of the survey of state institutions conducted by Helen's committee. The paper also commended Helen for two good bills, "one aimed at the owners of immoral houses and one broadening the power of the minimum wage commission." But the general assessment of the legislative session was dismal:

> Its bad deeds stand out like sore thumbs and almost conceal the little good it did.
>
> Revenge, ill-feeling; a desire to serve the few, instead of the many; destruction instead of construction—these are the motives which were found back of the major number of important bills this session . . . Steam-rolling, gagging, every other trick of unfair politicians—all these characterized its session . . . Shagging, expulsion of reporters, expulsion of [Representative] W. W. Howland for perjury, charges of graft, fraud, grand jury investigations. These things . . . made the Silly Twentieth a stench in the nostrils of the public.[126]

After such an experience in the minority party, Helen's decision against running for reelection was not surprising. In a *New York Times* article written from Denver, Helen said that because she talked less in her second session, she accomplished more, an experience shared by many new legislators.

> "They say it is hard, you know, for a woman to refrain from talking," said Senator Robinson. "I admit it is. It took me nearly two years to learn how to keep still. In my first session I liked to make speeches. I orated and talked and talked. I did not talk much in the present session. Experience, you see, had brought me wisdom. It had taught me one of the most valuable lessons given to me to learn in my political career. I learned when and how to hold my tongue."[127]

After this session ended, even though Helen decided not to run for reelection, she continued to grow in stature as a national and international leader for suffrage and peace.

6

Citizen of the World

After she left the senate, Helen continued to advocate for women while broadening her activities in other areas. In 1917 she headed a committee that met with the new Democratic governor, Julius C. Gunter, to ask him to appoint a woman to the state Industrial Commission. This was the board created in the 1915 session for the purpose of investigating labor disputes before a strike could take place. Since many workers were women, having a woman among the three members of the board seemed reasonable. The committee's efforts were unsuccessful, however.[1]

Another one of Helen's interests was family planning, and she was an early ally of pioneers in that field. She served on the national council of the Voluntary Parenthood League along with Judge Ben Lindsey, and her membership is cited in Margaret Sanger's *Family Limitation*.[2] In an article written in November 1918, just as an armistice was declared ending the Great War, Helen commented on the reduction in the number of births in the United States. This was the consequence, she said, of women finding other outlets for their creativity. The story of civilization is "the story of subordinating natural forces to human intelligence," she believed. Whereas men wanted more births for the machinery of war, women were asking, what has happened to "the babies we gave you?" Helen called for better "conditions of life of babies already born."[3]

In addition to her strenuous efforts for woman suffrage, she was active in the peace movement. That commitment was quickly converted to fervent work for victory after the United States entered the Great War.

FINAL BATTLE FOR WOMAN SUFFRAGE

Though Colorado women had voted since 1893, the federal battle for woman suffrage continued another twenty-seven years. As late as the spring of 1918 only ten western states and New York had woman suffrage, though by 1919 there were twenty-seven states.[4] Helen continued to be an important spokeswoman for the issue. She even contributed a recipe to *The Suffrage Cookbook,* put out by the Equal Franchise Federation of Western Pennsylvania.[5] In August 1915 she made a lecture tour through New York and New Jersey "to refute the charges made against women legislators and voters of the state [Colorado]."[6] She also gave four days to the Indiana Suffrage Association.[7] While Helen was in New York, a gentleman who was president of the Man Suffrage Association Opposed to Woman Suffrage foolishly asserted that "women politicians of Colorado are so unscrupulous in their abuse that they have driven some of the best men out of politics." Senator Robinson demanded the names of the women and men in question and when the event he mentioned had taken place.[8] At about the same time she brought a lawsuit seeking $5,000 in damages against a Summit, New Jersey, newspaper for the libel against her in a letter in the paper that said she had "introduced into the Colorado Senate a bill to re-establish race-track gambling in the state."[9] This was particularly ironic given her opposition to betting on horse races at county fairgrounds. Helen's husband, Ewing Robinson, said the letter was published as part of New Jersey's fight against woman suffrage. Helen was to speak in New Jersey the following week.[10]

In her speeches she indignantly defended Colorado against the "incessant criticism of the suffrage States by Eastern people."

> "I am tired of these constant slurs," she said. "I am tired of being used as an anti-suffrage argument. We have a more humane Legislature in Colorado than in the non-suffrage States. Our canning industries are as important as those of New Jersey. In New Jersey's canning factories the workers may keep at their work as long as flesh and blood will stand it. In Colorado we have an eight-hour day for the workers in the canneries. Colorado women stand as a unit for humane laws.
>
> "The last Colorado General Assembly passed an Industrial Disputes act which has already prevented one strike that threatened Denver. By this act both sides in a dispute between employer and employes [sic] must appear before an industrial commission. This is the most advanced industrial legislation now in force in any State in the Union. It is time other States stopped pointing their fingers at Colorado and began to think of following her example."[11]

At this time Helen believed in a state-by-state suffrage strategy, and she urged the leaders of the national suffrage organizations to focus on one state at a time, particularly those where there was a good prospect of passage.[12] In the same article one of Helen's rare references to her husband occurs. She claimed she was able to see more of him after she was elected to the senate because they had lunch together downtown every day. She also said she would return to Colorado shortly so her daughter could leave for college and Ewing would "not be left companionless." The next year an editor reported a telephone conversation in which a voice on the phone said, "This is Ewing Robinson." The editor replied, "Who?" Ewing replied, "Ewing Robinson, better known as the husband of Mrs. Helen Ring Robinson, state senator from Colorado." The article concluded, "Ewing Robinson is known to his friends as a fine fellow and a brilliant wit."[13]

This story ran in another newspaper in a more humorous form: "A man giving his name as Ewing Robinson has popped up with the assertion that he is the husband of Helen Ring Robinson, the woman state senator from Colorado. The old story of wife developing too fast for her husband to keep pace, for nobody ever heard of Ewing. Some rainy afternoon we are going to write a book to be called 'Obscure Husbands of Famous Women.'"[14]

In February 1916 Helen was in Atlanta promoting municipal suffrage, proving once again her tireless advocacy.[15]

In the 1916 presidential election, Helen publicly endorsed Woodrow Wilson even though some suffragists opposed him because his party—the Democrats—had not passed the federal suffrage amendment. Helen did not support the Woman's Party because she believed it was being used by anti-suffrage forces. In an article on the subject, she explained the complex relationship between the Woman's Party and the two established political parties.[16] Both parties had platform provisions favoring the extension of the vote to women on a state-by-state basis, provisions that in many cases had been enacted into law through the efforts of the National Suffrage Association, which favored either state or federal action. In contrast, the newer Congressional Union for Woman Suffrage, or Woman's Party, concentrated on passing a federal amendment through Congress. Its leverage was the bloc of women voters in the twelve states that already had the vote, states representing ninety-one electoral votes in the presidential contest.[17]

In 1914 the Congressional Union had opposed all Democratic candidates—even though the Democrats had long worked for suffrage—on the grounds that though they were the party in power, they had not yet passed a federal amendment. With the singleness of purpose typical of single-issue groups, the Woman's Party again in August 1916 passed a resolution to oppose President Wilson in his reelection bid because he and his party opposed the passage of the federal suffrage amendment while the Republican candidate, Charles Evans Hughes, had endorsed it.

Helen was concerned that the Woman's Party would peel off women who would otherwise have voted for Wilson and other Democrats down the ticket. The work of the new party was purely destructive, what today would be called negative. Helen did not believe this was an appropriate basis for a political party. Also, to hold the Democrats responsible for the failure of the constitutional amendment was unreasonable since Democrats did not have the two-thirds majority in either house that was necessary for passage. It was particularly unreasonable to assume that the Democrats could convince Republicans to vote for the amendment. In the event that the Republicans did win the majority of the members of Congress, it would be foolish to expect the remaining Democrats to support woman suffrage after the Congressional Union had defeated many of their colleagues. Helen's means of expressing this is particularly colorful: "But there are those who think it might be too exciting to ask a corpse to oblige with a jig at its own wake—just to please the man who made him a corpse."[18]

Helen shared Wilson's support for the rights of the common man. Her way of excoriating the moneyed interests and their former influence on government was to say that Wilson had moved the capitol of the country from Wall Street back to Washington. She claimed that Hughes wanted to move the capitol to Berlin.[19] Helen was enthusiastic enough about Woodrow Wilson to campaign for him and the entire Democratic ticket in Maine as well as Colorado.[20] In Colorado she campaigned by train, "on the trail of the Hughes Special" of Charles Evans Hughes.[21] Wilson was reelected, aided by a narrow victory in California that gave him all of that state's electoral vote.

During the winter of 1917–1918 the Congressional Union picketed the White House. The women were arrested, imprisoned, and force-fed, drawing much attention to their cause.[22]

In the US Senate debate on woman suffrage, one senator "reminded the assembly that there were eight states where men with nothing more than first citizenship papers were allowed to vote" while native women were denied that right.[23] After the amendment finally passed through the Congress on June 4, 1919, it had to be ratified by three-fourths of the states. Helen was active at this stage of the process, too, going to Connecticut with women representing the other forty-seven states in an effort to persuade the governor to call a special session to ratify the suffrage amendment. The Nineteenth Amendment to the US Constitution, giving women citizens the vote, was finally ratified on August 26, 1920.[24]

VOTER EDUCATION FOR WOMEN

After the passage of the suffrage amendment, women needed political education to become intelligent voters. Helen's second book, *Preparing Women for Citizenship,* was her effort to do just that.[25] Part of the material in the book had appeared earlier in articles published in the *Pictorial Review.* She dedicated the book to the memory of B.J.R., who was probably her brother, Judson B. Ring (or B. Judson Ring), who had apparently died by 1918. Two years older than Helen, Judson was her closest sibling, and he had given her away in her wedding.

In the book Helen insisted on the close relationship between the home and politics. She believed "the family should be put in the center of politics." The retail price of household commodities was a "practical political question."[26] "White coal," or electricity, was the fuel she thought the Public Utilities Commission should force all cities to provide at a reasonable rate because it would free housewives from many hours of labor.[27] She also wanted government price fixing to continue after the war and government-owned packing houses and cold storage facilities for food to be established.[28] At the same time that she wanted to make life easier for housewives, she scorned idle "parasite" women who were not contributing to their homes or their communities.[29] When Helen talked about women who worked outside the home, she argued for "equal pay for equal work"[30]—a goal women are still fighting for, though now, at least, overt discrimination against women in the workplace is illegal.

The book is full of political observations drawn from Helen's legislative experience; for example, she said "men are more likely to think in terms of human profit when they get behind legislation,

while women are more likely to think in terms of human need."[31]
Women, she believed, "have brought a new impulse to political life"
because they "cultivate fields that men alone might never think of cultivating."[32] Women citizens focus on three areas: dependents, such as
orphans; defectives, such as the feeble-minded; and delinquents, such
as those in detention schools.[33] She noted regretfully that the laws
stressed that a married woman merely reflected the citizenship of her
husband; that is, if an American woman married an Italian citizen, she
would lose her American citizenship.[34]

She encouraged political party membership because of the common principles uniting a party, but she pointed out that one did not
have to vote for that party's candidates all the time.[35] She opposed the
Woman's Party because women "for 70 years have been trying to fight
a sex-line at the ballot box,"[36] and the Woman's Party effectually reas-
serted that line. (The Woman's Party also worked against the reelection of Democrats even though they had supported woman suffrage,
as discussed earlier.) When the Democratic National Committee
appointed a committee of women advisers, she called the powerless
group "a Ladies Aid Society."[37]

In a chapter on women as office holders, she pointed out the irony
of Montana electing a woman to the US Congress while Massachusetts
and other states "refuse women the privilege of acting as notary pub-
lics."[38] A woman has to be better than a man "in order to be as good."
She made fun of the male effort to "protect" women from holding
office. This was motivated, she said, "because of a feeling of tenderness
for themselves. There has never yet been offices [sic] enough to supply
the regular male demand."[39]

Many women ran boardinghouses to support themselves and
their families. Managing a small city, she said, is not "half so hard as
to run a boarding house."[40] Therefore, Helen predicted, many women
would hold municipal offices in the future, which has proven to be
true in modern Denver, though the city is yet to have its first woman
mayor.

Women, Helen believed, needed to radically change their own
perceptions of themselves. Helen reviewed the mythic structure of the

fairy tale to illustrate how women have thought of themselves from early childhood. The prince typically had to do something, achieve some quest, but the princess had no task "except to be more beautiful than in the morning."[41] Typically, until the war, women who worked "belonged to an inferior order."[42] Boys were educated "democratically" in our country, while the average girl was educated "away from democracy."[43] Girls saw that the roles established for men and women either elevated women as angels, which limited their opportunities, or demeaned them as inferior.

> All about her she [the young girl] saw men either kneeling to women or pulling them round by the hair. She heard men calling women angels—locking them up. Women were "queens"—but they had to eat out of the hands of men.
>
> No wonder her idea of democracy was often adled [sic]. She heard men declaiming that "woman is infinitely better than man" and then she found those same men unwilling to treat women as if they were as good, barring them away from the democracy of the vote.[44]

As for the accusation that women are too emotionally unstable to hold office, she observed that she had seen "male legislators who were too hysterical or emotional to meddle in politics, who shed tears when a favorite bill was killed."[45] Representing the woman's point of view and defense of women, she believed, was the peculiar responsibility of women office holders. She told the story of a woman senator, obviously herself, saving the eight-hour day for women. When a male senator urged an exception for canneries because the fruit was perishable, she urged her colleagues to "think first of perishable girls," and the senate "voted almost unanimously for the girls instead of the tomatoes."[46]

Though Jeanette Rankin had been elected to Congress and women had been elected state senators in Arizona, Colorado, Utah, and Washington by the time Helen wrote her book, there were never enough of them to pass the laws that would have realized the women's agenda.[47] She urged people to lobby governors to appoint more women to boards of the institutions women were interested in, to prepare them for public office.[48]

Much of what Helen argued for was designed to make life more just—a living wage for women; a little tolerance, even for pacifists; parallel treatment for female and male prostitutes; and thinking of the people as "we," not "they."[49] She recognized that among the problems America needed to solve were those of poverty and race. Perhaps because of the knowledge she gained as the adapter of *Uncle Tom's Cabin,* she perceptively described the subtlety of our underlying race problem: "it gibbers in the wilderness and it can never be settled by lynchings."[50]

The worldview of Americans changed radically with World War I, Helen observed. In response to Wilson's promise to "make the world safe for democracy," she argued that people cannot be safe in the world while they perceive the state "as an entity quite apart from the people who compose it."[51] She argued that the law must be followed by states as well as by individuals, which leads into her arguments in support of the League of Nations.[52]

The choice of Helen as one of six suffrage delegates to represent the United States at an international women's gathering in Madrid in May 1920 was logical because she was one of the few American women to have achieved high elective office, and she was also a superb speaker and writer on woman suffrage.[53] The following month she was an American delegate in Geneva for what Carrie Chapman Catt called the most important woman suffrage conference ever held. Helen traveled with her stepdaughter, Alcyon, and Alcyon's aunt, Nellie B. Graham, the sister of Ewing's first wife.[54] Among the other delegates to the Geneva conference were Lady Astor, the first woman member of the British House of Commons, and Mrs. Josephus Daniels, wife of the American secretary of the navy.[55]

The program of that meeting lists Helen as one of the women members of parliaments who would report to the conference at an evening meeting. There were other members from Finland, Denmark, and Wurtemberg and Helen's too-familiar acquaintance from the Ford Peace Ship, Rosika Schwimmer from Hungary (described later).[56]

The conference considered a charter of rights for womanhood that included issues that are still sources of conflict in many countries: political suffrage, abolition of slavery of women, equal nationality rights for married women, equal guardianship of children, a single moral standard for both sexes, equal pay for equal work, pensions for mothers' aid, and civil rights for married women.[57]

On the conference program Helen's home address is listed as 1441 Pennsylvania Avenue in Denver, Colorado. The 1920 census data had her husband and her stepdaughter as lodgers at that address, but strangely Helen is not listed there or anywhere else that year, perhaps because she was out of the country when the census was taken. Ewing is listed as a sixty-two-year-old lawyer in general practice, while Alcyon, twenty-three, is described as a newspaper reporter. We don't know why Ewing and Alcyon moved into a hotel or large boarding-house, which is what 1441 Pennsylvania appears to have been at the time. In contrast, the *Denver City Directory* for 1920 has Ewing living at 1441 Josephine Street.[58]

One newspaper story suggests that Helen and Ewing did not always get along. They were both at a meeting of the Woman's Club of Denver when they rose at the same time to be recognized by the chair. The article begins, "If you want to know what happens in a suffrage state when a man and wife—both voters—want to talk at a public political meeting at the same time, read the following true story." The article claims that Ewing was known as Mr. Helen Ring Robinson. It continues:

> "Mr. Chairman!" they both cried simultaneously. They both stood side by side, Mr. Robinson much the taller and bigger.
>
> Mrs. Robinson looked at the person who challenged her right to the floor, and without waiting for the chairman to recognize her, she pushed Mr. Robinson back into his seat, and proceeded to deliver a few remarks.[59]

The first appearance of this story has a Denver dateline, and the text claims the story is true. Though there might be a seed of truth in the story, it seems unlikely that Helen would treat her husband this way in public, but it does suggest the tensions between Helen and her husband. Then, too, Ewing might not have had the right to speak at a Woman's Club meeting, unless it was open to the public.

AMERICA AND THE GREAT WAR

In addition to continuing her efforts for woman suffrage, Helen was involved in the peace movement until the United States entered the war. Though at first neutrality was the official US position, Americans became more and more involved in the conflict in Europe, which began in the summer of 1914 after the assassination of Archduke Franz Ferdinand, heir to the Austro-Hungarian throne. Within a month Austria-Hungary had declared war against Serbia, Russia had declared against Austria, and Germany had given Russia and France an ultimatum. Germany attacked France through neutral Belgium, and Turkey and Bulgaria joined Germany and Austria-Hungary. American sympathy for the allies—Britain, France, and Russia—gradually shifted to a determination to intervene.[60]

Before the United States declared war, women led the peace movement, beginning with the International Congress of 2,000 women at The Hague in 1915. At that conference Julia Grace Wales suggested a plan for continuous mediation among the warring powers, to be staffed by experts from the neutral nations who would propose one solution after another until the warring nations worked out their differences—a proposal that expressed great confidence in the power of reason. The women's congress sent delegates to the belligerent and neutral countries to see how they responded to such an idea, and they returned to report their favorable reception.[61] In fact, according to historian Eric Hobsbawm, no European government wanted a general war.[62]

This idea inspired Henry Ford, who first attempted to convince President Wilson to invite the belligerents to the United States to participate in continuous mediation as suggested by the women's International Congress—a kind of fledgling League of Nations before that idea had been formed—but Wilson refused to limit his options in this way. A Hungarian woman, Rosika Schwimmer, met with Ford, and the two created the idea of a "Peace Ship" to carry notable American leaders to Europe. The purpose of the trip was to visit the neutral nations and enlist them in "continuous mediation" until the differences were settled.[63] Ford announced his plans for the Peace Ship just nine days before the December 4 sailing of the *Oscar II.*

In spite of the several declarations of war and the Germans' 1915 sinking of the British ship *Lusitania,* drowning nearly 1,200 people, Helen accepted Henry Ford's invitation in November 1915. After the *Lusitania* disaster, there had been a diplomatic agreement between the United States and Germany that no American ships in British waters would be sunk by submarines, an agreement that lasted until January 1917.[64] Still, the trip was not without danger.

Helen was joined on this journey by her friend Judge Ben Lindsey and his wife, Henrietta, and 100 other prominent American men and women. Judge Lindsey commented, "I heartily approve Mr. Ford's efforts to stop the slaughter which has been going on in Europe for more than a year. If I can do anything to put an end to the war, I shall be only too glad to do it." Helen said she had accepted the invitation but commented that she would not be sure she would be going "until I have talked the matter over with my husband. In all probability I will be a member of the party," she added.[65] This is one of the few times she mentioned her husband in all her speaking and writing. Her going on the trip meant separation from Ewing and Alcyon over the Christmas holidays.

The other invited passengers—all of whom were guests of Henry Ford—included Helen Keller, who ultimately decided not to go, and Mrs. Helen Loring Grenfell, former Colorado state superintendent of schools.[66] Senator John F. Shafroth got passports and had them sent to the Hotel Biltmore in New York to await the arrival of Helen Ring Robinson and Helen Grenfell, but the latter stayed in Denver and learned too late on December 3 (the ship was to sail December 4) that the passports had arrived in New York. Former secretary of state and presidential candidate William Jennings Bryan was to join the party in three weeks.[67] Helen was considered one of the leaders of the group, as is indicated by her selection as one of ten members from whom five delegates to the Conference for Continuous Mediation were to be elected on January 15.[68] She lost the election, however, perhaps because another prominent person from Denver, Judge Lindsey, was selected. The conference did meet in Stockholm for a year after the peace voyage.[69]

The ambassadors of peace who began with such hope for bringing a "righteous peace for blood-soaked" Europe fell into bitter dissension shortly after the ship was under way, as revealed in Helen's article "Confessions of a Peace Pilgrim."[70] The forceful Madame Schwimmer controlled the expedition, which Helen thought was unfortunate—not only because of Schwimmer's strong personality but, in part, because her country, Hungary, was one of the belligerents. The Dutch actually protested to Henry Ford about Mme. Schwimmer.[71] Helen said the super-pacifists gave the peace pilgrims the third degree one night. Mme. Schwimmer and a committee created a platform with three planks, of which the first two were harmless platitudes. But the third plank "pledged the unyielding opposition of all members of the Ford Peace Expedition to any increase whatever, under any circumstances whatever, of the naval or military forces of the United States, and called upon all good Americans everywhere to oppose the recommendations of President Wilson's message on preparedness, lately delivered to Congress." Just two nights earlier, Wilson had asked for an increase in the standing army.[72] The committee expected all members of the delegation to sign the declaration; in fact, Ford and twenty-three others did sign it.[73] Lindsey and Helen threatened to leave the ship at the first port because of this pressure.

Ford became ill and realized at about the same time that it was impossible to achieve his peace plan. He came home shortly after the ship docked at the first European port: Christiana, Norway.[74]

This experience destroyed Helen's hope for a miracle. However, she concurred with Ford's idea that it pays to advertise; that is, the forces for peace needed to make themselves heard. Helen said, "We advertised that the soul of America was peace." Norway, she added, answered that its soul was peace also. The ship had similar effects in

Sweden and Denmark, though public meetings in Denmark had been forbidden. Helen gave the major address the second night they were in Christiana. She also spoke in Stockholm, where the lord mayor gave a reception in her honor, and in Copenhagen, where the staff of the country's greatest newspaper honored her with a reception.[75] The Germans allowed the peace pilgrims to cross their territory in a sealed train from Denmark to their last stop, The Hague.[76] Though initially Europeans accused Americans of being war profiteers, they learned that most of them wanted peace.[77]

Proof of the danger of the trip was clear when a sister ship to the *Rotterdam,* which sixty-seven members of the expedition were taking home, was crippled by a mine near England. The explosion on the *Ryndam* on its way from New York to Rotterdam killed three crew members, but none of the passengers was injured.[78]

In evaluating the trip, the expedition members had harsh words for the "autocratic leadership"; some had left the group early at the first port. Senator Helen Ring Robinson asserted that "certain ideas fostered by leaders of the party, and which they attempted to impose on the delegation, created discord." The author Herman Bernstein, in a statement for the press, said that an important blunder was made when the members were forced to declare their opposition to President Wilson's policy of national defense.[79]

Historians commented on Henry Ford's "ill-fated" attempt to "get the boys out of the trenches before Christmas." A less pacifistic assortment of pacifists would be hard to imagine. Interminable quarrels and personal vendettas haunted the Atlantic passage. Helen commented that "the leaders did not measure up to the bigness of the idea." Journalists were relieved that "the comedy of errors is over."[80] William C. Bullitt, a journalist who accompanied the pilgrims, thought the expedition needed more forethought:

> Now, had the purpose of the expedition been defined by the delegates to themselves at the beginning, and had those purposes been studied and reinforced by exhaustive thinking along every line of thought which must be considered by those who propose

the establishment and possible accomplishments of a neutral congress, we should have arrived in Scandinavia with a scientific program and speakers who could have defended that program from every point of view, historical, practical, psychological, diplomatic, etc.[81]

Instead, the Americans could only speak in generalities because this hard work had not been done.[82] Though the press made great fun of the expedition at the time, historians Robert Riegel and David Long observed that it was harmful to the entire peace movement.[83] On the more positive side, President Wilson may have used a kernel of this idea in his proposal for the League of Nations. If so, the Peace Ship was a very worthwhile effort.

In January 1917 Germany notified the United States that it was terminating the Sussex pledge *not* to sink US ships around the British Isles, forcing President Wilson's hand. He asked Congress for a Declaration of War, which passed the Senate on April 4 and the House on April 6, 1917, by overwhelming votes.[84] The country was quickly mobilized. American men ages twenty-one through thirty were registered for the armed services on May 18, 1917, and men eighteen through forty-five were registered in August 1918. By the time of the Armistice in November, 2 million Americans had gone overseas.[85] Of these, 116,000 died, a modest number compared to the 1.6 million French, 800,000 British, and 1.8 million Germans who lost their lives in the Great War.[86]

Helen quickly converted from pacifist to patriot and threw herself into war projects with great energy, to such an extent that she blamed her physical breakdown leading to her death six years later on overwork during the war.[87] On September 3, 1917, the governor of Colorado had created the State Council of Defense, to carry out the war plans of the federal administration, and the Woman's Council of Defense. Helen was a member of the Executive Committee of the Woman's Council, which was to help raise money in four Liberty Bond drives and campaigns to conserve food.[88] Helen was the Woman's Club of Denver chair of Liberty Loans, which required her to travel throughout the state urging women to support the war effort.[89] A historian of the war quoted her as saying "we can not win this war by shutting up women's energies in a garbage can."[90] In August 1918 Helen was speaking in Fort Collins and urging the women to organize because the men, who were currently doing it, would soon be going to war. Here is a moving excerpt from her volunteer recruitment speech:

> Not long ago I was down in the Cripple Creek region. As the train rolled along I would see large white spots and as I came close to them I saw they were flowers on the mountain side. Two years ago I was in France and I saw the same kind of white spots but when I reached them they were not flowers, but they were the crosses over the graves of the hundreds of thousands who had given their lives. British, Belgians, and French were buried there. The dead were forced to lay down the torch of liberty and we Americans have taken it up. We will carry it, and the women must work to provide the funds for the men who are going to Europe to fight this war out to a finish.[91]

The following month, as state chair, Helen led a Liberty Loan conference in Denver at the Brown Palace Hotel, at which county chairwomen gave their reports on the Third Campaign and their expectations for the Fourth.[92]

The *Rocky Mountain News* reported that Helen had just returned from a three-day trip to Grand, Jackson, and Routt Counties. In the previous two weeks she had visited twenty-two counties and roused women to buy more bonds.[93]

Helen's attractive twenty-two-year-old stepdaughter, Alcyon, emulated her devotion to war work by serving on a flying squadron that helped Colorado fruit growers harvest their crops, replacing the men who had joined the army. She was pictured in several Colorado newspapers.[94]

Helen was also a member of the Navy Commission on Training Camp Activities,[95] whose goal was to provide a wholesome environment for the sailors. Ever a hands-on kind of leader, she visited the

Great Lakes Naval Training Station near Chicago to see how the young men were living. This visit inspired her article published in *The Independent*.[96] Her visit was eased by "a friendly introduction from the Secretary of the Navy." She was pleased to meet one volunteer there from Denver who had often danced with Alcyon. This young man gave her a definition of the democracy that prevailed at the camp: "Democracy . . . is just folks thinking together and feeling together and working together, without any swank or privilege and with a chance for everybody. And that's the sort of thing we have here at Great Lakes." He went on to explain that the many ranks among the men "are not the badges of caste and personal glory but of service. That's the only true democracy . . . the democracy of opportunity and service."[97]

During the war a prayer of Helen's was printed in a book on faith published by Pastor Harry E. Fosdick, with no explanation of the source. The prayer is the clearest statement we have of Helen's sympathies and the vision that motivated her.

O God, our Father, our souls are made sick by the sight of hunger and want and nakedness; of little children bearing on their bent backs the burden of the world's work, of motherhood drawn under the grinding wheels of modern industry; and of overburdened manhood with empty hands, stumbling and falling.

Help us to understand that it is not Thy purpose to do away with life's struggle, but that Thou desirest us to make the conditions of that struggle just and its results fair.

Enable us to know that we may bring this to pass only through love and sympathy and understanding; only as we realize that all are alike Thy children—the rich and the poor, the strong and the weak, the fortunate and the unfortunate. And so, our Father, give us an ever-truer sense of human sisterhood; that with patience and steadfastness we may do our part in ending the injustice that is in the land, so that all may rejoice in the fruits of their toil and be glad in Thy sunshine.

Keep us in hope and courage even amid the vastness of the undertaking and the slowness of the progress, and sustain us with the knowledge that our times are in Thy hand. Amen.[98]

HELEN AS COMMUNITY LEADER

In 1918 Helen succumbed to the siren call of politics once again when she ran for Colorado lieutenant governor. At least one other woman had run for the nomination to that office on a minor party ticket in 1894. At the state Democratic Convention in the Denver Auditorium, Harry Churchill won the nomination with 657 votes, while W. K. Lockhart of Garfield County received 205 votes and Helen just 52. She fell short of the 95 votes required to gain a place on the Democratic primary ballot. Apparently the delegates could not see a woman in this role, while at the same convention Mary C.C. Bradford was unanimously endorsed for reelection to the office of superintendent of schools, which since 1910 had been seen as reserved for a woman. Women had occupied that office since 1895, but it was soon seen as exclusively a woman's office.[99]

After her years in the senate, Helen continued to serve the Denver Woman's Press Club as legislative chair and as a member of the Contest Committee (1918–1919), and she chaired a meeting in 1919–1920. According to the bylaws, the role of the Legislative Committee, which was formed in 1905,[100] was to "study the legislative problems that the State Federation is interested in, attend the meeting of the State Committee [a joint committee with representatives from many women's clubs] while the legislature is in session, and be prepared to give intelligent information upon bills presented to the club for indorsement [sic]."[101]

In 1920–1921 Helen's stepdaughter, Alcyon Robinson, was also listed in the *Denver Woman's Press Club Year Book* as a member, but, after Helen became ill, neither of them was listed in 1921–1922. The next year (1922–1923) Helen was a nonresident member living in Palm Springs, California, where, because of her poor health, she had moved to live with Alcyon. The town where she lived was Ocean Park, California, according to one obituary.[102]

FINAL WRITINGS

Helen became more outspoken on social and feminist issues as she grew older. Related to her battle for woman suffrage was her view of the equality of the sexes. She complained, "Men still believe in the Divine Right of their sex. Men think if they aren't the head of the family, there is no point in marriage." She wanted a single standard of "sex thought" that would "assert the equal dignity of the masculine and feminine personalities." The result would get rid of the "sex arrogance of men" and the "sex subserviency" of women. Men are not going to give women "a fair field" in sex, she said. Rather, women will have to take it.[103] Fathers of children born out of marriage should be held equally as responsible as the mothers for their support. Prostitution, she believed, was moral chaos and created a cesspool that needed to go.[104]

Helen wanted economic justice for all people, but particularly for women and children. Always ahead of her time, in 1919 she called for "brain power" and "heart power." The heart power was "to demand old age pensions . . . to provide state-controlled sickness insurance . . . to bring about just industrial conditions for all and decent housing for all."[105] Unfortunately, she did not live to see Social Security, state-regulated health insurance, or Federal Housing Administration—which address some of these problems.

"Women have always had an inalienable right to do the world's dirty work as well as its poorly paid work," Helen observed sardonically in a 1918 article.[106] She believed women should receive the same pay as men for equivalent work, whereas until recent times employers believed a wife did not need as large a salary as a husband. Helen thought sharing the family income should be part of the marriage contract.[107] It was unfortunate, she commented, that women only become their husbands' economic partners in the divorce courts, through alimony. In a more traditional vein, she held that the first job of women in the state is "to make motherhood safe, and the home stable."[108]

To open more fields of work to women, Helen advocated a law to ensure the right of women to have free access to all trades and professions. She wanted to strengthen the unions and put women in leadership positions in those unions.[109] One impediment to women's success in alternative jobs was their lack of rigorous education. They needed to be educated, Helen insisted, both as future housewives and as future working women. Unlike many modern feminists, Helen did not believe a woman could be both a working woman and a housewife at the same time, perhaps because the duties of a housewife were so much more strenuous and time-consuming in her era. She cited a woman who succeeded as the head of an insurance company because she had a "wife," her sister, who took care of her household.[110] Though she believed a woman could not be a worker and a wife and mother at the same time, Helen thought women should have the right to choose. Meanwhile, husbands, she thought, should help working wives with the housework.[111] In applying this stricture to herself, she may not have thought of herself as a worker, perhaps because her social position allowed her to hire help. If she did consider herself a worker, she had clearly chosen public work over being a mother and wife, providing another cause of friction between herself and her husband. This tension still pulls working women and stay-at-home moms in two directions at once, even as economic necessity often requires women to work.

LAST THINGS

When Helen returned to Denver from California in 1922 she lived at Heartsease, a sanitarium connected with Oakes Home; she died there on July 10, 1923.[112] Just before her death she wrote her stepdaughter, asking her to personally visit all the editors of the Denver papers to tell them her death was brought about by her work in the war effort: "Will you please see personally all the editors. I had no idea it [death] was coming so quickly. I want the brief story of my days to make plain the fact that it was the overworking of war days that made me an invalid."[113] She apparently had a complete physical breakdown.

We can only wonder why Helen didn't ask her husband to do this. Adding to the questions is the fact that Helen and Ewing were living apart at this time. For 1921, Ewing's home address was the Huntington at 1624 Grant Street and Alcyon is not listed, probably because she had moved to California. In 1922 Ewing's residence was "rms 321 17th Ave," perhaps a boardinghouse. In 1923, at the time of

Helen's death, Ewing and Alcyon were living at 1035 Emerson Street. Alcyon apparently returned to Denver during her stepmother's last illness, but she was out of town at the time of Helen's death, as indicated by the fact that funeral arrangements were postponed until she arrived.[114]

According to the *Denver Times,* crowds filed past Helen's bier as she lay in state in the Colorado State Capitol rotunda from noon to 2:00 p.m. on July 12. Her honor guards included members of the Denver Woman's Press Club and the League of Women Voters, who stood for the entire two hours. Helen was only the second woman to lie in state in the Capitol; Mrs. Julia V. Wells, wife of Judge A. M. Wells, was the first.[115] Reverend Frederick W. Oakes, the same minister who had married Helen and Ewing, officiated at the funeral at 3:00 p.m. in the chapel at Heartsease, a chapel that still exists in the Gardens at St. Elizabeth's. The pallbearers included Morrison Shafroth.[116]

Ewing was the executor of Helen's estate, valued for tax purposes at $3,777. The probate record indicates that her siblings B. J. Ring (Judson), Etta and Annie Ring, and Matilde Ring MacNair were deceased. The shakiness of Ewing's signature on these papers suggests that he himself was ill. In addition to Ewing and Alcyon, Helen's sister, Eva (Mrs. Albert G.) Thurston of Los Angeles, survived her.[117] In a will signed on July 7, 1923, three days before her death, Helen left her household belongings to Alcyon, except for anything Ewing might want for his personal use. These items were all packed in boxes and barrels, perhaps from the period during which she had lived in California. She left her sister Eva $200.[118]

Helen's body was cremated at Riverside Cemetery, and many months later her cremains were buried at Fairmount Cemetery in Denver.[119] Exhibiting great economy, her husband inscribed her name on the back of the tombstone he had erected for his first wife, Cora Ballard. Cora's side reads "Cora Ballard / wife of / Ewing Robinson / 1859–1897," and across the bottom of this side is "Robinson" in capital letters. Helen's side does not mention Ewing. The inscription is "Helen Ring Robinson, 1923 / I Follow the Gleam."[120] No birth date was given, so Helen's age was concealed to the end. *Time* magazine, in fact, reported her age as forty-five and erroneously called her the first woman senator in the country.[121] She was actually sixty-three.

The inscription on Helen's tombstone, "I Follow the Gleam," refers to a poem by Alfred, Lord Tennyson, "Merlin and the Gleam." In this poem the wizard Merlin represents the poet and the Gleam is "the higher poetic imagination."[122] The entire narrative is a metaphor for Tennyson's career. The last of the nine stanzas, which follows, ends with the command to "Follow the Gleam."

> Not of the sunlight,
> Not of the moonlight,
> Not of the starlight!
> O young Mariner,
> Down to the haven,
> Call your companions,
> Launch your vessel
> And crowd your canvas,
> And, ere it vanishes,
> Over the margin,
> After it, follow it,
> Follow the Gleam.[123]

Just two years after Helen's death, Ewing died at the Tours Hotel on Lincoln Street near Colfax Avenue on April 12, 1925. He was approximately sixty-seven years old, though one article claimed he was sixty.[124] The obituaries said he had been a practicing attorney until his death and that the funeral service would take place after Alcyon came from Los Angeles, where she lived.[125] After the service at St. John's Cathedral, presided over by Dean Benjamin Dagwell, he was cremated at Riverside.[126] Though there was room in the plot he owned at Fairmount, he was not buried with Helen and Cora. Instead, his cremains were taken to Ohio, probably by his sister Alice Robinson, who came to the service in Colorado.[127] One can only speculate why he was not buried in Fairmont, but this suggests again that Helen and Ewing were not close at the end of their lives.

Alcyon, who had graduated from the University of Colorado with a degree in journalism, returned to California, where she married

Martin Carlson, a Los Angeles engineer and businessman. They had a daughter, Alcyon Martia Carlson, born on Helen's birthday, February 21, 1926.[128]

Just six years later, on April 21, 1932, the young mother died after a year's illness. She suffered a "nervous breakdown," though her daughter did not know the exact cause of her death.[129] Alcyon Martia Carlson married journalist Fred Weybret, who, interestingly, was the son of a California state senator, Frederic Weybret.[130]

THE LEGACY OF HELEN RING ROBINSON

Helen followed the gleam of justice throughout her life, particularly justice for unfortunate women and children. In an extensive eulogy praising Helen, the *Denver Times* cited the breadth of view and deep human sympathy and understanding revealed in her writing. The paper credited her with being instrumental in the success of the woman suffrage movement. Further, it said that "her public career was always marked by vigorous indorsement [*sic*] of all humane and social welfare measures which have had as their objects opportunity for the underprivileged and justice to the oppressed." The paper concluded that "not only have Denver and Colorado lost an honored and distinguished citizen in her passing, but the cause of women and children a brilliant advocate and friend."[131]

Helen wanted a long list of reforms: the woman's vote to help bring about the reforms that were needed, women's share of offices at every level of government, adequate women's and children's wages, a limited number of hours for all workers, equal pay for comparable work, women members of juries, and nothing less than world peace through continuous mediation. She was a leader who fought tirelessly no matter how discouraging the fight for the changes she believed her society needed. These goals are so ambitious that she cannot be faulted for failing to achieve some of them.

As a writer and as a politician, Helen proved that a woman can be feminine and still be politically effective. She embraced her role as a housewife and saw that experience as an asset in her political efforts.

Before, during, and after her service in the senate, she worked vigorously for her vision of justice because she knew society cannot be healthy when women and children are suffering.

The memorial resolution passed by the Denver Woman's Press Club said she served as president, "lending luster to that organization by her brilliant mind and widely recognized work as a journalist and woman of letters," and that "she was unified with the club in spirit and purpose." The members added that in the senate she earned "a reputation for indomitable courage, and an invincible determination to accomplish the thing in which she believed."[132]

One newspaper was no less laudatory:

> Not because she desired office but because she believed that a principle was at stake, Mrs. Robinson entered the race for state senator and was elected. Her presence in the senate chamber was not taken kindly by the old fogey element, but to her this mattered little; what she was interested in was to prove to the world that in the legislature there were things for women to do. Her supporters believe that she gained her point. She had the sincerity and the altruism of a born crusader. Always with her the question was not whether the cause was popular but whether it was right in itself.[133]

Women senators and, indeed, all legislators would do well to "follow the gleam," emulating this courageous crusader.

AFTERWORD

WOMEN IN COLORADO
STATE POLITICS, 1894–2011

Stephen J. Leonard

As Pat Pascoe has shown, Helen Ring Robinson earned her place in Colorado history. Upon her death in 1923, Coloradans recognized that they had lost a trailblazer, but without the advantage of a long historical view they could not adequately assess her legacy. Did her 1912 election to the state senate herald a new era in Colorado, one in which women would increasingly occupy significant political posts? Or was she a fluke, a temporary phenomenon, a lucky lady who seized an opportunity to snatch a senate seat?

If the past were prologue, the likelihood of her being a fluke was high. In November 1894 three Republicans—Clara Cressingham, Frances S. Klock, both of Denver, and Carrie C. Holley of Pueblo— became the first women elected to Colorado's house of representatives. Although the house remained overwhelmingly male, the election of three women, a year after equal suffrage had been approved, suggested that Coloradans would see increasing numbers of women enter the halls of political power.

Such was not to be. For the next twenty years women suffered paltry representation in the General Assembly. Cressingham, Klock, and Holley each served one term. Between 1895 and 1918 only thirteen other women held assembly seats, eleven in the sifty-five-member house, and two—Helen Ring Robinson and Agnes Riddle—in the thirty-five-member senate.

Robinson's election to the senate did nothing to change the pattern. After Republican Agnes Riddle, the second woman elected to the senate, left office in 1920, no women graced the upper house until Democrat Eudochia Bell Smith in 1941. After Smith's exit in 1946, the senate was without a woman until Democrat Hestia Wilson was appointed in 1958 to replace her deceased husband. In the six decades between 1894 and 1954 only three women—Robinson, Riddle, and Smith—served in the senate. The scene changed slightly in the late 1950s and early 1960s when three women—Thelma Finley, Allegra Saunders, and Rena Mary Taylor—garnered senate slots. Between 1894 and 1964 more women were elected to the house of representatives than to the senate, but in the house as in the senate, men consistently dominated by wide majorities.

SLOW AS A TORTOISE: FROM SUFFRAGE TO THE 1960s

Chronicling women's pokey political pace is easier than explaining it. Why didn't equal suffrage rapidly bring Colorado women into the political sphere as officeholders? An early explanation advanced by an anonymous source, reported in the *Rocky Mountain News* on July 16, 1894, suggested that women were too delicate for political campaigning, "This is going to be an awfully hot campaign, don't you know, and there will be lots of mud-slinging . . . Now the women aren't used to mud; not yet. They don't know how to take it philosophically, as men do."

Political reality, rather than fear of mud, better explains why equal suffrage failed to bring women significant representation. Women could vote, but they could not wrest control of the major parties from men. Had women's issues been stronger than the other political issues of the mid-1890s, then women might have tried to break away from the Republican, Democratic, and Populist Parties to form an independent party, a party run by women, dedicated to electing women to office and to advancing women's causes. But to have even attempted that would have been an enormous, indeed impossible, logistical and financial task, especially when women enjoyed the right to vote in only Colorado and Wyoming.

Colorado's women, who had united to win the good fight for equal suffrage in 1893, divided along party lines in 1894 and usually remained that way thereafter. If they were to gain office, they had to work through the established parties. To women's misfortune, male politicos, accustomed to the power, plums, prestige, and in some cases plunder and pelf of office, jealously guarded their marbles.

The Republicans, many of whom had supported equal suffrage in 1893, saw a big difference between women voting and women having influence in the party or being nominated for office. In September 1894, for example, the Arapahoe County Republican Central Committee, the most powerful Republican county organization in the state, voted 98 to 23 to deny women equal rights on the committee. According to the *Rocky Mountain News* of September 4, 1894, one committee member argued that "the proposition to have women on the committee was absurd . . . they had no more right there than the Irish or Germans or Negroes or Catholics."

A year later, the *Rocky Mountain News* of September 18, 1895, reported that a Republican woman gave her sisters a harsh dose of reality when she told them that even if they did get representation on the county committee, "It isn't because they want us. It will simply be throwing a sop to get our votes." Such candor proved prophetic not only for the Republicans but also for the Democrats. Even as women took increasingly active roles in grassroots politics and expanded their roles in county political organizations, the major parties rarely offered them more than a few sops. Each party was willing to nominate a few women for assembly positions usually in the house of representatives, but the paltry numbers indicate that neither party thought it necessary, let alone desirable, to nominate more than a handful. Such stinginess limited women's chances of obtaining statewide offices because a seat in the assembly often provided a springboard for would-be governors and members of the US Congress.

To the legislative sops both parties also usually added a few additional sweeteners to attract women voters. Often women's supposed affinity for the schoolroom got them elected as county superintendents of schools and State Superintendent of Public Instruction. And by the mid-twentieth century women had a good chance to be elected county clerks and treasurers, parsnip posts in the garden of political delights. A few women, such as Agnes Mason Giddings of Fort Collins, who cast an electoral vote for Calvin Coolidge in 1924, were feebly rewarded for party work by being allowed to run for presidential electors—a fleeting honor without clout. On infrequent occasions a woman got to be a mayor. Until the second half of the twentieth century neither major party took kindly to the notion of running a woman for significant statewide posts—governor, lieutenant governor, attorney general, secretary of state, treasurer—or for seats in the US Congress.

Perhaps because capturing a significant office was so difficult for women, those who attempted it were often persons of extraordinary talent, able to slug it out in the male-dominated, sometimes mud-filled political arena. Although often overlooked by scholars, some of these women have occasionally caught historians' notice.

Minnie C.T. Love

Both Robert Goldberg in *Hooded Empire: The Ku Klux Klan in Colorado* (1982) and Phil Goodstein in his book *In the Shadow of the Klan: When the KKK Ruled Denver 1920–1926* (2006) report on the career of Minehaha C.T. Love, who thankfully went by the name "Minnie." Love, who grew up in Washington, DC, in the mid-nineteenth century, did not let the era's prejudice against women in medicine prevent her from becoming a doctor. She capitalized on Howard University's willingness to admit women to its medical school and in 1887 graduated with a MD. In the early 1890s, she, her husband Charles, and their family came to Denver banking on the city's atmosphere and sunshine to cure Charles's tuberculosis.

Charles died; Minnie thrived. She fought for women's suffrage; won appointment to the State Board of Charity and Corrections, and battled, as many women did, for temperance. In 1908, after years promoting the health of mothers and their babies, she pushed creation of Denver's Children's Hospital. In 1920 as a Republican she was elected to the state house of representatives. Losing in her 1922 bid for reelection, she bounced back to win a house seat in 1924. An intrepid joiner and networker, Love spun her connections with the Women of Woodcraft, the Daughters of the American Revolution, and the anti-Catholic Ladies' Loyal Orange Association into votes.

In the November 1924 election she won the backing of the state's powerful Ku Klux Klan. Later that year she gilded her Klan credentials by helping organize the Colorado Women of the Ku Klux Klan. Klan ties brought her additional rewards in 1925, when she was elected to the Denver Board of Education. An advocate of sterilizing women who were likely to bear feeble-minded progeny, Love failed to convince the General Assembly to sanction her point of view. She did, however, succeed in pressing legislation to protect the white and lavender-blue Columbine, Colorado's state flower.

Josephine Aspinwall Roche

In *A Wide-Awake Woman: Josephine Roche in the Era of Reform* (2003) Elinor McGinn tells the story of one of Love's younger contemporaries. Like Love, Josephine Aspinwall Roche boasted an education far beyond that of many male politicians. Daughter of a wealthy mine owner, she attended Vassar and New York's Columbia University, from which she received an MA in 1912. Like Love, Roche swam in reform soup serving as a police officer in Denver's red light district and as a probation officer for Juvenile Court judge Benjamin B. Lindsey. Eventually taking control of her father's coal empire, she insisted on paying workers decent wages even as the Great Depression of the 1930s prompted other companies to slash pay and jobs.

Unlike Love, Roche set her sights on high office. In 1934, backed by her friend Edward P. Costigan (US senator from Colorado, 1931–1937), she tried to run for governor—an audacious move at the time. In a 1974 interview, John A. Carroll (US senator, 1957–1963) explained to me that no one of stature within the Democratic Party was willing to nominate her at the state Democratic convention, so he, then a neophyte in the Costigan camp, accepted the task.

Roche won enough convention votes to get her name before the public as a primary election rival to Edwin C. Johnson, only to be easily bested by Big Ed. Coloradans were not ready for a woman governor. On the other hand, President Franklin D. Roosevelt was prepared to include a woman of Roche's talents in the top tier of his administration. In 1934 he appointed her Assistant Secretary of the Treasury, a post that made her the second highest ranking woman in the federal government.

Betty Eyre Pellet

Like Roche, Elizabeth "Betty" Eyre Pellet led something of a soap-opera life. A Broadway actress, she traded big-city glamour for marriage to a Colorado mine operator and life in the rugged San Juan Mountains. In her book *"That Pellet Woman!"* (1965), which she wrote with Alexander Klein, she recalled that as a county delegate to the 1934 state Democratic Convention she had intended to cast most of Dolores County's votes for Big Ed Johnson even though she personally favored Roche. Shortly before the vote "a key party official" told Pellet, "Don't you dare vote for her [Roche]." The threat so angered Pellet that she gave all of the county's votes to Roche.

Pellet survived crossing Big Ed. In 1940 she was elected to the Colorado house of representatives and, although out of office between 1943 and 1948, she resumed her house service in 1949 where she remained until 1964. Her term as house minority leader (1955–1956) made her the first women to hold that leadership position.

Her risky support of Josephine Roche in 1934 reflected Pellet's stubborn willingness to buck the odds. Seven years later such doggedness paid handsomely when after twenty-seven days of lobbying in Washington, DC, Pellet helped rescue the Galloping Goose, one of the strangest railroads ever to operate in the United States. Property of the Rio Grande Southern Railroad, the Goose was a weird contraption of regular railcars pulled by an automobile—sometimes a Pierce Arrow, sometimes a Cadillac, sometimes a Rolls Royce—mounted on railroad wheels. It ran on 162 miles of narrow-gauge track though the San Juan Mountains, hauling passengers, mail, ore, and other freight. Decades of poor earnings and high costs cooked the Goose into bankruptcy. By 1941 it was honking its last—an ugly blast that blew death to the mines and towns that depended on the little engine that could no more. Pellet's skillful lobbying helped get the Goose federal loans as if it were a foreign country eligible for Lend-Lease money, and the plumped up bird kept galloping through World War II.

Euodchia Bell Smith

Euodchia Bell Smith's many causes kept her galloping most of her life. Her election to the Colorado house of representatives in 1936, her reelection in 1938, and her election to the Colorado state senate in 1940, where she served until 1946, put her among the most successful Colorado women politicians during the first half of the twentieth century. Generally Smith has remained in the historical shadows, but Phil Goodstein, in *From Soup Lines to the Front Lines: Denver during the Depression and World War II, 1927–1947* (2007), gives a glimpse of her career by focusing on her anti-Communism in the late 1930s. Her biographer, should she ever get one, will no doubt mention Smith's chapter on Colorado women in volume 2 of LeRoy Hafen's *Colorado and Its People* (1949) and will emphasize her push to amend Colorado's constitution so that women could sit on juries—a measure that voters approved in 1943.

SPEEDY AS A HARE: 1970 TO 2010

When the General Assembly convened in early 1963 six women took seats in the house—Jean K. Bain, Ruth B. Clark, Kathleen P. Littler, Elizabeth "Betty" E. Pellet, Ruth S. Stockton, and Betty Kirk West. No woman served in the senate that year. In the nearly seventy years since women first won representation in the Colorado legislature their assembly representation had inched up from 3 percent to 6 percent. When the 100-member assembly met in 2011, the picture had radically changed with forty-one of its members being women. That gave Colorado boasting rights as the state with the highest percentage of women lawmakers in the nation.

As women's representation in the assembly skyrocketed in the 1970s and 1980s, and as their seniority increased, so did their ability to gain leadership positions. Republican Ruth S. Stockton, who served in the house (1961–1964) and the senate (1965–1984), emerged as one of the state's most powerful lawmakers, holding such posts as president pro tem of the senate and chair of the Joint Budget Committee. Her long-effective service brought her special honor—a stained glass window portrait in the Colorado capitol. In 2003 Republican Lola Spradley took the top house job by becoming speaker and the same year Republican Norma Anderson became the senate majority leader. In 2005 Democrat Joan Fitz-Gerald won election as president of the senate.

When Democrat Elizabeth "Betty" L. Benavidez took a seat in the house in 1971 she became the first Latina in that chamber, and two years later the outspoken Democrat Arie Parks Taylor became the first African American woman in the house. Six years later Democrat Pauline "Polly" Baca-Barragán landed a spot in the senate—the first Hispanic woman to do so. In 1994 Gloria Tanner accomplished a similar feat by becoming the first African American woman in the senate.

As yet there has been no woman governor of Colorado, although Democrat Gail S. Schoettler came within a few thousand votes of defeating Bill Owens in 1998. A place in the US Senate has also eluded Colorado women. Democrat Nancy E. Dick lost to Republican William

160

Armstrong in 1984. Democrat Dottie Lamm failed to unhorse Senator Ben Nighthorse Campbell in 1998. And in 2010 Jane E. Norton could not buck Ken Buck in the primary election that selected the Republican senatorial nominee.

Although the governorship and US senatorships have been beyond their grasp, many women have served in significant statewide posts. In 1966 Republican Virginia Neal Blue became the first woman to be elected Colorado state treasurer, thereby making it easier for others, such as Democrats Gail S. Schoettler and Cary Kennedy, to target that post. Nancy E. Dick, who in 1978 became the state's first woman lieutenant governor, similarly paved the way for Republican Jane E. Norton and Democrats Gail S. Schoettler and Barbara O'Brien—to pluck that often mainly ceremonial honor. Mary Estill Buchanan's 1974 election as secretary of state, after nearly a century of male ownership of that office, led to more than twenty years of Republican women in the position, including Natalie Meyer, Victoria "Vicki" Buckley, Donetta Davidson, and Gigi Dennis.

Women have also proven adept at getting work in the US House of Representatives. When Betty Pellet caught congressional fever and ran for the House in 1942, she found that many men, particularly in western Colorado, bridled at the thought of sending a woman to Congress. Thirty years later when Democrat Patricia Scott Schroeder ran, her male opponent dismissed her as "little Patsy." Such patronizing might have been effective decades earlier, but it backfired in 1972. Schroeder won and kept winning until she retired in early 1997. Her successor from Colorado's First Congressional District, Diana L. DeGette, was first elected in 1996 and has remained in Congress since. Outside of Denver women have fared less well in garnering congressional seats, although Republican Marilyn Neoma Musgrave (2003–2009) and Democrat Elizabeth "Betsy" Helen Markey (2009–2011) found the sprawling eastern Colorado Fourth Congressional District hospitable to their ambitions.

Other women have used Colorado posts as launching pads to high appointive offices. Republican Anne Gorsuch Burford cut her sharp political teeth in the Colorado house of representatives before her controversial stint as head of the Environmental Protection Agency in the early years of Ronald Reagan's administration. Republican Gail Ann Norton, Colorado's first woman attorney general (1991–1999), gained a cabinet post as George W. Bush's Secretary of the Interior (2001–2006). That brought her the distinction of being the first woman to head the Department of the Interior and the first Colorado woman to hold a cabinet post.

Helen Ring Robinson may have been a fluke, but she was more than a successful woman politician born before her time. Her years in the senate did not lead to a rush of women into the assembly, but by keeping the torch of women's involvement in Colorado politics brightly lit, she illuminated the way for hundreds of other women who came, slowly at first and eventually in waves, after her. If for that reason alone, the Robinson story deserves telling. Thanks to Pat Pascoe for telling it.

SELECTED WRITINGS BY HELEN RING ROBINSON

"Agnes Riddle, Dairywoman-Legislator." *Good Housekeeping* 55 (August 1912): 168–172.

"Bernhardt's L'Aiglon Shows Actress Still Has Marvelous Art." *Rocky Mountain News*, May 15, 1911, p. 10.

"A Big Brother of the Joyous Heart: Stevie of Clayton." *Rocky Mountain News*, April 2, 1911, sec. 3, p. 5.

"Books: Their Makers and Their Readers." *Denver Times*, January 10, 1903, p. 8.

Book Section of Saturday Magazine (editor), *Denver Times*, January 10, 1903, p. 8.

"Confessions of a Peace Pilgrim." *Independent*, February 14, 1916, vol. 85, pp. 225–226.

"A Fair Field in Labor." *Pictorial Review*, July 1919, p. 45.

"A Fair Field in Sex." *Pictorial Review*, May 1919, p. 21.

"A Fair Field in the State: For Mothers of Women." *Pictorial Review*, August 1919, p. 24.

" 'Hats That May Have Been Used for Ballot Boxes,' Seen by a Woman in Convention." *Rocky Mountain News*, July 8, 1908, p. 5.

"In the Homes of the Dreamers: Glimpses into the Domestic Circle of Maurice Maeterlinck, George Bernard Shaw, Marion Crawford, and Gabriele D'Annunzio." *The Scrapbook*, October 1907, pp. 581–588.

" 'Less Attentive Sex' Takes Notice, Really, as Convention Shows." *Rocky Mountain News*, July 9, 1908, p. 3.

Letter to Mrs. N. M. Jaeger of the Political Equality Club of Minneapolis, May 31, 1914. Luth and Nanny Jaeger Papers, Collection A.J22, Box 1, Minnesota Historical Society Library, St. Paul.

Letter to Judge Ben B. Lindsey supporting W. D. Wright for Jury Commissioner, December 17, 1912. Library of Congress, Ben Lindsey Collection, Box 41, December 1912.

"Making the World Safe for Monogamy." *Pictorial Review*, November 1918, p. 5.

"On Being a Woman Senator." *Independent*, April 20, 1914, vol. 78, pp. 130–132.

"Prayer." In *The Meaning of Faith* in Harry E. Fosdick's trilogy *The Meaning of Prayer, Faith, and Service*, pp. 257–258. Garden City, NY: Garden City Books, 1951 [1917]. (This prayer was found on Jim McGuiggan's website: jimmcguiggan.com.)

Preparing Women for Citizenship. New York: Macmillan Co., 1918.

"Preparing Women for the Ballot: Second Article; Women's Work as Wholesale Housekeepers." *Pictorial Review* vol. 19, no. 9 (June 1914): 2, 48.

"Preparing Women for the Ballot." *Pictorial Review* vol. 19, no. 8 (May 1918): 23, 78.

"Putting Her House in Order: No Woman Can Manage More Than One Business at a Time." *Pictorial Review*, January 1919, p. 11.

"Releasing Women for the Top: Being Some Meditations on the Work of Women after the War." *Pictorial Review*, December 1918, p. 24.

"The St. Augustine of Our Century: Views and Reviews." *Rocky Mountain Daily News*, November 21, 1910, p. 12.

"Sex Equality and Brass Tacks." *Delineator*, November 1923, vol. 103, p. 2.

"The Sorrows of Miranda and Me." *Independent*, January 22, 1921, vol. 105, pp. 83–84.

"Squads Right! Squads Left!" *Independent*, July 27, 1918, vol. 95, pp. 120–121.

"The Time Has Come to Consider Birth Politics." *Pictorial Review*, February 1919, p. 27.

Uncle Tom's Cabin for Children by Harriet Beecher Stowe, adapted by Helen Ring Robinson. Philadelphia: Penn Publishing Company, 1908.

"Views and Reviews." *Rocky Mountain News*, November 27, 1911, p. 10.

"Visions of Sarah Platt Decker Guide Mrs. Robinson's Pathway." *Rocky Mountain News*, November 8, 1912, p. 6.

"The War in Colorado." *Independent*, May 11, 1914, vol. 78, pp. 245–247.

"What about the Woman's Party?" *Independent*, September 11, 1916, vol. 87, pp. 381–383.

"Wilson Moved Capitol Back from Wall Street." *Alamosa Journal*, October 19, 1916, p. 8. www.coloradohistoricnewspapers.org.

"Woman Senator Tells Both Sides in Mine Warfare." N.p., unidentified newspaper clipping dated May 2, 1914. Archives, University of Colorado at Boulder Libraries, Boulder.

CHAPTER 1

1. The fact that Helen was not always forthright about her age in later years means we cannot work backward from that information either. Helen submitted two different birthdates on her passport applications. In 1915 she said she was born on February 21, 1866; in 1920 she said she was born on February 21, 1864. Both applications give her birthplace as Eastport, Maine. Ancestry.com; Patricia R. Lambart letter to the Colorado Historical Society, November 22, 1965.

2. US Bureau of the Census, Ninth and Tenth Census of the United States, 1870 and 1880 (Washington, DC: National Archives and Records Administration, 1870 and 1880), http://content.ancestry.com. On this website, images of the original survey documents are available. There is conflicting information about her mother, who is named variously as Mary Prescott Ring or Mary Margaret Thompson, daughter of Peter Thompson of Sweden. The support for the latter as Helen's mother arises from a letter writ-

ten to the Colorado State Historical Society in 1965 by Patricia R. Lambart (Mrs. E. C. Lambart Jr.). Lambart's letter stated that she was Helen's relative, although she did not give the specific relationship, and it asserted that Helen was born in about 1863 to Thomas Warren Ring (1800 to about 1874) and that Helen's mother was Mary Margaret Thompson, or at least that Helen's siblings called this Mary Margaret their mother. According to Lambart's letter, Thomas Warren Ring's father (Helen's grandfather if Thomas was indeed her father) was William Ring (about 1775–1820). William Ring in addition had a stepson, Richard Warren (1786–1865), who represented his town in the state legislature and also became a state senator and town selectman in Maine. Thomas Warren Ring, though not related by blood to the Warrens, had been named after Richard Warren's father, Thomas Warren. If Helen was born into this family, she may have heard her father talk about state senator Richard Warren. Mary Margaret Thompson (not Mary Prescott), whom Lambart named as Helen's mother, was, according to Lambart, born along the Maine border in what is now New Brunswick, Canada, and was the daughter of Peter Thompson of Sweden. In later years Helen did claim she was a descendant of the old Norse pirates. "Mrs. Helen Ring Robinson Dies of Ailment Incurred by Overwork during War," *Denver Post*, July 10, 1923, p. 5.

3. The editors of *The Woman's Who's Who of America* claim the information given was submitted by the biographees themselves; thus it should be reliable. *Woman's Who's Who of America: A Biographical Dictionary of Contemporary Women of the United States and Canada, 1914–15*, ed. John William Leonard (New York: American Commonwealth, 1914); *Who Was Who in America*, vol. 1, 1897–1942 (Chicago: A. N. Marquis, 1943). Helen's obituary in the *Denver Post* (July 10, 1923) also gave her birthplace as Eastport, Maine, as did *Pictorial Roster: Twentieth General Assembly* (Denver: Pictorial Roster, 1915), http://www.genealogybug.net/colorado/040.htm.

4. US Bureau of the Census, 1870 and 1880.

5. "Mrs. Helen Ring Robinson Dies of Ailment Incurred by Overwork during War"; "Colorado's Woman Senator Is Here," *Providence Journal*, June 16, 1913, p. 2.

6. The family was living in the household of Emerson P. Blake, forty-five, and his wife, Sally C. Blake, forty-three.

7. 1880–1881 Wellesley catalog and letter provided by Wilma R. Slaight, archivist, Wellesley College Archives, Wellesley, MA, August 18, 2004.

8. *The Annual Bulletin of Colorado College,* March 1894, gives as part of her biography "Wellesley College, '81–'83; Columbia College Annex, '86"; information provided by Jessy Randall, curator and archivist, Colorado College, Special Collections, Colorado Springs.

9. See, for example, Mae Bradley, "Colorado's First Woman Senator," *Rocky Mountain News,* January 12, 1913, sec. 5, p. 4.

10. Letter from Donald Glassman, Barnard College archivist, New York, NY, October 22, 2004.

11. Information from *Annual Bulletin of Colorado College,* March 1894, provided by Jessy Randall, curator and archivist, Colorado College, Special Collections, Colorado Springs.

12. *Pictorial Roster: Twentieth General Assembly.*

13. *Annual Bulletin of Colorado College,* March 1894, gives the specifics about Cleveland; "Helen Ring Robinson Is Paid High Tribute," *St. Louis Star,* reprinted in the *Denver Republican*, March 23, 1913, part 3, p. 2, claims she taught in Yonkers and Cleveland. *Pictorial Roster: Twentieth General Assembly* also says she taught school in New York and was associate principal of the Hathaway-Brown School.

14. Hathaway-Brown sources were cited in a letter of August 29, 2005, from Virginia P. Dawson, PhD, History Enterprises, Inc., Cleveland, who received my inquiry from the headmaster of the school, Bill Christ.

15. Sometime during Helen's first years in Colorado she won a reputation as a horsewoman during a summer spent at Wagon Wheel Gap, near Creede. She mastered a rebellious horse named Dutchy, which had thrown all previous would-be riders, according to Mae Bradley, "Colorado's First Woman Senator."

16. Isma Dooly, "Suffrage and Some Suffragettes: Sidelights on a Growing Movement," *Atlanta Constitution,* March 2, 1913, p. 7M.

17. *A Century of Colorado Census,* compiled by Suzanne Schulze, 1976, rev. 1977 by Robert Markham (Greeley: Michener Library, University of Northern Colorado), vol. I, table 17; Colin B. Goodykoontz, "The People of Colorado," in *Colorado and Its People: A Narrative and Topical History of the Centennial State,* vol. 2, ed. LeRoy Hafen (New York: Lewis Historical Publishing, 1948), p. 86.

18. While Helen migrated to the West, many members of her family remained in Providence. Mary Ring and Helen's brothers, "B. Judson, compositor" and "Gustavus B." (no occupation given), and two sisters, "Eva T., teacher" and "Rebecca L., teacher," were living together in Providence in

1889. According to the Providence, Rhode Island, Directory of 1889, they all lived at 47 Wood. Two of Helen's sisters were in Providence at the 1910 census: Etta Ring was fifty-five, single, a dressmaker, and a lodger and Annie L. Ring, thirty-eight (should be forty-three), was single, a boarder, and a teacher in public school (US Bureau of the Census, Thirteenth Census of the United States, 1910 [Washington, DC: National Archives and Records Administration, 1910]). Another sister, Eva A., Mrs. Albert G. Thurston, survived Helen in 1923, as did "a brother living in Newark, N.J." This may be the husband of her sister Matilde, R. J. or R. O. MacNair, whom she visited in 1913 and referred to as her brother. "Mrs. Helen Ring Robinson Dies Following Breakdown from Her Work during World War," *Denver Times,* July 10, 1923, p. 1; "Colorado Woman Senator Is Here."

19. "Women in a Rage at Mayor Gaynor; Will Entertain Bernhardt, Suffragists to Have Her as a Special Guest Next Wednesday," *New York Times,* May 17, 1913, http://query.nytimes.com.

20. *Colorado College Catalogue,* 1886, Colorado Historical Society, Denver.

21. J. Juan Reid, *Colorado College: The First Century, 1874–1974* (Colorado Springs: Colorado College, 1979).

22. The *Colorado College Annual Bulletin,* published in March 1894, also lists her as an instructor of English and elocution.

23. Map of the City of Colorado Springs, City Engineers' Office, 1909, available in Western History and Genealogy, Denver Public Library. The "College Reservation" is a four-block area east of Cascade, whereas Colorado College was west of Cascade.

24. *Directory of Colorado Springs, Colorado City and Manitou* (Colorado Springs: Gazette Printing, 1894). Jessy Randall, curator and archivist, Colorado College Special Collections, letter of November 8, 2004, provided the information about the 1894 *Annual Bulletin*; the advertisement in the *Colorado Springs Gazette* ran sporadically sixteen times between September 23 and October 13, 1894; http://content.ancestry.com.

25. Colorado College "Commencement Program," 1893, Colorado Historical Society, Denver.

26. "Lectures at Colorado College in 1894," brochure, Colorado Historical Society, Denver.

27. Elinor Bluemel, *One Hundred Years of Colorado Women* (Denver: Elinor Bluemel, 1973); *The Banner,* 1896, Wolfe Hall and Jarvis Hall Collection #681, Box 3, Colorado Historical Society, Denver; Robert I.

Woodward, archivist, St. John's Cathedral, Denver, letter of October 27, 2004.

28. Carl Abbott, Stephen J. Leonard, and David McComb, *Colorado: A History of the Centennial State*, rev. ed. (Boulder: Colorado Associated University Press, 1982), p. 195; Allan DePont Breck, *Episcopal Church in Colorado, 1860–1963* (Denver: Big Mountain, 1963), p. 78.

29. Wolfe Hall and Jarvis Hall Collection, Box 3, Scrapbook, p. 34, Colorado Historical Society, Denver.

30. *Denver City Directory*, 1896, 1897, and 1898.

31. *The Banner*, 1896, and brochures, '95–'96 and '96–'97, both in Wolfe Hall and Jarvis Hall Collection, Colorado Historical Society, Denver.

32. Wolfe Hall brochure, 1893–1894, Wolfe Hall and Jarvis Hall Collection, Box 3, Scrapbook, p. 20, Colorado Historical Society, Denver.

33. Wolfe Hall *Banner* for Christmas 1897, cited by Robert I. Woodward, archivist, St. John's Cathedral, Denver, letter of October 27, 2004.

34. *The Banner*, June 1896, Wolfe Hall and Jarvis Hall Collection, Box 2, folder 26, Colorado Historical Society, Denver; *Wolfe Hall, 1895–1896* and *Wolfe Hall, 1896–1897* (booklets), Wolfe Hall and Jarvis Hall Collection, Box 2, folder 27, p. 4, and Box 3, Scrapbook, p. 60, Colorado Historical Society, Denver. Miss LeFevre was listed on the 1897 graduation program as part of "The Muses Dower," whose job was giving appropriate gifts to the graduates.

35. Undated clipping, *Wolfe Hall, 1893–1894*, Wolfe Hall and Jarvis Hall Collection, Box 3, Scrapbook, p. 20, Colorado Historical Society, Denver.

36. Bradley, "Colorado's First Woman Senator."

37. *Denver City Directory*, 1899. Descriptions of the trustees come from Stephen J. Leonard and Thomas J. Noel, *Denver: Mining Camp to Metropolis* (Boulder: University Press of Colorado, 1990), pp. 29–30, 35, 37, 47–49, 78, 240, 300; "Joel Frederick Vaile" [obituary], *Rocky Mountain Herald*, April 8, 1916, p. 5.

38. Undated clipping, Wolcott School Clippings File, Western History and Genealogy, Denver Public Library.

39. Kristen D. Iverson, *Molly Brown: Unraveling the Myth* (Boulder: Johnson Books, ca. 1999), pp. 122, 134–135.

40. "Wolfe, Wolcott, and Jarvis," *Denver Times*, September 12, 1898, p. 2.

41. Undated clipping, Wolcott School Clippings File, Western History and Genealogy, Denver Public Library.

42. Miss Wolcott School, *The Annual*, June 1904, Western History and Genealogy, Denver Public Library.

43. *The Social Year-Book* (Denver: Carson-Harper, 1898).

44. See Sylvia Pettem, *Separate Lives: The Story of Mary Rippon* (Longmont, CO: Book Lode, 1999), 75–76, 129. A poll by the National Education Association indicated that as late as the 1920s, half of the school districts forced women teachers to resign if they married (p. 155). See also Miss Wolcott School, *The Annual*. As late as 1915, Helen Wixson, Denver Public Schools board member, had to propose that the rule against married women teaching be waived on a case-by-case basis (*Denver Express,* March 25, 1915, p. 2).

45. *Denver Times*, February 14, 1902, p. 5.

46. "Helen Ring Robinson, First Woman to Be Senator in Colorado, Dies," *Rocky Mountain News,* July 11, 1923, p. 9.

47. *Silverton Standard*, January 29, 1898, http://www.cdpheritage.org. Roy's father, Ralph, and Ewing's father, Samuel, were brothers. According to Ann Hofstetter Delaney, the great-granddaughter of Roy Robinson, Ewing's first move to Iowa, where his Uncle Ralph lived, and then to Colorado, where Ralph's son Roy and his wife lived, suggests the ongoing contact with this part of the family. Delaney's grandmother and Roy's daughter, Ramona Rose Robinson Elder, talked to her often about her beloved cousin Alcyon, as both girls were without siblings and very close in age. Alcyon Robinson was born March 15, 1896, in Denver, whereas Ramona Robinson was born in September 1897 in Silverton. US Bureau of the Census, Twelfth Census of the United States, 1900 (Washington, DC: National Archives and Records Administration, 1900); letters from Ann Hofstetter Delaney to the author, August 18 and August 20, 2005.

48. Marriage Certificate, May 1, 1895, and Death Certificate, July 19, 1897, Colorado State Archives, Denver. Cora died of typhoid at St. Luke's Hospital. Alcyon Robinson was born March 15, 1896, according to letter of July 11, 2005, from Fred Weybret, husband of Alcyon Robinson's daughter, Alcyon Martia Carlson Weybret, to the author. He responded for his wife, who was in poor health.

49. Cora Ballard Robinson Abstract of Probate, August 13, 1897, Colorado State Archives, Denver.

50. In 1870 Ewing's older sister was teaching school, while "Ewing G." and four siblings were at school and two others were at home. The value of his father's real estate had increased to a comfortable $25,000. His mother died in 1871 and his father died in 1878, probably leaving some of his money

to Ewing, who had just turned twenty-one. US Bureau of the Census, Eighth and Ninth Census of the United States, 1860 and 1870 (Washington, DC: National Archives and Records Administration, 1860 and 1870, http:// content.ancestry.com). The Family Search International Genealogical Index gives Ewing's father's birth date as February 15, 1815, and his mother's name as Caroline Dodge, born May 3, 1826. Ewing's siblings were Mary Robinson, William Patterson Robinson, Allie Robinson, and Louis Clark Robinson. All, including Ewing, are buried in Beverly, Washington County, Ohio. Death dates of his parents are also from this source, which was submitted by an unnamed relative who was a member of the LDS Church (International Genealogical Index, v. 5.0, http://www.familysearch.org). In the census data, first and middle names are often reversed.

51. He lived in the household of Emma Oades. See US Bureau of the Census, 1880, where Robinson is misread as Robinsen; also Ewing Robinson obituary, *Rocky Mountain News*, April 13, 1925, p. 8.

52. *Rocky Mountain News*, April 13, 1925, p. 8.

53. Roll of Attorneys, *Colorado Reports Cases Adjudged in the Supreme Court of Colorado*, vol. 28 (Denver: Mills, 1902). I am indebted to David Erickson for providing this information in an e-mail of May 25, 2005.

54. *Denver City Directory*, 1901, 1902, 1903. Frank L. Grant was admitted to practice on September 15, 1900 (Roll of Attorneys, *Colorado Reports*, vol. 28, 1902). This last information was provided by David Erickson in an e-mail of May 25, 2005. Ewing continued to practice law up until his death in 1925. His office was in the Equitable Building in Denver from about 1894 to at least 1910, and he was regularly listed in the *Denver City Directory*. In 1912 he is listed in the Empire Building at the corner of 16th Street and Glenarm. Ewing attended the annual Bench and Bar Banquet put on by the Denver Bar Association in 1900, and he was listed as a member of the Colorado Bar Association, a voluntary association, in the 1904 list of members but not in the 1910 or 1924 lists. Banquet information provided by David Erickson (e-mail of May 25, 2005) is from the *Denver Evening Post*, February 24, 1900, p. 3. Additional information was provided by Diane Hartman, Colorado Bar Association, phone conversation, October 27, 2004.

55. *The Social Year-Book, a Social Directory of the Men and Women Who Make up the Social Life of Denver; Together with a Club Directory Embracing the Membership of the Principal Clubs of Denver and Diagrams of Churches and Theatres* [hereafter *The Social Year-Book*] (Denver: Carson-Harper, 1898, 1899, 1901–1902).

56. An associate membership probably allowed them to avoid the requirement for "active" membership: the submission of an example of work to be approved before admission. Jerome C. Smiley (ed.), *History of Denver, with Outlines of the Earlier History of the Rocky Mountain Country* (Denver: Times-Sun, 1901). *The Social Year-Book, 1901–1902* listed them both as associate members of the Artists' Club. In the same year Helen's address is 1638 Pennsylvania and Ewing Robinson's is "Wolfe Hall," which is probably an error. Their names appear immediately beside each other on the list. *The Social Year-Book, 1901–1902,* p. 101.

57. US Bureau of the Census, 1900. Also see US Bureau of the Census, 1870, where father, Oscar L. Ballard, and wife, Jane Ballard, of Malone, New York, have two children of the right ages, Cora M., twelve, and Nellie, fourteen. In the plot owned by Ewing Robinson at Fairmount Cemetery, his first wife, Cora, and a Perley Graham, who died at age thirty-three in 1899, are buried. Perley, usually a man's name, may have been Nellie Graham's husband or a relative of her husband.

58. *Denver Times,* February 14, 1902, p. 5.

59. Jean Bogaert, *The Story of All Saints Parish 1874–1964* (Denver: All Saints Parish, 1964). Reverend Oakes served as rector of All Saints from 1893 through 1896 (see chart on last unnumbered page). Oakes may have known Helen when she taught in Yonkers because while he was rector of All Saints, his wife, Mabel Oakes of Yonkers, New York, was added to the rolls (*All Saints Parish Register,* All Saints Episcopal Church, Denver). Reverend Oakes also officiated at her funeral in the chapel at Oakes Home.

60. Phil Goodstein, *Denver from the Bottom Up: From Sand Creek to Ludlow,* vol. 1 (Denver: New Social Publications, 2003), p. 233; Robert E. Riegel and David E. Long, *The American Story* (New York: McGraw-Hill, 1955), vol. 2, p. 55.

61. Marriage Certificate, February 13, 1902, Colorado State Archives, Denver.

62. Marriage Certificate of Ewing Robinson and Cora M. Ballard, May 1, 1895, Colorado State Archives, Denver; letter from Robert I. Woodward, archivist, Saint John's Cathedral, Denver, to the author, November 1, 2004.

63. Harriet Beecher Stowe, *Uncle Tom's Cabin for Children,* adapted by Helen Ring Robinson (Philadelphia: Penn Publishing, ca. 1908), Library of Congress e-Book. A copy was given to Alcyon and inscribed "To Alcyon, Love Mother, '08" and to Alcyon's cousin, Ramona Robinson, inscribed "For my dear Ramona from the Adapter." Ramona was Roy Robinson's

daughter, who was raised in Denver. Fred Weybret reported that a copy of the book is still in the family's possession (letter from Fred Weybret, July 11, 2005). The inscription to Ramona is reported in a letter from Ann Hofstetter Delaney, a descendant of Ramona's, August 18, 2005. Delaney has Ramona's copy.

64. At the time of Alcyon's death in 1932 she was employed as a reporter for the *Los Angeles Record* (letter from Fred Weybret, July 11, 2005). Alcyon married Martin Carlson, and they had one child, Alcyon Martia Carlson (later Weybret), born February 21, 1926. "Mrs. Helen Ring Robinson Dies Following Breakdown from Her Work during World War"; Colorado State Archives, Denver, Probate Case Index, Helen Ring Robinson, Case #32621, July 24, 1923.

65. "Robinson Accused of Dispossessing Client," *Denver Times,* June 8, 1903, p. 8.

66. The case, known as *The People ex rel. The Colorado Bar Association v. Ewing Robinson,* can be found in *Colorado Reports: Covering Cases Reported in Pacific Reporter,* vol. 75P (St. Paul, MN: West Publishing, 1962), pp. 922–924. The case was decided March 7, 1904.

CHAPTER 2

1. Phil H. Goodstein, *Robert Speer's Denver: The Mile High City in the Progressive Era* (Denver: New Social Publications, 2004), p. 1.

2. For the Populist role in Colorado and its influence on progressivism, see James E. Wright, *The Politics of Populism: Dissent in Colorado* (New Haven, CT: Yale University Press, 1974), especially pp. 264–265.

3. Phil H. Goodstein, *Denver from the Bottom Up: From Sand Creek to Ludlow,* vol. 1 (Denver: New Social Publications, 2003), p. 198.

4. William Chafe, "Women's History and Political History: Some Thoughts on Progressivism and the New Deal," in *Visible Women: New Essays on American Activism,* ed. Nancy Hewitt and Suzanne Lebsock (Urbana: University of Illinois Press, 1993), pp. 101–118.

5. Paula Baker, "The Domestication of Politics," *American Historical Review* 89 (June 1984): pp. 620, 625, 631.

6. Ibid., p. 632.

7. Rheta Child Dorr, quoted in ibid.

8. Molly Ladd-Taylor, *Mother-Work: Women, Child Welfare and the State, 1890–1930* (Urbana: University of Illinois Press, 1994), p. 7.

9. Theda Skocpol, *Protecting Soldiers and Mothers: The Political Origins of Social Policy in the United States* (Cambridge, MA: Harvard University Press, 1993), pp. 2, 10.

10. Ladd-Taylor, *Mother-Work,* p. 92.

11. Helen Sumner, *Equal Suffrage: Results of an Investigation in Colorado Made for the Collegiate Equal Suffrage League of New York State* (New York: Harper and Brothers, 1909), pp. 200–202.

12. On the cooperation between Lindsey and progressive women, see Todd Laugen, *The Gospel of Progressivism: Moral Reform and Labor War in Colorado, 1900–1930* (Boulder: University Press of Colorado, 2010), pp. 125–151. See also the introduction by Stephen J. Leonard in Ben B. Lindsey and Harvey J. O'Higgins, *The Beast* (Boulder: University Press of Colorado, 2009 [1910]).

13. Rebecca J. Mead, *How the Vote Was Won: Woman Suffrage in the Western United States, 1868–1914* (New York: New York University Press, 2004), p. 2.

14. Colorado College page of *Directory of Colorado Springs, Colorado City and Manitou* (Colorado Springs: Gazette Printing, 1894); also *Colorado College Annual Bulletin,* March 1894.

15. For detailed accounts of that election, see Stephen J. Leonard, " 'Bristling for Their Rights': Colorado's Women and the Mandate of 1893," in *Western Voices: 125 Years of Colorado Writing,* ed. Steve Grinstead and Ben Fogelberg, Colorado Historical Society (Golden, CO: Fulcrum [from *Colorado Heritage*], Spring 1993), pp. 226–233; Goodstein, *Denver from the Bottom Up,* pp. 219–229; Suzanne M. Marilley, *"Why the Vote?" Woman Suffrage and the Origins of Liberal Feminism in the United States, 1820–1920* (Cambridge, MA: Harvard University Press, 1996), pp. 126–189.

16. Mead, *How the Vote Was Won,* p. 2. Utah women were disenfranchised by the US Congress in 1887 and then re-enfranchised when Utah was admitted as a state in 1896. The women of Washington Territory were also briefly enfranchised by the territorial legislature in 1883 but lost the vote by a decision of the Territorial Supreme Court in 1888, according to Mead, p. 15.

17. Ibid., p. 53, citing Coloradan Ellis Meredith, who was quoting Sarah Platt Decker in "What It Means to Be an Enfranchised Woman," *Atlantic Monthly* (August 1908): pp. 196–197.

18. Robert S. Morrison, "Legislation in Colorado," in *Semi-Centennial History of the State of Colorado,* vol. 1, ed. Jerome C. Smiley (Chicago: Lewis, 1913), p. 642.

19. Quoted in Stephen J. Leonard and Thomas J. Noel, *Denver: Mining Camp to Metropolis* (Boulder: University Press of Colorado, 1990), p. 97.

20. Sumner, *Equal Suffrage,* pp. 194, 196.

21. Robin Muncy, *Creating a Female Dominion in American Reform, 1890–1935* (New York: Oxford University Press, 1991), p. 4; Carl N. Degler, *At Odds: Women and the Family in America from the Revolution to the Present* (New York: Oxford University Press, 1980), pp. 314, 655; Janet Zollinger Giele, *Two Paths to Women's Equality: Temperance, Suffrage, and the Origins of Modern Feminism* (New York: Twayne, 1995), pp. 80, 158.

22. "Women's Clubs Delegates Discuss Suffrage," *Colorado Springs Gazette,* September 10, 1909, p. 3, http://content.ancestry.com.

23. Mae Bradley, "Colorado's First Woman Senator," *Rocky Mountain News,* January 12, 1913, sec. 5, p. 4. The first paragraph was quoted verbatim in an article by Isma Dooly, "Suffrage and Some Suffragettes: Sidelights on a Growing Movement," *Atlanta Constitution,* March 2, 1913, p. 7M, www.ancestry.com.

24. "Women Legislators Should Be Womanly," *New York Times,* November 23, 1913, p. 12, www.proquest.com.

25. "Woman Legislator Defends Suffrage," *New York Times,* May 10, 1913, p. 9, www.proquest.com.

26. Helen Ring Robinson, "Preparing Women for the Ballot," *Pictorial Review* (May 1918): pp. 23, 78. Helen's views and articles on suffrage were gathered into a volume published in 1918 titled *Preparing Women for Citizenship* (New York: Macmillan, 1918).

27. "Colorado's Woman Senator Is Here," *Providence Journal,* June 16, 1913, p. 2. Xerox and transcript provided by Providence Public Library.

28. Helen Ring Robinson, "Preparing Women for the Ballot," *Pictorial Review* (June 1918): pp. 2, 48.

29. "Colorado's Woman Senator Is Here," p. 2.

30. Helen is quoted in "Colorado's 'Lady Senator' Jars East because She's No Freak," *Denver Republican,* July 10, 1913, p. 1.

31. Robinson, *Preparing Women for Citizenship,* pp. 12–13. See Gail M. Beaton's "The Literary Study and Philanthropic Work of Six Women's Clubs in Denver, 1881–1945" (master's thesis, University of Colorado–Denver, 1987).

32. Ibid., p. 14.

33. "Pioneer Women," in *History of Denver, with Outlines of the Earlier History of the Rocky Mountain Country,* ed. Jerome C. Smiley (Denver: Times-Sun, 1901), pp. 784–786.

34. Robinson, *Preparing Women for Citizenship,* pp. 45–46.

35. Skocpol, *Protecting Soldiers and Mothers,* p. 329.

36. Cora V. Collett, *A History of the Woman's Club of Denver* (Denver: the Club, 1930), pp. 5, 8, 9.

37. *Annual,* Denver Woman's Club, 1912–1913 through 1917–1918.

38. Helen Ring Robinson, "Visions of Sarah Platt Decker Guide Mrs. Robinson's Pathway," *Rocky Mountain News,* November 8, 1912, p. 6.

39. *The Social Year-Book* (Denver: Carson-Harper, 1899).

40. *Denver City Blue Book,* 1908–1909; Gail M. Beaton, "The Literary Study and Philanthropic Work of Six Women's Clubs in Denver, 1881–1945," *Essays in Colorado History* 13 (1992): p. 63.

41. *Who's Who in Denver Society* (Denver: W. H. Kistler, 1908).

42. Booklet, *History of the Denver Woman's Press Club, 1898–1899–1900,* Denver Woman's Press Club Collection, Box 2, Western History and Genealogy, Denver Public Library.

43. *The Women Who Made the Headlines: Denver Woman's Press Club, the First Hundred Years* (Lakewood, CO: Western Guideways, 1998), pp. 4–5.

44. Jerome C. Smiley (ed.), *History of Denver, with Outlines of the Earlier History of the Rocky Mountain Country* (Denver: Times-Sun, 1901), p. 788.

45. *Denver Woman's Press Club Year Book,* 1900–1901, 1901–1902, and 1903–1904.

46. *Denver Woman's Press Club Minutes,* Box 2, January 30, August 6, and October 17, 1907; October 21, 1909, all in Western History and Genealogy, Denver Public Library. The 1910 census listed Ewing and Helen at 1222 Gaylord. She was described as a writer for a newspaper and he as an attorney in general practice. His age was fifty; her age is illegible. US Bureau of the Census, *Thirteenth Census of the United States,* 1910 (Washington, DC: National Archives and Records Administration, 1910), http://ancestry.com.

47. *History of the Denver Woman's Press Club, 1898–1899–1900,* Denver Woman's Press Club Collection, Box 2, Minutes, January 17 and January 30, March 14, April 18, May 2, and May 16, 1907, Western History and Genealogy, Denver Public Library. I am also a member of the Denver Woman's Press Club, having served as president in 2005–2006.

48. *Denver Woman's Press Club Minutes,* Box 2, March 4, 1909; January 20, 1910; January 19, 1911; November 21, 1912.

49. Ibid., April 16, April 22, and June 24, 1908. The minutes are in the Denver Public Library collection cited above, but the yearbooks cited here are in the care of the club.

50. Ibid., April 22, 1908; Certificate of Incorporation, p. 40.

51. Beaton, "Literary Study," pp. 68, 71, 73; Sharon Snow Carver, *Club Women of Three Intermountain Cities of Denver, Boise and Salt Lake City between 1893 and 1919* (Ann Arbor: University of Michigan Press, 2000), pp. 13, 314–315.

52. For example, see Helen Ring Robinson, "Books: Their Makers and Their Readers," *Denver Times,* January 10, 1903, p. 8.

53. Helen Ring Robinson, "The St. Augustine of Our Century; Views and Reviews," *Rocky Mountain News,* November 21, 1910, p. 12.

54. Helen Ring Robinson, "Views and Reviews," *Rocky Mountain News,* November 27, 1911, p. 10.

55. Helen Ring Robinson, "In the Homes of the Dreamers: Glimpses into the Domestic Circle of Maurice Maeterlinck, George Bernard Shaw, Marion Crawford, and Gabriele D'Annunzio," *The Scrapbook* (October 1907): pp. 581–588.

56. Dooly, "Suffrage and Some Suffragettes," p. 7M.

57. Harriet Beecher Stowe, *Uncle Tom's Cabin for Children,* adapted by Helen Ring Robinson (Philadelphia: Penn Publishing, [ca. 1908]).

58. Ibid., "Afterword."

59. Helen Ring Robinson, "Hats That May Have Been Used for Ballot Boxes," *Rocky Mountain News,* July 8, 1908, p. 5.

60. Helen Ring Robinson, " 'Less Attentive Sex' Takes Notice, Really, as Convention Shows," *Rocky Mountain News,* July 9, 1908, p. 3.

61. Helen Ring Robinson, "A Big Brother of the Joyous Heart," *Rocky Mountain News,* April 2, 1911, p. 5.

62. Helen Ring Robinson, "Bernhardt's L'Aiglon Shows Actress Still Has Marvelous Art," *Rocky Mountain News,* May 15, 1911, p. 10.

63. Helen Ring Robinson, "Agnes Riddle; Dairywoman-Legislator," *Good Housekeeping* (August 1912): pp. 168–172.

64. "Local Happenings," *Steamboat Pilot,* June 2, 1909, p. 13; Dee Richards, *Steamboat Round the Bend* (Steamboat Springs, CO: Steamboat Pilot, 1976), p. 134.

65. *Ballinger and Richards Thirty-Second Annual Denver City Directory for 1904* (Denver: Ballinger and Richards, 1904) and subsequent directories; US Bureau of the Census, 1910. Denver County Assessor's records indicate

that Ewing bought 1441 Josephine, which had a house on it, on October 28, 1902; he owned it until November 23, 1908. Helen bought the land at 1222 Gaylord where the house was to be built on October 17, 1903, for $1,750; she owned it until November 20, 1919 (Western History and Genealogy, Denver Public Library).

66. *Denver Woman's Press Club Year Book,* each year from 1899 to 1923.

67. "Woman's Duty to Study up Civics," *Trenton Evening Times,* May 31, 1913, p. 5, www.newspaperarchive.com.

68. Sharon Powers, "Colorado's Foremothers Were First Women Elected to Any State Legislature in the Nation," paper, Denver Legislative Council Library, August 16, 1994, p. 2.

69. Billie Barnes Jensen, "The Woman Suffrage Movement in Colorado" (master's thesis, University of Colorado–Boulder, 1959). Appendix E summarizes the bills influenced by women legislators in their first years in the legislature.

70. Powers, "Colorado's Foremothers," p. 4.

71. Jensen, "Woman Suffrage Movement," appendix E.

72. Sumner, *Equal Suffrage,* pp. 124–125.

73. Marcia Tremmel Goldstein, *Meet Me at the Ballot Box: Women's Innovations in Party and Electoral Politics in Post-Suffrage Colorado, 1893–1898* (Ann Arbor: University of Michigan Press, 2007), pp. 12, 198.

74. Jensen, "Woman Suffrage Movement," appendix E.

75. Robyn Muncy, "Women Demand Recognition: Women Candidates in Colorado's Election of 1912," in *We Have Come to Stay: American Women and Political Parties, 1880–1960,* ed. Melanie Gustafson, Kristie Miller, and Elisabeth I. Perry (Albuquerque: University of New Mexico Press, 1999), p. 46.

76. Sumner, *Equal Suffrage,* p. 27.

77. *Women Who Have Served in the Colorado General Assembly* (Denver: Legislative Council, 1978), Government Documents, Denver Public Library.

78. When I was elected to the Colorado State Senate in 1988, I was one of seven women in the thirty-five-member body. In the 2008 session there were still only ten women.

79. Rachel R. Dennis and Sally R. Hayden, *A Guide to the Papers of Ellis Meredith* (Denver: University of Denver, 1979), p. 4.

80. Rheta Childe Dorr, *What Eight Million Women Want* (1910), part 3 of 4, chapter 10 (unnumbered pages), www.fullbooks.com.

81. Elinor Bluemel, *One Hundred Years of Colorado Women* (Denver: Elinor Bluemel, 1973), pp. 53–55; "Share Honor as First Woman Delegate," *Colorado Prospector*, a history newspaper with reprints of original accounts, March 1988, p. 8, p.r. [reprint from *Rocky Mountain News*, July 7, 1908].

82. "Miss Anna L. Wolcott," *Denver Republican*, October 26, 1910, p. 5; "Shafroth's Plurality Now Placed at 18,000, Gunter also Gaining," *Denver Post*, November 10, 1910, p. 1. Anna was one of two regents elected.

83. Laugen, *Gospel of Progressivism*, pp. 31–32.

84. Dorr, *What Eight Million Women Want*, chapter 10.

85. Fred Greenbaum, *Fighting Progressive: A Biography of Edward P. Costigan* (Washington, DC: Public Affairs Press, 1971), pp. 27–28.

86. "Senator Helen Robinson," *Literary Digest*, February 15, 1913, p. 368.

87. Laugen, *Gospel of Progressivism*, pp. 32–34.

88. James Baker and LeRoy Hafen, *History of Colorado* (Denver: Linderman, 1927), vol. 3, p. 1114, cited in Brenda Morrison, "Their Hats in the Ring," *Colorado History* 10 (Denver: Colorado Historical Society, 2004), p. 3.

89. "What Women Are Saying about Mrs. Robinson," *Rocky Mountain News*, September 10, 1910, p. 6.

90. Ibid.

91. Alice Rohe, "Women Aroused by Plan to Pledge State Teachers' Body to Mrs. Cook," *Rocky Mountain News*, September 15, 1910, p. 16.

92. Alice Rohe, "Women Clash in Democratic Convention," *Rocky Mountain News*, September 16, 1910, p. 14.

93. For the description of the 1910 convention and election, see Morrison, "Their Hats in the Ring," pp. 9–12. Ellis Meredith wrote the first suffragist novelette, called "Sharp Arrows," using this election as her inspiration ("Ellis Meredith's Suffragist Novelette, 'Sharp Arrows' Depicts Colorado Characters," *Rocky Mountain News*, February 8, 1913, p. 3).

94. "The St. Augustine of Our Century: Views and Reviews by Helen Ring Robinson," *Rocky Mountain News*, November 21, 1910, p. 12.

95. "State Politics," *Alamosa Journal*, July 26, 1912, p. 4, http://gunnison.aclin.org.

96. Robinson, "Visions of Sarah Platt Decker," p. 6.

97. "Both Assemblies Dominated by Same Machine's Headless Ballot and Recall Stabbed: Democratic Gang Throws Sop to Reform at County

Meet; Names Lindsey, Hicks and Mrs. Robinson," *Rocky Mountain News,* August 9, 1912, pp. 1, 3; "Field Forces Judge Allen before Democratic Primary," *Denver Express,* August 9, 1912, p. 3.

98. Muncy, "Women Demand Recognition," p. 51.

99. Ibid.

100. "A List of Nominations," *Denver Times,* November 2, 1912, p. 8; "Progressive Democrats Bolt, Name Ticket; Tynan at Head," *Denver Republican,* August 10, 1912, p. 1; "Platform Crowd Endorses Tynan for Governor," *Denver Express,* August 9, 1912, p. 7.

101. Alice Rohe, "State Needs Women in Law-Making Body, Says Mrs. Robinson," *Rocky Mountain News,* September 4, 1912, p. 12.

102. Ibid.

103. Muncy, "Women Demand Recognition," p. 51; Rohe, "State Needs Women in Law-Making Body," p. 12.

104. Letter dated December 17, 1912, Ben Lindsey Collection, Box 41, labeled "November 1912," Library of Congress, Washington, DC.

105. "Evans-Speer Gang Picks Candidates to Support at Tomorrow's Primary: Purpose Is to Let Henchmen Know Who Are 'Right': Action Is an Unparalleled Outrage and a Challenge That People Must Meet," *Rocky Mountain News,* September 9, 1912, p. 1.

106. *Rocky Mountain News,* September 6, 1912, p. 3.

107. James B. Pearce (secretary of state), *Abstract of Votes Cast at the Primary Election . . . and at the General Election Held on the Fifth Day of November, A.D. 1912* (Denver: Smith-Brooks, 1913), in Colorado State Archives, Denver.

108. Carl Ubbelohde, Maxine Benson, and Duane A. Smith, *A Colorado History,* 5th ed. (Boulder: Pruett, 1982), p. 282.

109. Sample ballot, Ben Lindsey Collection, Box 288, "Political File" [1912], Library of Congress, Washington, DC.

110. Ibid.

111. *Abstract of Votes,* 1912.

112. "Colorado Democrats Control Legislature; 77 to 23 Is Working Majority of Party," *Denver Post,* November 8, 1912, p. 1.

113. Laugen, *Gospel of Progressivism,* pp. 50–51.

114. Robinson, "Visions of Sarah Platt Decker," p. 6.

115. *Utah History Encyclopedia,* ed. Allen Kent Powell (Salt Lake City: University Press, University of Utah, 1994), Utah state website, http://www.media.utah.edu/UHE.

116. James J. Lopach and Jean A. Luckowski, *Jeannette Rankin: A Political Woman* (Boulder: University Press of Colorado, 2005), p. 8.

117. United Kingdom Parliament website, http://www.parliament.uk/parliamentary_publications_and_archives/. According to Elise Boulding, only Finland had women members of its legislative body before 1912. Elise Boulding, *The Underside of History: A View of Women through Time* (Boulder: Westview, 1976), appendix 13-1, p. 792. Women made up 10 percent of Finland's legislative body in 1907 and 13 percent in 1908. Then there were none until 1930.

CHAPTER 3

1. *Laws Passed at the Nineteenth Session of the General Assembly of the State of Colorado* (Denver: Western Newspaper Union, 1913), pp. 669–696; Carl Ubbelohde, Maxine Benson, and Duane A. Smith, *A Colorado History*, 5th ed. (Boulder: Pruett, 1982), pp. 281–283.

2. "She Calls Herself 'Housewife of Colorado Senate' and Will Work for Women and Children," *Denver Republican*, November 8, 1912, p. 10. The *Denver Republican* was the mouthpiece of the Republican machine, according to Fred Greenblum in *Fighting Progressive: A Biography of Edward P. Costigan* (Washington, DC: Public Affairs Press, 1971), p. 23.

3. Quoted in an article by Frances Melrose, "Helen Robinson Left Political Mark," *Rocky Mountain News*, January 8, 1989, p. 16M.

4. Mae Bradley, "Colorado's First Woman Senator," *Rocky Mountain News*, January 12, 1913, sec. 5, p. 4.

5. Ibid. In the following session Helen passed a bill that addressed prostitution by declaring it a public nuisance to own, lease, or maintain property for immoral use (*Digest of the Session Laws*, 1915, p. 16). A similar bill by house member Felix Tait was killed, revived, and killed again ("The Week in the Legislature," *Denver Express*, April 5, 1913, p. 3). Helen was shocked to learn in a hearing about the contested election of Senator Casimiro Barela that prostitutes in Trinidad's red light district paid Trinidad authorities for protection. They were also herded to the polls and forced to vote Republican ("Barela Starts Defense Today," *Rocky Mountain News*, February 8, 1913, p. 3).

6. "Woman Dons Her Toga," *Washington Post*, January 3, 1913, p. 1, www.ancestry.com.

7. The actual presiding officer of the senate was the lieutenant governor until a 1974 constitutional amendment. Now the senate elects its president

after he or she is nominated by the majority party caucus ("Helen Ring Robinson Is Paid High Tribute," *St. Louis Star,* reprinted in *Denver Republican,* March 23, 1913, part 3, p. 2). "Senatorial courtesy" is still practiced in the senate, as even bills that have been killed are brought back as a courtesy to give the sponsor an opportunity to correct their shortcomings and try to pass them again. Appeals on the floor to senatorial courtesy to gain votes for a motion are common.

8. "Four Go Back on Adams; Is Beaten," *Denver Express,* January 6, 1913, p. 1; "Republicans Help Adams Win Seat," *Denver Express,* January 8, 1913, p. 7. Helen opposed the seating of Senator Barela after the majority of a legislative investigative committee said the election was won "by fraud and conspiracy" ("Majority Finds Barela Fraud," *Rocky Mountain News,* March 15, 1913, p. 4).

9. "Adams Is President," *Bayfield Blade,* La Plata County, January 17, 1913, p. 3; "Heard and Seen at the Capitol," *Denver Express,* January 8, 1913, p. 7.

10. Colorado Department of State, *Legislative Manual* (Denver: Smith-Brooks, 1903), p. 60.

11. *Senate Journal of the Nineteenth General Assembly of the State of Colorado* (Denver: Smith-Brooks, 1913) (henceforth cited as SJ). A "session" lasts two years, but there is a separate journal for each year the General Assembly meets. In this era the legislature typically met only in the odd-numbered years unless an Extraordinary Session was called.

12. Elias M. Ammons, *Inaugural Address of Elias M. Ammons, Governor of Colorado before the Nineteenth General Assembly,* January 14, 1913 (Denver: Smith-Brooks), Colorado State Archives, Denver. The following Ammons quotes are from this speech.

13. *Laws Passed at the Nineteenth Session,* pp. 517–518.

14. "Ammons to Let Ax Fall; Many Heads Drop," *Rocky Mountain News,* January 26, 1913, p. 1; "Two Bills Give Governor Way to Economize," *Rocky Mountain News,* January 30, 1913, p. 1.

15. "Ammons Promises Fairness to Women in Giving Positions," *Denver Express,* January 9, 1913, p. 3.

16. This is the same senator who suggested in 1911 that Colorado rescind women's right to vote. Stephen J. Leonard, "'Bristling for Their Rights': Colorado's Women and the Mandate of 1893," in *Western Voices: 125 Years of Colorado Writing,* ed. Steve Grinstead and Ben Fogelberg, Colorado Historical Society (Golden, CO: Fulcrum [from *Colorado Heritage*], Spring 1993), p. 233.

17. "Insists Women Drink More: Colorado Senator Repeats 'Insult' Denounced by Feminine Member," *Washington Post,* February 6, 1913, p. 1. See also "Attack on Women Brings Response," *Nevada State Journal,* February 6, 1913, p. 4, www.ancestry.com; "Says Women Drink More," *New York Times,* February 6, 1913, p. 7, http://query.nytimes.com/gst/abstract. html?res=9A04E0D81E3AE633A25755C0A9649C946296D6CF.

18. "Woman Senator Defends Denver Women against Charge of Highball Drinking," *Denver Express,* February 5, 1913, p. 1. *The Express* was generally very favorable in its coverage of Helen.

19. "Helen Ring Robinson Defends Women and Threatens Hecker with Expulsion from Senate," *Rocky Mountain News,* February 6, 1913, p. 2. The speech was quoted approvingly and at length in the paper's editorial the following day.

20. "Flowers Sent to Woman Senator," *Denver Express,* February 7, 1913, p. 3. The Woman's Senatorial League was Helen's campaign committee.

21. SJ, 532.

22. Cora V. Collett, *History of the Woman's Club of Denver* (Denver: the Club, 1930), p. 27, Western History and Genealogy, Denver Public Library.

23. "Lindsey Plans Laws: Judge Has Twelve Bills for Colorado Legislature to Raise Legal Standing of Women," *LaCrosse Tribune,* January 9, 1913, p. 6, www.newspaperarchive.com.

24. Ben Lindsey letter to Helen Ring Robinson, January 2, 1913, Ben Lindsey Collection, Box 41, January 1913, Library of Congress, Washington, DC.

25. January 1913 (date is unclear on Xerox copy; may be January 18), Ben Lindsey Collection, Box 41, January 1913, Library of Congress, Washington, DC.

26. "Utilities Bill Is Passed," *Rocky Mountain News,* February 28, 1913, p. 10. The reference to a platform bill is reminiscent of the ambitious Progressive Democratic platform of 1908 and 1910 under Governor John Shafroth, much of which was enacted.

27. "Minimum Wage Passes Senate," *Denver Express,* March 7, 1913, p. 1. One reluctant vote for the bill was from Senator Hecker, who explained that he was opposed to the measure from the start but he knew it was unconstitutional and that his vote would do no harm ("Women's Minimum Wage Bill Passes," *Rocky Mountain News,* March 7, 1913, p. 4).

28. "Girls' Wages Low in Denver; Law Needed," *Denver Express,* March 13, 1913, pp. 1, 3.

29. "Sudden Driving Out of Redlight Women by Mayor Is Denounced,"
Denver Express, February 24, 1913, p. 7; Josephine Roche, "Girls Driven
to Wrong in Denver by Ignorance, Low Pay, and Fatigue," *Denver Express,*
March 15, 1913, p. 1; "Denver Profits from Vice Total 10 Millions Year,"
Denver Express, March 29, 1913, p. 1; "Ammons to Aid in Vice Probe after
Session," *Denver Express,* March 27, 1913, p. 2.

30. "Girls' Wage Probe in Colorado Is Proposed," *Denver Express,*
March 10, 1913, p. 1. The Colorado Constitution limits bills to one subject; the title limits amendments only to those considered germane. A title
and the bill may be narrowed in scope but not broadened. A bill with a
very broad title, such as "Concerning Education," would be open to extensive amendments. The chair rules whether each amendment fits under the
title.

31. "Denounce Fight on Minimum Wage," *Denver Express,* March 31,
1913, p. 1.

32. "Minimum Wage Bill Is Passed," *Denver Express,* April 14, 1913, p.
1; *Laws Passed at the Nineteenth Session,* pp. 407–411. The bill was rewritten
several times with "strike-below" amendments; each one struck the whole
bill and replaced it with a new one. See SJ, 226, where it was introduced
and sent to the Labor Committee; SJ, 749, 763–766, and 775, where it was
heard on Second Reading; SJ, 793, where it passed Third Reading; and SJ,
1404–1407, where it passed the house after another "strike-below" amendment. The conference committee did another strike-below (SJ, 1645), and
the senate readopted the bill, SJ, 1648–1649.

33. "Ammons Takes up the Wage Bill," *Denver Express,* April 25, 1913,
p. 3; *Laws Passed at the Nineteenth Session,* p. 411.

34. *Laws Passed at the Nineteenth Session,* pp. 407–411.

35. *List of Bills, 1913.* SB 471 is missing from the collection of bills in
the Colorado State Archives.

36. Theda Skocpol, *Protecting Soldiers and Mothers: The Political Origins of Social Policy in the United States* (Cambridge: Harvard University
Press, 1993), pp. 401, 404–406, 411–412, 423; Todd Laugen, *The Gospel of
Progressivism: Moral Reform and Labor War in Colorado, 1900–1930* (Boulder: University Press of Colorado, 2010), p. 52. For Supreme Court decision
finding minimum wage unconstitutional, see Laugen, p. 118.

37. Record on the bill, Colorado State Archives, Denver.

38. SB 111, SB 112, and all other bills are available in the Colorado
State Archives, Denver; SJ, 207.

39. Helen's two bills were introduced the same day, SJ, 207; *Laws Passed at the Nineteenth Session,* pp. 510–515.

40. Ben Lindsey letter to Agnes Riddell [*sic*], January 17, 1913, Ben Lindsey Collection, Box 41, January 1913, Library of Congress, Washington, DC.

41. "Woman's Jury Bill Is Killed," *Rocky Mountain News,* February 1, 1913, p. 2. Colorado district attorneys opposed giving women the right to sit on juries ("Lawyers Oppose Women Juries," *Rocky Mountain News,* February 16, 1913, p. 2).

42. SJ, 401.

43. See constitutional amendment passed November 7, 1944, in *Laws Passed at the Thirty-Fifth Session of the General Assembly of the State of Colorado* (Denver: Bradford-Robinson, 1945), Art. II, sec. 23, p. 424.

44. SJ, 398–401.

45. This entire incident is reported in the *Denver Express,* February 1, 1913, p. 7. The subsequent quotation is taken from that article.

46. *House Journal of the Nineteenth General Assembly of the State of Colorado* (Denver: Smith-Brooks, 1913) (henceforth cited as HJ), 845; "Woman Jury Act Killed in House," *Denver Express,* February 27, 1913, p. 1. The committee claimed that the subject was covered under HB 176, but that bill does not extend the right to serve on juries to women (HJ, 1396–1397). In later years constitutional amendments were always concurrent resolutions (SCRs or HCRs).

47. SJ, 757.

48. SJ, 612–613.

49. Bradley, "Colorado's First Woman Senator," sec. 5, p. 4.

50. "Platform Bills Picked for Calendar," *Denver Express,* March 3, 1913, p. 7. A minimum salary for teachers was also endorsed by the Federation of Women's Clubs ("House Bars Speech by Judge Lindsey," *Rocky Mountain News,* February 25, 1913, p. 8).

51. SJ, 1182–1183.

52. The bill itself in the State Archives shows no further action after the striking of the enabling clause, but it erroneously indicates that action took place on February 2, 1913, rather than April 2, 1913.

53. "Senate Passes Pamphlet Bill," *Denver Express,* April 4, 1913, p. 1.

54. SJ, 1183.

55. Helen Robinson, "On Being a Woman Senator," *Independent,* April 20, 1914, pp. 130–132.

56. Ibid.; *Laws Passed at the Nineteenth Session,* pp. 603–605.

57. SB 313, Colorado State Archives, Denver.

58. SJ, 675.

59. SJ, 527.

60. Records on SB 178, HB 262, and SB 199, Colorado State Archives, Denver.

61. SJ, 1789.

62. *Denver Women's Press Club Minutes* (August 6, 1907), Western History and Genealogy, Denver Public Library.

63. "Summary of Laws Passed," *Blue Valley Times,* Dillon, CO, May 30, 1913, p. 6, http://www.cdpheritage.org.

64. *Laws Passed at the Nineteenth Session,* p. 653; US Department of Education, www.ed.gov/about/landing.jhtml?src=gu.

65. SJ, 239.

66. SJ, 1715. Another bill on the subject, HB 91 by Mr. Elmore, had minimum hours and wages for men working for public service corporations. It passed 54 to 1 (HJ, 605). Helen was added as a sponsor in the Labor Committee report (SJ, 570) in the last reference to this bill.

67. *Laws Passed at the Nineteenth Session.*

68. Ibid., p. 151.

69. "Ammons Signs Utility Bill: Governor also Signs Four Other Measures Passed by Legislature," *Summit County Journal and Breckinridge Bulletin,* April 18, 1913, p. 2.

70. SJ, 561.

71. *Laws Passed at the Nineteenth Session,* pp. 73 (HB 84) and 74 (HB 157).

72. SJ, 561.

73. SB 110 had passed Third Reading on a 25 to 0 vote while Helen, the sponsor, was among the 10 absentees (SJ, 1466–1467); "Summary of Laws Passed," p. 6.

74. SJ, 517.

75. "Bill to Regulate Minors Approved," *Denver Express,* February 8, 1913, p. 1.

76. SJ, 81–82.

77. "Urge Haste in Asylum Probe," *Denver Express,* January 20, 1913, p. 7. The bill had been held up for a report on state institutions.

78. SJ, 242.

79. "Asylum Condition Disgrace, Says Senator: Senate Votes Probe," *Denver Express,* January 22, 1913, p. 1.

80. HJ, 296.

81. "Asylum Probe Is Forced through by Women Members," *Denver Express*, January 28, 1913, p. 7.

82. "Asylum Probers Named; 2 Women Are on Committee," *Denver Express*, February 1, 1913, p. 1; "Lock Doors on Probing of Asylum," *Denver Express*, February 5, 1913, p. 1.

83. "Fight to Oust Senator Barela," *Rocky Mountain News*, February 5, 1913, p. 5.

84. See SJ, 849–851 for their report.

85. SJ, 756.

86. SJ, 1287–1288.

87. SJ, 1350.

88. SJ, 1358–1359.

89. SJ, 1786.

90. The house passed the resolution the same day (SJ, 1790). See chapter 5 for the committee report in the 1915 session.

91. *List of Bills, 1913.*

92. SJ, 900.

93. SJ, 1351.

94. "Colorado Legislative Doings, the Senate," *Blue Valley Times*, Dillon, CO, March 21, 1913, p. 2, cdpheritage.org.

95. SJ, 928.

96. *Laws Passed at the Nineteenth Session*, pp. 1–7.

97. See the constitutional amendment in ibid., pp. 678–681.

98. "Judicial Decision Recall Bill Killed by Senators," *Denver Express*, February 13, 1913, p. 7. SB 76 by Senator Affolter died 16 to 15 the first time it was heard on Third Reading on February 11 (SJ, 518). It failed on reconsideration on February 13 on a 17 to 17 vote (SJ, 553). See the bill in Colorado State Archives, Denver.

99. SJ, 1789.

100. "Senator Helen Robinson," *Literary Digest*, February 15, 1913, pp. 367–369. Phil Goodstein says Helen Ring Robinson sponsored such a bill and that the reason for it was to avoid bringing unfit children into the world. He said she emphasized eugenics, but I did not find evidence to substantiate this idea. Phil H. Goodstein, *Robert Speer's Denver: The Mile High City in the Progressive Era* (Denver: New Social Publications, 2004), p. 307.

101. "Tubercular Bill Passes Senate," *Denver Express*, February 24, 1913, p. 1; *Laws Passed at the Nineteenth Session*, pp. 457–462; "Sena-

tors Indignant over House Methods," *Rocky Mountain News,* February 25, 1913, p. 6.

102. "Woman Senator Likes Boxing, but Votes against Bill," *Rocky Mountain News,* March 6, 1913, p. 6.

103. SJ, 1232.

104. HJ, 1853; "The Week in the Legislature," *Denver Express,* April 5, 1913, p. 3.

105. SB 331, Colorado State Archives, Denver.

106. "Libel Measure Dies in Senate," *Rocky Mountain News,* March 14, 1913, p. 5.

107. SJ, 859; Bill back of SB 332, Colorado State Archives, Denver.

108. "Little Bladelets," *Bayfield Blade,* March 21, 1913, p. 1, http://gunnison.aclin.org.

109. "Use Recall if You Don't Get Utility Bill," *Denver Express,* March 7, 1913, p. 3.

110. "Telephone Trust Bids for Legislative Favor," *Denver Express,* January 4, 1913, p. 3; "Field's Free Phone Bribe Riles Members," *Denver Express,* January 7, 1913, p. 1.

111. "Corporations Watch Public Utility Bill," *Denver Express,* January 24, 1913, p. 7; "Utility Measure Is Before Senate," *Denver Express,* January 28, 1913, p. 7; Phil H. Goodstein, *Denver from the Bottom Up: From Sand Creek to Ludlow,* vol. 1 (Denver: New Social Publications, 2003), p. 302.

112. "Seventeen Spineless Senators Deny Right of People to Rule," *Denver Express,* February 28, 1913, p. 1; "Plan to Repair the Injury to Public Utilities Bill," *Denver Express,* March 1, 1913, p. 3. Progressives in the house planned to reinstate the provision.

113. "Plan to Meet State Senators," *Rocky Mountain News,* February 13, 1913, p. 7.

114. "Wolves of Privilege Shed Sheep's Clothing," *Denver Express,* March 6, 1913, p. 1; "Governor Ammons Comes out Openly as Tool of Interests," *Denver Express,* March 13, 1913, p. 1.

115. "Hilts Attacks Referendum Law," *Rocky Mountain News,* February 16, 1913, p. 8.

116. "Seven Anti-Adams Democrats Stand Firm by Party Pledges Despite Ostracisms in Senate," *Rocky Mountain News,* February 27, 1913, p. 3.

117. "Public Utilities Bill Is Passed," *Rocky Mountain News,* February 28, 1913, p. 10.

118. "The People Win," *Denver Express,* March 18, 1913, p. 1; "Protect Cities in Utility Bill," *Denver Express,* March 20, 1913, p. 3.

119. "Committee Kills Home Rule Section in the Utilities Bill," *Denver Express,* April 2, 1913, p. 1; "The Week in the Legislature," *Denver Express,* April 5, 1913, p. 3.

120. SJ, 242–244.

121. "Seek Probe by State in Coal Fields," *Denver Express,* January 15, 1913, pp. 1, 3.

122. SJ, 485.

123. SJ, 1781.

124. SJ, 1511.

125. "Denounce Coal Operators for 3-Year Strike," *Denver Express,* April 12, 1913, p. 1.

126. "8-Hour Mine Bill Passed by Senate," *Denver Express,* March 4, 1913, p. 7. According to Stephen J. Leonard and Thomas J. Noel, the passage of an eight-hour-day statute weakened militant unionism. *Denver: Mining Camp to Metropolis* (Boulder: University Press of Colorado, 1990), p. 174. For the ballot issue passed in 1912, see *Laws Passed at the Nineteenth Session* at the end of the volume.

127. "Labor Fares Well in Assembly by Passage of Important Bills," *Denver Express,* April 1, 1913, p. 2; "The Week in the Legislature," p. 3.

128. "Legislators Obey People in Choice of U.S. Senators," *Denver Express,* January 14, 1913, p. 1; "Direct Election Bill Passed," *Denver Express,* April 12, 1913, p. 1. See *Laws Passed at the Nineteenth Session,* pp. 640–641.

129. SJ, 223.

130. The last reference to the memorial in the *Senate Journal,* 1637, indicates that it was referred to the Committee of the Whole.

131. "Democratic Caucus Kills 'Pork Barrel,'" *Rocky Mountain News,* January 30, 1913, p. 6; *Laws Passed at the Nineteenth Session,* pp. 286–295.

132. SJ, 1915; HJ, 1915.

133. Robinson, "On Being a Woman Senator," pp. 130–132.

134. Ibid., p. 131.

135. Ibid., p. 132.

136. "Helen Ring Robinson Is Paid High Tribute." Though Colorado gave women the vote in 1893, most other states in the nation had not yet done so.

CHAPTER 4

1. Suzanne M. Marilley, *"Why the Vote?" Woman Suffrage and the Origins of Liberal Feminism in the United States, 1820–1920* (Cambridge: Harvard University Press, 1996), p. 212. For the earlier sequence of states and countries granting suffrage, see Marcia Tremmel Goldstein, *Meet Me at the Ballot Box: Women's Innovations in Party and Electoral Politics in Post-Suffrage Colorado, 1893–1898* (Ann Arbor: University of Michigan Press, 2007), note 3, p. 192.

2. Janet Zollinger Giele, *Two Paths to Women's Equality: Temperance, Suffrage, and the Origins of Modern Feminism* (New York: Twayne, 1995), pp. 149, 162.

3. *Pictorial Roster: Twentieth General Assembly* (Denver: Pictorial Roster Publishing Company, 1915), http://www.genealogybug.net/colorado/040.htm.

4. "Suffrage Is Live Issue," *Grand Traverse Herald and Traverse Bay Eagle,* July 31, 1913, p. 1, www.newspaperarchive.com. She addressed a rally in Baltimore before the presentation of a suffrage play ("Pleads to Throw Lemon at Suffragette Meeting," *Indianapolis Star,* June 1, 1913, p. 5, newspaperarchive.com).

5. "Colorado's 'Lady Senator' Jars East because She's No Freak," *Denver Republican,* July 10, 1913, p. 1.

6. *Wellesley College News,* January 22, 1914, p. 8.

7. This speech was scheduled for November 19. Ibid., November 17, 1913, p. 7.

8. The quote is from *A History of Woman Suffrage,* ed. Ida Husted Harper (New York: National American Woman Suffrage Association [1922]), vol. 5, p. 366. The meeting ran from November 29 to December 5, 1913. See also "Women to Urge Vote Amendment," *Atlanta Constitution,* November 30, 1913, p. 4A, www.ancestry.com.

9. "Women to Seek Wilson's Favor," *Indianapolis Star,* December 1, 1913, p. 1, www.ancestry.com.

10. Amanda MacKenzie Stewart, *Consuelo and Alva Vanderbilt: The Story of a Daughter and a Mother in the Gilded Age* (New York: HarperCollins, 2005), p. 339; Rebecca J. Mead, *How the West Was Won: Woman Suffrage in the Western United States, 1868–1914* (New York: New York University Press, 2004), p. 165.

11. Marilley, *"Why the Vote?"* p. 212.

12. "Senator Helen Ring Robinson Talks on 'Woman Suffrage in Practice,'" *Portsmouth Herald,* Portsmouth, NH, December 10, 1913, p. 4.

13. *Wellesley College News,* March 12, 1914, p. 7; "Talk on Suffrage Stirs Eager Crowd," *New York Times,* January 20, 1914, p. 18, http://query.nytimes.com/gst/abstract.html?res=9400EFDC1730E733A25753C2 A9679C946596D6CF.

14. "The Church," *Colorado Springs Gazette,* February 14, 1914, p. 8, http://gunnison.aclin.org, www.newspaperarchive.com; "Equal Suffrage News," *Nevada State Journal,* February 23, 1914, p. 4, www.newspaperar-chive.com.

15. "Women Legislators Should Be Womanly," *New York Times,* November 23, 1913, p. 12.

16. Ibid.; "Woman Legislator Defends Suffrage," *New York Times,* May 10, 1913, p. 9. This speech was presented before the Equal Suffrage League at the Hotel Astor in New York City.

17. "Women Legislators Should Be Womanly," p. 12.

18. "Colorado's Woman Senator Is Here," *Providence Journal,* June 16, 1913, p. 2.

19. See Stewart, *Consuelo and Alva Vanderbilt.*

20. "Colorado's Woman Senator Is Here," p. 2.

21. "Little Bladelets," *Bayfield Blade,* February 13, 1914, p. 1, http://gunnison.aclin.org.

22. *Colorado Springs Gazette,* February 14, 1914, p. 8, http://gunnison.aclin.org.

23. "Woman vs. Woman for State Senator," *New York City Mail,* February 24, 1914, n.p., Archives, University of Colorado at Boulder Libraries; Molly Brown House Museum, http://mollybrown.org, accessed 2003.

24. "Colorado Woman for Congress," *Pathfinder,* Washington, DC, June 13, 1914, n.p.; "Senator's Toga Would Fit Her," *New York City Mail,* July 23, 1914, n.p., Archives, University of Colorado at Boulder Libraries.

25. Phil Goodstein, *Denver from the Bottom Up: From Sand Creek to Ludlow,* vol. 1 (Denver: New Social Publications, 2003), p. 356.

26. Barron Beshoar narrates the dramatic events of those two years in *Out of the Depths: The Story of John R. Lawson, a Labor Leader* (Denver: Colorado Labor Historical Committee of the Denver Trades and Labor Assembly, 1942), p. 57.

27. Ibid., p. 92.

28. Ibid., p. 96.

29. Rick J. Clyne, *Coal People: Life in Southern Colorado Coal Towns, 1890–1930* (Denver: Colorado Historical Society, 1999), p. 11.

30. Beshoar, *Out of the Depths*, p. 113.

31. Beverly E. Stimson, "Outward and Visible Signs: The Trinidad Legacy of Reverend John O. Ferris," *Colorado Heritage* (Winter 2004): p. 21.

32. "Conditions in Rockefeller War on Unions: A White Slavery Camp, Says Colorado's Woman Senator: Gunmen Hired by State to Crush Organized Labor," *New York American,* April 11, 1914, p. 1.

33. Helen Ring Robinson, "The War in Colorado," *Independent,* May 11, 1914, pp. 245–247.

34. Helen Ring Robinson, "Woman Senator Tells Both Sides in Mine Warfare," n.p., unidentified newspaper clipping, May 2, 1914, Archives, University of Colorado at Boulder Libraries.

35. "Bigger than His Dad," undated and unidentified news clipping, 1915, Archives, University of Colorado at Boulder Libraries.

36. "Full Responsibility for Strike and Tyranny of Operators Placed on Rockefeller by U.S. Report," *Denver Express,* August 27, 1915, p. 1; United States House of Representatives (1916), Commission on Industrial Relations, 1912–1915, Final Report of the Commission on Industrial Relations (Washington, DC: US Government Printing Office, 64th Cong. 1st sess., 1916), S. Doc. 415 (http://books.google.com/books?id=NU2VAAAAIAAJ), pp. 59, 7212, 7216.

37. Letter from James H. Brewster to Helen Ring Robinson, December 23, 1914, Archives, University of Colorado at Boulder Libraries; "Law Professor Is Fired from University of Colorado for Telling Truth," *Denver Express,* June 23, 1915, p. 1.

38. "Denver Women Demand Relief for Riot Zone," *Denver Times,* April 22, 1914, Archives, University of Colorado at Boulder Libraries; Scrapbook of Helen Tobin Kosure, Vollrath Collection, cited in Kristen D. Iverson, *Molly Brown: Unraveling the Myth* (Boulder: Johnson Books, ca. 1999), p. 200. William Vollrath married the daughter of Grace Tobin Carroll, a niece of Molly Brown. Their descendants inherited this family scrapbook. Iverson, p. 248.

39. Beshoar, *Out of the Depths*, pp. 164–165.

40. Robinson, "Woman Senator Tells Both Sides in Mine Warfare."

41. Ibid.

42. Stimson, "Outward and Visible Signs," p. 22.

43. Ibid., pp. 22–24.

44. "Militia Destroys Victims' Bodies at Ludlow," *Denver Express,* April 22, 1914, p. 1.

45. "State News: Of Interest to All Colorado People," *San Juan Prospector,* May 2, 1914, p. 4.

46. Stimson, "Outward and Visible Signs," p. 22.

47. "Mine Owners Blamed for Ludlow Battles: Helen Ring Robinson, Just Back from Strike District, Calls Killing of Women an Outrage," unidentified, undated newspaper clipping, Archives, University of Colorado at Boulder Libraries.

48. Colorado State Constitution, Article V, Section 7, and Article IV, Section 9, *Colorado Revised Statutes,* 2002, vol. I, ed. Charles W. Pike (Denver: Bradford, 2002), pp. 349, 325.

49. "Women of Colorado Called to Protest Horrors at Ludlow," *Rocky Mountain News,* April 24, 1914, p. 1.

50. Todd Laugen, *The Gospel of Progressivism: Moral Reform and Labor War in Colorado, 1900–1930* (Boulder: University Press of Colorado, 2010), p. 55.

51. "Thousands of Denver Women to March to the Capitol," *Denver Post,* April 24, 1914, p. 1.

52. "10,000 Women Rise Up for Every Slain Sister: Meeting Pledges Itself That Warfare on Children Shall Pass Away," *Denver Express,* April 24, 1914, p. 2.

53. "500 Women Storm Capitol, Corner Squirming Governor and Demand Strike War End," *Denver Post,* April 25, 1914, p. 1.

54. Beshoar, *Out of the Depths,* p. 200. Helen says in her article that it was a committee of five women ("The War in Colorado," *Independent,* May 11, 1914, p. 247). The *Denver Post* added Mrs. J. C. Herlinger, with an eight-month-old baby, and Mrs. J. J. Ryan, omitting Senator Robinson ("500 Women Storm Capitol," *Denver Post,* April 25, 1914, p. 1).

55. Beshoar, *Out of the Depths,* p. 200.

56. Ibid., p. 201.

57. Ibid., p. 203; "Punish the Guilty for Ludlow Massacre, Cry Women . . .," *Denver Express,* April 25, 1914, p. 1.

58. Beshoar, *Out of the Depths,* p. 203. Much of this narrative is in "500 Women Storm Capitol."

59. Robinson, "War in Colorado," p. 247.

60. Ibid.

61. Beshoar, *Out of the Depths,* pp. 204–205.

62. Ibid., p. 198.

63. Letter from Helen Ring Robinson to Mrs. N. M. Jaeger of the Political Equality Club of Minneapolis, May 31, 1914, Luth and Nanny Jaeger

Papers, Collection A.J22, Box 1, Minnesota Historical Society Library, St. Paul.

64. "Denver Women Brave Storm to Probe Slaughter at Ludlow," *Denver Express,* May 1, 1914, p. 3.

65. "Mine Owners Blamed for Ludlow Battle," unidentified, undated newspaper article, Archives, University of Colorado at Boulder Libraries.

66. "Garment Workers Deny Mrs. Brown Aided Them," *Denver Express,* February 4, 1915, p. 2.

67. Robinson, "War in Colorado," p. 247.

68. *Laws, Extraordinary Session of the Nineteenth General Assembly* (Denver: Western Newspaper Union, 1914).

69. "Mine Owners Blamed for Ludlow Battles."

70. "Special Session Cannot Enact Arbitration Laws," *Rocky Mountain News,* May 6, 1914, p. 1.

71. *Senate Journal of the Nineteenth General Assembly of the State of Colorado: Extraordinary Session* (Denver: Smith-Brooks, 1915) (henceforth cited as SJ), pp. 5–8.

72. "Ammons Grilled for Strike War in State Senate," *Denver Post,* May 7, 1914, p. 1.

73. SJ, 73, 86, 89.

74. SJ, 95; "Woman Senator Protests," *Woman's Journal,* June 6, 1914, Archives, University of Colorado at Boulder Libraries.

75. SJ, 86.

76. SJ, 115.

77. "Plea for Strike Kids Heard in Senate as Persons Hits 'Gag,'" undated, unidentified newspaper article, Archives, University of Colorado at Boulder Libraries; later identified as from the *Denver Express,* May 7, 1914, p. 3.

78. SJ, 36; "Senate Orders Report upon Arbitration Bill," *Denver Post,* May 11, 1914, p. 3.

79. SJ, 59. At some point, according to the *Laws, Extraordinary Session,* Senators Sherman Bellesfield and Hubert Reynolds resigned, but a majority of those elected would then have been 17.

80. *House Journal of the Nineteenth General Assembly of the State of Colorado: Extraordinary Session* (Denver: Smith-Brooks, 1914) (henceforth cited as HJ), p. 98.

81. SJ, 92; (No headline), unidentified, undated newspaper article, Archives, University of Colorado at Boulder Libraries.

82. SJ, 138.

83. "Battle Royal to Come in Strike Special Session in Attempt to Break Limit Ammons Put in Call," *Denver Post,* May 6, 1914, p. 1.

84. "End of Strike by Legislative Committee, Demand of Senate," *Denver Post,* May 14, 1914, p. 1.

85. SJ, 88–89.

86. "End of Strike by Legislative Committee."

87. SJ, 92.

88. "Payment of Strike Bills Will Be Chief Work of Extra Session: Machine Men Grab Control of the Legislature," *Rocky Mountain News,* May 5, 1914, p. l. Seven progressives among the twenty-four Democratic senators elected in 1912 held out against the machine.

89. "Women Legislators Take Hand in Strike," *Rocky Mountain News,* May 5, 1914, p. 3.

90. "Three Arbitration Measures to Go before Senate," undated, unidentified newspaper article, Archives, University of Colorado at Boulder Libraries; "Constabulary Is Doomed . . .," *Rocky Mountain News,* May 7, 1914, p. 4.

91. SJ, 45.

92. SJ, 194, 46–47; "House Deadlock Now Threatened on Militia Bill," *Rocky Mountain News,* May 9, 1914, p. 1. The last time the bill appeared in the journal (on p. 62), it was laid over and does not appear again.

93. SJ, 101.

94. *Laws, Extraordinary Session,* 1914, pp. 17–20, 22; "Legislature Will Quit This Afternoon," *Denver Post,* May 16, 1914, p. 1.

95. SJ, 114.

96. SJ, 53; *Laws, Extraordinary Session,* p. 211.

97. SJ, 65; "Senate Kills Constabulary Bill—7 to 21," *Rocky Mountain News,* May 12, 1914, p. 2.

98. SJ, 44; *Laws, Extraordinary Session,* pp. 11–13; "Senate Smothers Resolution Attacking Ammons' Interests," *Denver Post,* May 8, 1914, p. 1.

99. SJ, 113.

100. *Laws, Extraordinary Session,* pp. 4–5.

101. HB 8, ibid., p. 3.

102. SJ, 104.

103. SJ, 139.

104. "Plea to Wilson to End Strike Won in Senate," undated (May 15, 1914?), unidentified clipping, Archives, University of Colorado at Boulder

Libraries; also "Extra Session to End Today, Machine Wins," *Rocky Mountain News,* May 16, 1914, p. 1. The memorial was referred to the house, but on the last day of the session its members would not suspend the rule requiring resolutions to be laid over one day. Thus the memorial died when the session ended. Also see "Plan to Urge Aid by Wilson Lost in Senate," *Rocky Mountain News,* May 17, 1914, p. 3. This headline is misleading because the memorial passed in the senate and died in the house. An emergency clause avoided the possibility of referring a bill after it passed to a vote of the people.

105. SJ, 43.

106. "Ammons Grilled for Strike War in State Senate," *Denver Post,* May 7, 1914, p. 1. This resolution also claimed that the legislature had the right to modify existing coal leases and to guarantee a fair wage, proper living and working conditions; ensure the right to collective bargaining; and control the price of coal.

107. SJ, 43.

108. SJ, 91.

109. "House Deadlock Now Threatened on Militia Bill," *Rocky Mountain News,* May 9, 1914, p. 1; "Senate Smothers Resolution Attacking Ammons' Interests," *Denver Post,* May 8, 1914, p. 1; "Senators Save Ammons While House Fiddles," *Denver Express,* May 8, 1914, p. 1.

110. SJ, 111–112.

111. "President's Message," *Denver Express,* May 14, 1914, p. 1.

112. "Governor's Reply," *Denver Post,* May 17, 1914, p. 1.

113. Upton Sinclair, *The Brass Check: A Study of American Journalism* (Long Beach, CA, 1920), chapter 4, digitized for Project Gutenberg, http://www.teleread.org/brasscheckfull.htm.

114. Ibid.

115. Quoted in ibid.

116. Ibid.

117. Letter from Helen Ring Robinson to Mrs. N. M. Jaeger of the Political Equality Club of Minneapolis, May 14, 1914, Luth and Nanny Jaeger Papers, Collection A.J22, Box 1, Minnesota Historical Society, St. Paul.

118. "Senator Robinson," *Harper's Weekly,* May 23, 1914, p. 4.

119. United States Industrial Relations Commission, Document no. 415, 64th Congress, First Session (1916), V.VII, 7217, Laugen, *Gospel of Progressivism,* p. 209, note 8.

120. "Mrs. Catt Goes to London," *New York Times,* June 27, 1914, p. 13, http://query.nytimes.com.

121. Stewart, *Consuelo and Alva Vanderbilt*, p. 345; "Sacrifice for Suffrage: Women Set a Day for Raising Fund for Campaign States, Suffrage Day at Newport," *New York Times*, June 30, 1914, p. 4.

122. Stewart, *Consuelo and Alva Vanderbilt*, pp. 364–365, 369–370.

CHAPTER 5

1. Todd Laugen, *The Gospel of Progressivism: Moral Reform and Labor War in Colorado, 1900–1930* (Boulder: University Press of Colorado, 2010), p. 63.

2. *Abstract of Votes Cast at the Primary Election Held on the Eighth Day of September A.D. 1914 and at the General Election Held on the Third Day of November, A.D. 1914, for United States Senators, Congressmen, and State Legislative and District Officers, also the Proposed Constitutional Amendments, Initiatives, and Referred Measures,* by John Ramer, secretary of state, 1915, Denver.

3. "Senators Grab for Plums on Committees," *Denver Express*, January 11, 1915, p. 1.

4. *Senate Journal of the Twentieth General Assembly of the State of Colorado* (Denver: Smith-Brooks, 1915) (henceforth cited as SJ), 1272.

5. *Laws Passed at the Twentieth Session of the General Assembly of the State of Colorado* (Denver: Western Newspaper Union, 1915), pp. xxiv–xxv.

6. "Legislature Idle: Members Talk Committee Chairman," *Denver Express*, January 9, 1915, p. 1.

7. Elias M. Ammons, *Biennial Message before the Twentieth General Assembly* (Denver: Smith-Brooks, January 8, 1915), Box 13898, Colorado State Archives, Denver, pp. 7, 10–12, 15, 17.

8. George A. Carlson, *Inaugural Address before the Twentieth General Assembly* (Denver: Smith-Brooks, January 12, 1915), Box 13898, Colorado State Archives, Denver, p. 10.

9. Ibid., p. 8

10. Ibid., p. 4.

11. Laugen, *Gospel of Progressivism*, p. 95.

12. "Industrial Bill '99' Introduced in Senate by Senator Eaton," *Denver Express*, January 25, 1915, p. 2.

13. Laugen, *Gospel of Progressivism*, p. 98.

14. SJ, 182.

15. Candlish was later the Ku Klux Klan candidate for Denver chief of police appointed by Mayor Benjamin Stapleton in 1923. Stephen J. Leonard

and Thomas J. Noel, *Denver: Mining Camp to Metropolis* (Boulder: University Press of Colorado, 1990), pp. 198–199.

16. SJ, 577–578.

17. "Carlson Declares War on Dems as Labor Bill Loses," *Denver Express,* February 27, 1915, p. 1. The rule continues in the rules of the Colorado State Senate today (V, 3), according to Charlie Pike, director of Legislative Legal Services.

18. "Anti-Carlson Compensation Law Approved by Democrats," *Denver Express,* March 17, 1915, p. 1.

19. SJ, 1036.

20. SJ, 1063.

21. *House Journal of the Twentieth General Assembly of the State of Colorado* (Denver: Smith-Brooks, 1915) (henceforth cited as HJ), 1252–1253.

22. "Constitutional Convention Asked by Reactionaries in House; Primary Law Safe," *Denver Express,* March 31, 1915, p. 1.

23. "Industrial Bills Being Prepared; Both Have Teeth," *Denver Express,* March 8, 1915, p. 1; *Laws Passed at the Twentieth Session,* pp. 515–561.

24. Todd Laugen, "Struggles for the Public Interest: Organized Labor and State Mediation in Postwar America," *Journal of the Gilded Age and Progressive Era* (4:1) (2005): pp. 69–82. See *Laws Passed at the Twentieth Session,* pp. 562–587.

25. *Laws Passed at the Twentieth Session,* pp. 564–565.

26. "Civil Service Mutilation Completed by House and Industrial Bill Passes," *Denver Express,* March 29, 1915, p. 1.

27. "Legislators Take It Easy with Important Bills Waiting Action," *Denver Express,* March 2, 1915, p. 3.

28. HB 177, Colorado State Archives, Denver.

29. *Laws Passed at the Twentieth Session,* pp. 562–587.

30. Ibid., pp. 588ff.

31. "Here's Record of Betrayal by Solons," *Denver Express,* April 12, 1915, p. 2.

32. Laugen, *Gospel of Progressivism,* pp. 97, 99–100.

33. See the poem "The Rubaiyat of Pat, the Statehouse Janitor," *Denver Express,* April 12, 1915, p. 1.

34. "Grand Jury Is Asked to Probe Vicious Lobby," *Denver Express,* March 31, 1915, p. 1.

35. "G.O.P. Boat Hits Squalls and Is Rocking," *Denver Express,* February 16, 1915, p. 1.

36. All three of the coal company relief bills were later killed after a bitter fight in the house: SB 321 (HJ, 1691), SB 330 (HJ, 1690), and SB 430 (HJ, 1690); "Anti-Lindsey and Coal Relief Bills Pass Night Session of Legislature," *Denver Express,* April 10, 1915, p. 3; "Here's Record of Betrayal by Solons," p. 2. Representative Sabin proposed a similar relief bill, HB 516, for the Empire Coal Company that was killed in the House Appropriations Committee, HJ, 1663 ("Corporation Lobby Works Openly at Capitol and It's Up to Carlson to Save People's Rights," *Denver Express,* March 27, 1915, p. 1).

37. "Anti-Lindsey and Coal Relief Bills Pass Night Session of Legislature," p. 3.

38. "Woman Agent of 'Beast' Sent Money, She Says, but Messenger Boy Denies It; Roosevelt May be Called to Dispute 'The Beast' Charges," *Denver Express,* March 13, 1915, p. 1. Teddy Roosevelt sent a letter to Judge Lindsey confirming that Lindsey was in the East all through March 1912. The letter appeared in the *Denver Express* on March 30, 1915 ("T. R. Shows How Base Are Charges against Lindsey," p. 1).

39. "Carlson's 'Big Stick' Proves Toothpick; Howland Expelled by House, Leaves Jail under Bail; House Votes to Extend Graft Hunt," *Denver Express,* March 16, 1915, p. 1.

40. "Howland Gets Acquittal by Court Ruling," *Denver Express,* July 2, 1915, p. 1.

41. "Farrar Says Sabin Bill Curbs Cities," *Denver Express,* March 30, 1915, p. 1.

42. HJ, 1366–1367.

43. SJ, 1722.

44. "Women at Capitol Hero Worshipers," *Rocky Mountain News,* January 24, 1913, p. 7.

45. "Speaker Stewart Arrests Editor of Express on One Charge and Condemns Him on Different One before He Is Given a Hearing," *Denver Express,* April 3, 1915, p. 1. Charlie Pike, director of Legal Services at the State Capitol, says the rule still exists, though members of the legislator's family may sit in his or her chair during ceremonies (House Rules, V, 7).

46. "Representative Ardourel Is Arrested for Assault; C. H. Newell Sues Steward for $50,000 for Fake Arrest; Ardourel also Sued," *Denver Express,* April 5, 1915, p. 1; "Ardourel Is Found Guilty of Assault on Express Editor; Fined by Judge Rice," *Denver Express,* April 9, 1915, p. 1. Both Ardourel and Stewart tried to delay the trials in these civil cases by asking for all the articles Newell had printed that were critical of them and full written descriptions

of the incident. "Ardourel Seeks to Halt $10,000 Assault Hearing," *Denver Express,* April 22, 1915, p. 1; "Stewart Isn't in Hurry for Newell Trial," *Denver Express,* April 30, 1915, p. 1. See also, "Ardourel Contradicts Himself under Oath in Answering Newell Suit," *Denver Express,* May 12, 1914, p. 1; "Ardourel Admits Slugging Express Editor; Pays Fine," *Denver Express,* May 29, 1915, p. 1.

47. "Rep. Harris' Life Threatened in Note on Anti-Tipping Bill," *Denver Express,* March 4, 1915, p. 3.

48. "Legislative Wheels Are Clogged with 1092 Bills, Many of Reactionary Variety," *Denver Express,* February 5, 1915, p. 2.

49. "The Legislature Should Reform or Quit," *Denver Express,* March 15, 1915, p. 1.

50. "Freedom of Speech and Press Attacked in Vicious Bills," *Denver Express,* January 27, 1915, p. 1.

51. "House Votes to Wreck Homes and Break Hearts; 'Beast' Marks Every Bill Approved by Lindsey for Defeat and Plans 'to Get' Carlson," *Denver Express,* February 24, 1915, p. 1.

52. SJ, 1510.

53. SJ, 1460.

54. For the first two bills, see "A Senatorial Duty" (editorial), *Denver Express,* March 10, 1915, p. 4.

55. SJ, 1450.

56. SJ, 1460; "Anti-Lindsey Relief Bills Pass Night Session of Legislature," *Denver Express,* April 10, 1915, p. 3.

57. "Senatorial Duty," p. 4.

58. SJ, 1725.

59. "Stewart Violates House Rules to Kill Civil Service; Solons Throw Water before 'Gag Rule' Ends Opposition to Making Carlson King," *Denver Express,* March 24, 1915, p. 1.

60. "Civil Service Mutilation Completed by House and Industrial Bill Passes," p. 1.

61. SJ, 1478.

62. SJ, 20.

63. SJ, 345.

64. SJ, 326–344.

65. SJ, 327–329.

66. SJ, 329–330.

67. SJ, 330–331.

68. SJ, 331.

69. SJ, 332.

70. SJ, 332–333.

71. SJ, 334–335.

72. SJ, 336–337.

73. SJ, 338–339.

74. Helen Ring Robinson, *Preparing Women for Citizenship* (New York: Macmillan, 1918), p. 76.

75. SJ, 340.

76. SJ, 339–341.

77. SJ, 341.

78. SJ, 342.

79. SJ, 342–344.

80. SJ, 1411; *Laws Passed at the Twentieth Session*, pp. 459–461.

81. SJ, 1722; "Woman Senator Has Bills to Aid Her Sex," *Denver Times,* January 4, 1915, p. 2.

82. The Chicago vice commission in 1911 "concluded that the low returns [wages] of respectable labor were a contributing cause of prostitution." Theda Skocpol, *Protecting Soldiers and Mothers: The Political Origins of Social Policy in the United States* (Cambridge, MA: Harvard University Press, 1993), p. 413.

83. SB 48, Colorado State Archives, Denver.

84. SJ, 133.

85. HJ, 1670.

86. SJ, 1722.

87. SJ, 1725.

88. *Laws Passed at the Twentieth Session,* pp. 360–363.

89. SJ, 623; "Senate Passes Redlight Bill," *Denver Express,* March 3, 1914, p. 3. A call of the senate would send the sergeants out to find and return every member.

90. SJ, 1722.

91. *The Revised Statutes of Colorado, 1908* (Denver: Smith-Brooks, 1908), pp. 564–565. The bill amended section 2112 of chapter 16, wherein the causes for divorce included the husband's failure to provide for his family.

92. SB 152, Colorado State Archives, Denver.

93. Letter of Fred Weybret to the author, June 22, 2005. He is the husband of the daughter of Alcyon Robinson Carlson, Helen's stepdaughter.

Alcyon Carlson Weybret believed her mother died in Los Angeles on April 21, 1932, after "a nervous breakdown," although she did not know the immediate cause of death.

94. "Booze Bill Sure to Pass, Carlson Says; Vote Is On," *Denver Express,* February 1, 1915, p. 1.

95. SJ, 241ff.

96. SJ, 1533.

97. "Children and Mother or Hogs! Which? House Says Hogs; How about Senate?" *Denver Express,* February 25, 1915, p. 1. The editorial asserts that this bill was sponsored by Representative Evangeline Heartz, but there is no record of her introducing such a bill.

98. "Woman Senator to Keep up Her Fight to Deny Mothers' Right to Redeem Children in Court," *Denver Express,* February 26, 1915, p. 1.

99. "Here's Record of Betrayal by Solons," p. 2.

100. SJ, 507–508.

101. SJ, 1534.

102. "Four Bills to Be Initiated by New League," *Denver Express,* April 4, 1914, p. 1; SJ, 1319; HJ, 1683.

103. "Woman Senator Has Bills to Aid Her Sex," p. 2.

104. "Woman Senator Kills Bill to Limit Supreme Court," *Denver Express,* March 10, 1915, p. 1.

105. "Farrar Says Sabin Bill Curbs Cities," *Denver Express,* March 30, 1915, p. 1; "Sabin Water Co. Bill Won't Hurt Denver—Farrar," *Denver Express,* March 29, 1915, p. 1.

106. "Theft of Millions by Water Company Aided by Falsification of House Vote," *Denver Express,* April 2, 1915, p. 1; HJ, 1324.

107. SJ, 557.

108. HJ, 1366–1367.

109. "Express to Beat Water 'Grab' Bill Governor Carlson Plans to Sign and Leading Denver Men Approve Plans," *Denver Express,* April 6, 1915, p. 2.

110. "Here's Record of Betrayal by Solons," p. 2.

111. "Senate Shows It Is Still Owned by Corporations," *Denver Express,* February 25, 1915, p. 1. The Denver Union Water Company was eventually sold to the city of Denver for more than $13 million in 1918. Leonard and Noel, *Denver,* p. 139.

112. SJ, 880.

113. SJ, 1041–1042.

114. "Forgetful Solons 'Rest' from 'Labor,'" *Denver Express,* January 30, 1915, pp. 1, 3.

115. SJ, 225.

116. SJ, 267–268; *Laws Passed at the Twentieth Session,* pp. 232–234.

117. SJ, 1536.

118. SB 163, Colorado State Archives, Denver; "Bills Backed by Railroad Men Beaten," *Denver Express,* March 9, 1915, p. 3.

119. SB 405, Colorado State Archives, Denver.

120. SJ, 891–892.

121. SJ, 249.

122. *Laws Passed at the Twentieth Session,* p. 597.

123. "Damnable! Petition Wilson! Do It Now! Ammons Appeal against Conservation Policy," *Rocky Mountain News,* February 4, 1913, p. 5.

124. "Legislators Take It Easy with Important Bills Waiting Action," *Denver Express,* March 2, 1915, p. 3.

125. SJ, 1511.

126. "Here's Record of Betrayal by Solons," p. 2.

127. "Talked Less and Won," *New York Times,* April 12, 1915, p. 16, http://query.nytimes.com/gst/abstract.html?res=9C05E7D61238E633A25751C1A9629C946496D6CF.

CHAPTER 6

1. "Women Ask Industrial Board Member," *Summit County Journal,* February 24, 1917, p. 7, http://gunnison.aclin.org. The listing of the members of the Industrial Commission in 1917 and 1919 indicates that all members were men. *Laws Passed at the Twenty-First Session of the General Assembly of the State of Colorado . . . 1917* (Denver: Brook-Haffner, 1917), n.p., and *Laws Passed at the Twenty-Second Session of the General Assembly of the State of Colorado . . . 1919* (Denver: American Printing and Publishing, 1919).

2. Margaret Sanger, *Family Limitation,* in *American Feminism: Key Source Documents, 1848–1920,* 5th ed., ed. Janet Beer, Anne-Marie Ford, and Kathleen Joslin (New York: Voluntary Parenthood League, 1916).

3. Helen Ring Robinson, "The Time Has Come to Consider Birth Politics," *Pictorial Review* (February 1919): p. 27.

4. Sybil Downing, *The Vote: A Novel* (Albuquerque: University of New Mexico Press, 2006), p. 199. From 1870 to 1910 there had been 480 cam-

paigns in 33 states but only 17 actual referendum votes. Of these, only 2 passed, in Colorado and Idaho, and 2 new states allowed women to vote in their constitutions: Wyoming in 1890 and Utah in 1896. See Eleanor Flexner, *Century of Struggle: The Woman's Rights Movement in the U.S.* (Cambridge: Harvard University Press, 1973 [1959]), p. 222.

5. L. O. Kleber, *The Suffrage Cookbook* (Pittsburgh: Equal Franchise Federation of Western Pennsylvania, 1915), http://purl.galileo.usg.edu/uga fax/tx715xk63. The recipe was for shrimp wriggle, made of shrimp, rice, green pepper, Worchestershire sauce, catsup, butter, a pint of cream, and one wine glass of sherry or Madeira. Helen is listed as Miss Helen Ring Robinson, which is unusual for a married woman and a senator.

6. "Senator Helen R. Robinson Goes East," *Weekly Ignacio Chieftan,* August 20, 1915, p. 4, www.coloradohistoricnewspapers.org; "County Fair, Central Park, Dunkirk, New York," *Evening Observer,* Dunkirk, NY, August 28, 1915, p. 11, www.newspaperarchive.com.

7. "Suffragists to Use Corn Card," *Palo Alto Recorder,* Emmetsburg, IN, August 12, 1915, p. 6, www.newspaperarchive.com.

8. "Mrs. Robinson Asks Facts: Colorado Senator Demands Basis of Wheeler's Suffrage Charge," *New York Times,* September 25, 1915, p. 8, www.nytimes.com/gst/abstract.html?res=9904EFDB133FE233A25756C2A 96F9C946496D6CF.

9. "Helen Robinson Asks $5000 Libel," *Colorado Transcript,* September 16, 1915, p. 6, www.coloradohistoricnewspapers.org.

10. "Senator Robinson Asks $5000 for Gambling Story," *Denver Express,* September 8, 1915, p. 1.

11. "Woman Senator on Stump," *New York Times,* September 22, 1915, p. 1l, www.nytimes.com.

12. "Colorado Woman Senator Says Suffrage Is State Issue," *Galveston Daily News,* October 17, 1915, p. 7, www.newspaperarchive.com. This article reported Helen's second visit to Galveston that year.

13. "The the [*sic*] Editor Knew Him," *Lincoln Daily News,* August 12, 1916, p. 7, www.newspaperarchive.com.

14. "Pickings," *Kokomo Tribune,* Kokomo, IN, August 15, 1916, p. 4, www.newspaperarchive.com.

15. "Suffragists Ready for Tonight's Rally," *Atlanta Constitution,* February 25, 1916, p. 4, www.newspaperarchive.com.

16. Helen Ring Robinson, "What about the Woman's Party?" *Independent,* September 11, 1916, pp. 381–383.

17. The twelve states were Wyoming, Colorado, Utah, Idaho, California, Washington, Oregon, Arizona, Kansas, Illinois, Nevada, and Montana.

18. Robinson, "What about the Woman's Party?" p. 383. The Congressional Union organized the Woman's Party in the twelve states where women could vote in order to defeat Wilson in those states (Flexner, *Century of Struggle*, p. 276).

19. Helen Ring Robinson, "Wilson Moved Capitol Back from Wall Street," *Alamosa Journal,* October 19, 1916, p. 8, www.coloradohistoricnewspapers.org.

20. "Fifteen Progressives Will Aid Democrats in Maine," *Washington Post,* August 17, 1916, p. 2, www.ancestry.com.

21. "The Fame of 'That Special,'" *Alamosa Journal,* December 28, 1916, p. 8, www.coloradohistoricnewspapers.org; "The National Capital: The Fame of That Special," *Adams County Union-Republican,* January 3, 1917, p. 1, www.newspaperarchive.com.

22. Janet Zollinger Giele, *Two Paths to Women's Equality: Temperance, Suffrage, and the Origins of Modern Feminism* (New York: Twayne, 1995), p. 153.

23. Downing, *The Vote,* p. 209.

24. "Women Ready for Connecticut Drive," *New York Times,* May 2, 1920, p. E8, http://query.nytimes.com/gst/abstract.html?res=9506E2D7 133FE432A25751C0A9639C946195D6CF; "Woman Senator Speaks at Rally," *Bridgeport Telegram,* April 30, 1920, p. 30, www.newspaperarchive.com; Downing, *The Vote,* pp. 279–280.

25. Helen Ring Robinson, *Preparing Women for Citizenship* (New York: Macmillan, 1918).

26. Ibid., p. 6.

27. Ibid., p. 91.

28. Ibid., p. 94.

29. Ibid., p. 8.

30. Ibid., p. 98.

31. Ibid., p. 47.

32. Ibid., p. 122.

33. Ibid., pp. 74–75.

34. Ibid., pp. 21–22.

35. Ibid., p. 54.

36. Ibid., p. 60.

37. Ibid., p. 58.

38. Ibid., p. 63.

39. Ibid., p. 64.

40. Ibid.

41. Ibid., p. 104.

42. Ibid.

43. Ibid., p. 108.

44. Ibid., pp. 104–105.

45. Ibid., p. 66.

46. Ibid., p. 69.

47. Ibid., pp. 67–68.

48. Ibid., p. 79.

49. Ibid., p. 107.

50. Ibid., p. 128.

51. Ibid., p. 114.

52. Ibid., p. 117.

53. "Colorado News Notes," *Weekly Ignacio Chieftan,* March 5, 1920, p. 5, www.coloradohistoricnewspapers.org; (no headline), *Manco Times-Tribune,* March 5, 1920, p. 3, http://gunnison.aclin.org; "Senator Robinson" (editorial), *Denver Times,* July 11, 1923, p. 8.

54. "Woman Suffrage Party Sails for Conference," *Greeley Republican,* May 20, 1920, p. 1, www.newspaperarchive.com. This article also reports that Alcyon was a former society editor for the Greeley paper and that both Alcyon and Helen planned to write magazine articles about the trip.

55. "Geneva Conference Most Important Ever Held, Says Mrs. Catt," *Fort Collins Courier,* June 4, 1920, p. 5, www.coloradohistoricnewspapers. org.

56. *The International Woman Suffrage Alliance: Report of the Eighth Congress* (Geneva), June 6–12, 1920, http://www.aanioikeus.fi/pdf/iwsareport1.pdf.

57. "Charter of Rights for Womanhood," *New Castle News,* New Castle, PA, June 7, 1920, p. 11, www.newspaperarchive.com.

58. US Bureau of the Census, Fourteenth Census of the United States, 1920 (Washington, DC: National Archives and Records Administration, 1920), http://ancestry.com. Alcyon would have been twenty-four in 1920 after her birthday on March 15.

59. "Terse News Stories of Interest Concerning the Feminine World," *Washington Post,* May 23, 1915, p. 29; "No Chance for Mere Man When a Woman Talks," *Elyria Evening Telegram,* May 17, 1915, p. 1, newpaperar-

chive.com. I did not find such a story in the *Denver Post* for the week immediately preceding the *Elyria Evening Telegram* report.

60. Robert E. Riegel and David F. Long, *The American Story* (New York: McGraw-Hill, 1955), pp. 210–213.

61. Dorothy Schneider and Carl J. Schneider, *American Women in the Progressive Era, 1900–1920* (New York: Facts on File, 1993), pp. 198–203.

62. Eric Hobsbawm, *The Age of Empire, 1875–1914* (New York: Pantheon Books, 1987), p. 311.

63. Allan Nevins and Frank Ernest Hill, "Henry Ford and His Peace Ship," *American Heritage Magazine* (9:2) (February 1958), http://www.americanheritage.com/articles/magazine/ah/1958/2/1958_2_65.shtml.

64. Riegel and Long, *American Story,* pp. 217–218.

65. "Judge Lindsey Will Go; Helen Robinson of Colorado also Accepts Invitation," *New York Times,* November 26, 1915, p. 4; "Ford Asks Lindsey and Sen. Robinson to Make Peace Trip," *Denver Express,* November 24, 1914, p. 1.

66. "Ford Now Planning on Overflow Ship," *New York Times,* November 29, 1915, p. 1.

67. "Ford Peace Ship Weighs Anchor Tomorrow: Three Denverites Aboard Marine Fliver," *Denver Times,* December 3, 1915, p. 1.

68. "Ford Party Elects Peace Delegates," *New York Times,* January 14, 1916, p. 3.

69. Nevins and Hill, "Henry Ford and His Peace Ship."

70. Helen Ring Robinson, "Confessions of a Peace Pilgrim," *Independent* 85, February 14, 1916, pp. 225–226.

71. Nevins and Hill, "Henry Ford and His Peace Ship."

72. Ibid.

73. "War Opens on Henry's Peace Ship," *Denver Express,* December 13, 1914, p. 1.

74. "Judge Lindsey Made Head of Peace Party as Ford Comes Home," and "Ford Came Home because of Sickness, Is Official Excuse," *Denver Express,* December 24, 1915, p. 1.

75. Robinson, "Confessions of a Peace Pilgrim," p. 226; "Weatherly Says Ford Peace Party Has Accomplished Much," *Lincoln Daily Star,* January 23, 1916, p. 23, www.newspaperarchive.com; "Mrs. Helen Ring Robinson Dies of Ailment Incurred by Overwork during War," *Denver Post,* July 10, 1923, p. 1.

76. Nevins and Hill, "Henry Ford and His Peace Ship."

77. Robinson, "Confessions of a Peace Pilgrim," p. 226.

78. The information in this paragraph is from "Ryndam Was Crippled by External Explosion," *Atlanta Constitution,* January 30, 1916, p. A11, www.newspaperarchive.com.

79. Ibid.

80. Nivens and Hill, "Henry Ford and His Peace Ship." The statement from Helen is expressed slightly differently in "As Mail Is Seized Van Dyke Protests," *New York Times,* January 30, 1915, www.nytimes.com, wherein she is quoted as saying "the weakness of the undertaking was due to the fact that the leaders did not rise to the magnitude of the idea."

81. William C. Bullitt, "Autocratic Leader Split Ford's Party," *New York Times,* January 31, 1916, p. 2.

82. Ibid.

83. Riegel and Long, *American Story,* p. 219.

84. Ibid., p. 223.

85. Ibid., p. 227.

86. Eric Hobsbawm, *The Age of Extremes: A History of the World, 1914–1991* (New York: Vintage Books, 1996), p. 26.

87. "Mrs. Helen Ring Robinson Dies of Ailment Incurred by Overwork during War," p. 1.

88. James H. Baker and LeRoy R. Hafen, *History of Colorado,* vol. 3 (Denver: Linderman, 1927), pp. 1003–1004.

89. "Woman's Club of Denver Establishes Endowment for Museum Internships," *Colorado History News* (January 1996): p. 12. The *San Juan Prospector,* March 1, 1918, p. 1, contains a notice that Helen was appointed state chairman of the woman's committee for the next Liberty Loan drive, www.coloradohistoricnewspapers.org.

90. Ida Clyde Clarke, *American Women and the World War* (New York: D. Appleton, 1918), p. 1, www.lib.byu.edu/~rdh/wwi/comment/Clarke/Clarke01.htm.

91. "Women Must Work, Warns Senator Helen Ring Robinson," *Fort Collins Weekly Courier,* August 23, 1918, p. 8, www.coloradohistoricnews papers.org.

92. "Liberty Loan Conference in Denver," *Summit County Journal,* September 14, 1918, www.coloradohistoricnewspapers.org.

93. "Small Towns in State Eager to Boost Loan," *Rocky Mountain News,* October 14, 1918, p. 10.

94. Caption under photo of Alcyon Robinson, *Littleton Independent,* May 24, 1918, p. 6; also in *Akron Weekly Pioneer Press,* May 24, 1918, p. 1, www.coloradohistoricnewspapers.org.

95. Clarke, *American Women,* chapter 7, p. 1.

96. Helen Ring Robinson, "Squads Right! Squads Left," *Independent,* July 27, 1918, p. 120.

97. Ibid., p. 127.

98. Harry E. Fosdick, *The Meaning of Prayer, Faith, and Service* (Garden City, NY: Garden City Books, 1917), pp. 257–258. Fosdick was quoting from Ralph Diffendorfer's "Thy Kingdom Come." This prayer was first found on the website of Jim McGuiggan (jimmcguiggan.com).

99. "Name Gunter for Governor," *Akron Weekly Pioneer Press,* July 26, 1918, p. 1, www.coloradohistoricnewspapers.org.

100. *History of the Denver Woman's Press Club, 1898–1899–1900,* Denver Woman's Press Club Collection, Box 2, Minutes, February 16, 1905, Western History and Genealogy, Denver Public Library.

101. *Denver Woman's Press Club Year Book,* 1919–1920, p. 26.

102. *Denver Woman's Press Club Year Book,* 1920–1921, 1921–1922, 1922–1923; "Mrs. Helen Ring Robinson Dies Following Breakdown from Her Work during World War," *Denver Times,* July 10, 1923, p. 1.

103. Helen Ring Robinson, "A Fair Field in Sex," *Pictorial Review* (May 1919): p. 21. See also Robinson article, "Making the World Safe for Monogamy," *Pictorial Review* (November 1918): p. 5.

104. Helen Ring Robinson, "A Fair Field in the State: For Mothers of Women," *Pictorial Review* (August 1919): p. 24.

105. Robinson, "The Time Has Come to Consider Birth Politics," p. 27.

106. Helen Ring Robinson, "Releasing Women for the Top: Being Some Meditations on the Work of Women after the War," *Pictorial Review* (December 1918): p. 24.

107. Helen Ring Robinson, "Sex Equality and Brass Tacks," *Delineator* (November 1923): p. 2.

108. Robinson, "Fair Field in the State," p. 24.

109. Helen Ring Robinson, "A Fair Field in Labor," *Pictorial Review* (July 1919): p. 45.

110. Robinson, "Releasing Women for the Top," p. 54.

111. Helen Ring Robinson, "Putting Her House in Order: No Woman Can Manage More than One Business at a Time," *Pictorial Review* (January 1919): p. 11.

112. Francis Melrose, "Helen Robinson Left Political Mark," *Rocky Mountain News,* January 8, 1989, p. 16M.

113. "Mrs. Helen Ring Robinson Dies of Ailment Incurred by Overwork during War," p. 1.

114. *Denver City Directory* (Denver: Ballenger and Richards, 1921, 1922, 1923); "Mrs. Helen Ring Robinson Dies of Illness Caused by War Work," marked *Denver Post,* July 10, 1923; *Dawson Scrapbook, 67,* p. 217, Colorado State Historical Society, Denver; "Helen Ring Robinson, First Woman to be Senator in Colorado, Dies," *Rocky Mountain News,* July 11, 1923, p. 9.

115. "Crowds Pass before Mrs. Robinson's Bier at State Capitol," *Denver Times,* July 12, 1923, p. 4; "State Pays Tribute to the Memory of Helen Ring Robinson," *Denver Post,* July 12, 1923, p. 21.

116. "Crowds Pass before Mrs. Robinson's Bier at State Capitol," p. 4.

117. Eva and Albert Thurston had a daughter, Dorothy, born in 1895. Charles Albert Thurston, a publisher of *Thurston's Auto-highway, Mountain and Desert Map* (1915), died in 1941.

118. Probate Case #32621, July 24, 1923, Colorado State Archives, Denver.

119. The Riverside Interment Record says, "CREM OF Robinson, Helen Ring, Age 60, Color W, Sex F, July 12, 1923. CREM. #2513." (This was the day of the cremation.) Though the record also gives her age as sixty, census data indicate that she was sixty-three. July 10 is given as the date of death. The Fairmont Cemetery Interment Record in the Plat Book, 146, identifies the burial place of the ashes as Section W ½ (west half of lot), Lot 53, Block 4. The burial did not take place until April 22, 1924.

120. Ewing paid two dollars for this inscription, according to the Probate Record Case #32621, July 24, 1923, Colorado State Archives, Denver.

121. "Engaged," *Time* magazine, July 23, 1923 (no pagination), http://www.time.com/time/magazine/article/0,9171,716238,00.html.

122. George Benjamin Woods and Jerome Hamilton Buckley, *Poetry of the Victorian Period* (New York: Scott Foresman, 1955), p. 163.

123. Alfred, Lord Tennyson, *The Poetical Works of Tennyson,* published in 1898 under the title *The Poetical and Dramatic Works of Alfred, Lord Tennyson* (Cambridge edition) (Boston: Houghton Mifflin, 1898), p. 551.

124. The 1920 census estimated the year of his birth as 1857. The burial permit also gives his age as sixty-seven (*Rocky Mountain News,* April

18, 1925, p. 15); "Ewing Robinson, Denver Attorney, Dies in Hotel Here," *Rocky Mountain News,* April 13, 1925, p. 8, states that his age was sixty.

125. "Ewing Robinson, Denver Attorney, Dies in Hotel Here," p. 8.

126. Cremation was April 17, 1925. Robert I. Woodward, archivist of St. John's Cathedral, Denver, letter of October 27, 2004, to the author.

127. Ewing was buried in Beverly, Ohio, according to the Pedigree Resource File at www.familysearch.org.

128. California Birth Index, www.ancestry.com.

129. "Mrs. Alcyon Carlson Dies in California," *Denver Post,* May 6, 1932, p. 34; Fred Weybret letter to author, July 11, 2005.

130. Fred Weybret kindly responded to many of my questions because his wife was unable to do so as a result of ill health. The Weybrets live in Lodi, California.

131. "Senator Robinson," *Denver Times,* July 11, 1912, p. 8.

132. Helen Ring Robinson file, Denver Woman's Press Club.

133. "Protagonist in a Good Cause," *Denver News,* July 11, 1923, Dawson Scrapbook, 67, pp. 215–217, Colorado Historical Society, Denver.

Index